D1000407

Charles Booth

ON THE CITY:
PHYSICAL PATTERN
AND SOCIAL STRUCTURE

THE HERITAGE OF SOCIOLOGY

A Series Edited by Morris Janowitz

Charles Booth

ON THE CITY: PHYSICAL PATTERN AND SOCIAL STRUCTURE

Selected Writings

Edited and with an Introduction by

HAROLD W. PFAUTZ

THE UNIVERSITY OF CHICAGO PRESS

CHICAGO AND LONDON

Library of Congress Catalog Card Number: 67-28466

The University of Chicago Press, Chicago & London

The University of Toronto Press, Toronto 5, Canada

Published 1967

Printed in the United States of America

Contents

INTRODUCTION *by Harold W. Pfautz*

CHARLES BOOTH: SOCIOLOGIST OF THE CITY

1

THE TIMES, THE MAN, AND THE INQUIRY

ON THE OCCASION of Charles Booth's Opening Address as President of the Royal Statistical Society, November 21, 1893, the Chairman remarked:

The public were now well agreed that in Mr. Booth they had a gentleman to whom all classes of the community as well as the Society were greatly indebted. His public spirit had been manifested in so many ways that it could not be too highly appreciated. It was very rare indeed for a gentleman in Mr. Booth's position, not only to devote a great deal of money to investigations of this kind, but still more to devote a great deal of time and energy to see that those investigations were carried out. Mr. Booth having set so good an example, must be highly commended, and he should hope that in some way or other he would receive some public acknowledgement for the great services he had rendered. Very few people have shown so much candor in dealing with the facts investigated. He told them exactly what processes he used in arriving at the facts; there was no concealment of any kind; and he built up his conclusions with the utmost care, as a scientific investigator ought to do. In fact, he really stood at the very foremost rank of statistical investigators, and had investigated subjects which very few people would have the courage to attack, involving as they did so much arduous labor, and so much difficulty in finding a clue through the labyrinth.[1]

It is not an easy task to assess the role played by Charles Booth and his monumental study of the people in London at the close of the nineteenth century in the development of sociology. As far as general social science, so-called, is concerned, the inquiry

1 *Journal of the Royal Statistical Society*, 56 (November, 1893): 596.

undoubtedly was one of a number of efforts which served to establish the radical premise that environment rather than human nature is the primary cause of—and thus the potential cure for—man's social ills. Moreover, if Auguste Comte provided a vision of and a name for the discipline, Charles Booth, with his abiding concern "to get at things as they are," was one of the first to take seriously the positivist assumptions that human society should and could be made an object of secular study.

Booth's lack of formal academic training, his position outside the university, and his self-image as primarily a man of business conspired, despite his contacts with both the intellectuals and the intellectual currents of his day, to minimize his impact on the development of sociology as a special social science. He played little or no part in the development of British academic sociology, which adhered to the philosophic style set by Hobhouse. And, while his contribution to the social survey movement in both England and America has been well documented, the dissociation between the social work and sociological traditions that occurred in American universities was sufficient to undercut the interest of sociologists in his study. Further, given the drive toward empirical research which took root in the United States in the twenties, together with the abstract theoretical traditions imported from France and Germany, Booth's linkage with social reform—he was personally instrumental in the movement to provide state pensions for the aged and played a major role in the modern trend to substitute data for doctrine in the design of public policy—served, again, to minimize acquaintance with his massive inquiry on the part of practicing sociologists. Finally, the very scale of his classic study—seventeen volumes—suggests the truth of Ruth Glass's recent observation that Booth has always been "more admired than read."[2]

The inevitable result has been that few sociologists have had any conception of the vast scope, the methodological innovations, or the rich insights into the city as a spatial pattern and social structure which Booth's study involved, or the questions it raised

2 Ruth Glass, "Urban Sociology in Great Britain: A Trend Report," *Current Sociology*, 4 (1955): 46.

in these connections. While the inquiry has always been dutifully acknowledged as "a landmark of empirical research," most references have been either misleading, misinformed, or both in regard to its relevance for sociologists. Typically, Booth has been dismissed as a social reformer whose work had applicability only for the social survey, in contrast to social research. He has been described as unconcerned with generalization, uninterested in process or social change, having nothing to say about the social life of slum dwellers, and as paying little or no attention "to social, psychological, and ecological factors so prominent in sociological appraisals of community life."[3] Even Robert E. Park, who was familiar with the inquiry, was content to note Booth's contribution only on the impressionistic, descriptive level:

> It was not, however, Booth's statistics, but his realistic descriptions of the actual life of the occupational classes—the conditions under which they lived and labored, their passions, pastimes, domestic tragedies, and the life-philosophies with which each class met the crises peculiar to it—which made these studies a memorable and permanent contribution to our knowledge of human nature and society. What we have then, finally, in these volumes, is a minute and painstaking account of the phase of modern civilization at the end of the nineteenth century, as manifestations in the life of the London laborer. These volumes were a sociological study, they have become a historical document.[4]

To reinterpret a man's work from the perspective of another era is always a somewhat dubious and even dangerous endeavor: given the new ground, the transposition from things implicit to things explicit, while easily made, often involves the risk of spurious linkages. Again, it is impossible precisely to trace the intellectual paths which Booth's facts, generalizations, and methodological

3 J. F. Steiner, "The Sources and Methods of Community Study," in *The Fields and Methods of Sociology*, ed. L. L. Bernard (New York: Farrar & Rinehart, 1934), p. 304. See also, W. F. Whyte, "Social Organization in the Slums," *American Sociological Review*, 8 (February, 1943): 34.

4 R. E. Park, "The City as a Social Laboratory," in *Chicago: An Experiment in Social Science Research*, ed. T. V. Smith and L. D. White (Chicago: The University of Chicago Press, 1929), p. 46.

innovations took among those who followed him.[5] Booth was never interested in the development of a science of sociology involving a body of knowledge and articulated by a technical, conceptual scheme. His focus was pragmatic—the problem of poverty in the midst of urban plenty—and his approach was essentially on the common-sense level. He made no conscious effort to rationalize or to systematize most of the concepts he employed.

Nevertheless, while in one sense it may be a perversion of the materials to abstract them from the perspective of sociology as it developed after Booth, the relevance for sociologists of his findings, his methods, and his observations cannot be denied. In fact, contained in his classic survey are both theoretical and methodological contributions that make it one of the principal antecedents of the research methods and interests informing the rise of an empirical sociology of the city in America in the twenties, as well as of the study of community social stratifications and organizational structure and functioning, which became dominant motifs in the thirties and forties and continue as such to this day.

The Man and His Times: Origins of the Inquiry

THE EARLY YEARS Beatrice Webb once remarked of Charles James Booth that he symbolized "the mid-Victorian time Spirit." An examination of his life and times suggests that he also represented its raw nerve: that a wealthy captain of industry should organize and pursue at his own expense a seventeen-year inquiry into the condition of the working people of London, or that a Conservative in politics, wedded to the tradition of individualism, should become responsive to the social costs of laissez faire and advocate a scheme of non-contributory pensions for the

5 As Everett Hughes observed in a communication to the writer: "Park was such a prodigious reader and such a ruminator that he often did not know where he had got something. He never presented an idea until it had gone through the crucible of his own mind, and when it came out, he often did not know its source. He often asked me (and others with whom he talked—and they were many), where he had probably got an idea."

aged hints at the conflicts and paradoxes that marked both the man and his era.

The picture of Charles Booth revealed by his wife's *Memoir*, by his sometime colleague Beatrice Webb in her autobiography, and more recently by the Simeys (who had access to family letters and original manuscripts)[6] is that of a very remarkable man. Energetic yet reserved, sensitive but always determined, frail of constitution but robust of purpose, Booth was a man of many parts: "Charley" to his intimates; always "the Chief" to his business associates; and, finally, "the Rt. Hon." to a public for which his name became almost a household word. Yet the conflicting themes and strands of his life were somehow woven together into such a pattern of wholeness and wholesomeness as to present a very modern image of "success." Just as his avocation of social investigation foreshadowed the rise of twentieth-century empirical sociology, so, too, his vocation and life style adumbrated the twentieth-century urban man of business and public affairs.

Booth was born in 1840, the next-to-oldest of five children of a prosperous Liverpool corn merchant. The family traditions were Liberal in politics and Unitarian in religion, which provided a firm background for the growth of a character imbued with a strong sense of personal responsibility, coupled with acute social sensitivity. While replete with such private tragedies as the death of his mother when he was only thirteen, that of his father when he was twenty, and that of the young woman whom he planned to marry when he was twenty-two, the first forty years of Booth's life reveal a fairly conventional picture of a well-endowed young man's search for self and place in the world.

There never seemed to be any doubt about a commercial

6 Needless to say, the account of Booth's life and the history of his social research lean heavily on these sources: *Charles Booth: A Memoir* (London: Macmillan & Co., 1918); Beatrice Webb, *My Apprenticeship* (New York: Longmans Green & Co., 1926); and T. S. Simey and M. B. Simey, *Charles Booth, Social Scientist* (London: Oxford University Press, 1960). See also: Harold W. Pfautz, "Charles Booth's Contribution to the Theory and Method of Human Ecology and Social Organization" (Master's thesis, Department of Sociology, University of Chicago, 1947).

career. After the traditional Grand Tour, which followed on the completion of his formal schooling at the age of sixteen, Booth served his business apprenticeship in the shipping firm of Lampson and Holt from 1856 to 1862. This interest was simply a result of family contacts, since a sister had married one of the Holts.

Upon leaving the firm for another tour of the Continent (which was cut short by the death of his childhood sweetheart), Booth was catapulted into a fledgling commission business, dealing in hides, with his older brother, whose American partner had suffered a complete breakdown. As a result, Booth spent the next year and a half in America in an only moderately successful attempt to establish the new enterprise on a firm basis. On his return to Liverpool in 1864, he not only set up a Liverpool office but, with characteristic energy and with his own capital (as well as that of relatives and friends), expanded the business to include a shipping line. He had become fascinated with steam power while employed by Lampson and Holt and, in a fashion which was to become typical, he familiarized himself with every aspect of this novel type of power and played a major role in supervising both the design and construction of two cargo steamships for the new firm. In 1866 he accompanied the first ship on its maiden voyage to South America, not merely because of his own investment in the project but simply because he had come to know more than anyone else about steamships. At this time, too, Booth developed the habit of collecting basic data and attempting to state the relevant facts in the simplest terms as a preliminary to every business decision.

During this period he lived in the warm and even exciting context of a rather closely knit circle of extended and often overlapping groups of kin, close friends, and business associates. It was a lively collection of intelligent, educated, and well-to-do young people who sought to make better sense of the world in which they lived. And, for the next five years, while he was engaged in the trying task of establishing the still fledgling business venture, Booth also became deeply involved in a number of local political activities as well as in a constant and intense dialogue with his intimates—daily conversations, letters, and even a family magazine—concerning the issues of the day. Indeed, just as his business experience oriented him to the importance of data, his social life style forced him to argue his position cogently and to put his thoughts into writing. Both were excellent apprenticeships for what was to come.

His political adventures—an attempt to develop support for the extension of the franchise among the workers; an endeavor to make the extension real by organizing the workers politically; a concern to educate "the new masters" by raising funds for a trades hall to be used for their economic as well as political instruction; and a proposal to establish a program of universal secular education by means of public grants to school children of working-class parents—were, all of them, abysmal failures. They served only to disillusion him with politics as the path to social betterment. On the other hand, the intense dialogues concerning the rising conflict between the new science and the old religion and, especially, the discrepancies between the ideals of Christian philanthropy and individual responsibility which had been taught and the realities of life among the poor which were daily discovered ultimately led him to question most of the things he had taken for granted: the natural and moral superiority of the rich, poverty as but the rule of Divine Law in the affairs of men. Especially did they lead in Booth's case to increasing doubts about his religion and the relevance of his world view to the new and wider, often more exciting, often more depressing world which he had found as a result of his political forays among the workers. Understandably, a severe reaction followed: Booth gave up the religion of his fathers; he flirted with Positivism, which had swept English intellectual circles in the sixties; and he found himself increasingly alienated not only from the world in which he lived but also from those whom he loved and with whom he worked.

In the meantime he had met Mary Macauley, daughter of a civil servant, niece of the historian, and cousin to Beatrice Webb (then Beatrice Potter), whose more urbane background served further to introduce him to ideas and facts that challenged his basic assumptions. Despite their differences (his first proposal was rejected), they were married in 1871. But Booth was worn down by the press of his business affairs, the stress of his intense self-questioning, and his disillusionment with his political efforts on behalf of the working class. After the birth of his first child in 1873, he experienced the first of a number of breakdowns. For the next two years, he and his wife retreated to the Continent in an attempt to restore both his mind and body.

When the young couple returned in 1875, Booth's recovery was by no means complete, and he did not immediately play an active role in the affairs of his business. He did, however, make the fateful decision to establish his residence in London, and the following year he set up an office of his firm in the city. More important, his wife introduced him to the intellectual currents of the city to which she had access and which were in sharp contrast to those of his more provincial Liverpool. Here, happily for Booth, the problems of the day were dissociated from self and cast, rather, in impersonal and abstract terms. In this atmosphere, his interest in social problems began to revive.

In 1878 Booth was suddenly recalled to America, where he spent seven months reorganizing a bankrupt glove factory in which his firm had an interest. His success in this venture seemed to provide the tonic he needed. At any rate, from this point on, despite the fact that he was never again robust and experienced other breakdowns which involved other therapeutic retreats, the self-confidence and executive ability which followed upon and increasingly secured his success in business never deserted him. Indeed, they were to play a major role in his success in his avocation of social research, for the empirical orientation to social facts in Booth's case came not from any academic training but from long experience in business, where the analysis of trends and the organization of men were the modes he consciously adopted to meet the problems he encountered.

THE TIMES Just about the time the Booths returned to England, the social forces which were to destroy the complacent optimism of British social and economic life began to break to the surface. The first half of the century, indeed up to 1870, had been so full of material progress and increasing wealth that the optimism it engendered was sufficient to blind at least the dominant segment of the population to the existence of any pressing domestic problems. After the seventies, according to Lynd, social and economic trends fostered by the previous expansion in commerce and industry became visible and non-reversible.[7] The rural-agricultural basis of the economy had been destroyed and in its place had developed an industrial-commercial economy which emphasized impersonal profit-making in contrast to traditional concepts of livelihood. While the transition had brought about the political emancipation of the urban middle class, just as surely it had secured the poverty of an increasingly large number of the working class.

Indeed, the negative aspects of the new order became further objectified and magnified as England faced contracting markets owing to the competition of the newer industrializing nations, Germany and America. The agricultural depression of 1873–86 was a time of falling prices and profits as well as of increased unemployment. A new force was also at work: an economy based on coal and iron, steam, and the non-joint-stock company was in the throes of transition to an economy based on steel, electricity, and that economic wonder—the joint-stock company.

These material and structural changes were not without their correlates in the ideological realm. Until the last quarter of the nineteenth century, economic liberalism was the established philosophy: it assumed a natural order in society, the result of the operation of unalterable natural forces. Natural inequality and self-interest were taken for granted as the bases of a viable economic and social order. Faith in natural science, in progress, in rational individual effort, and in the liberty of person were the pillars of such a world view. Wealth was assumed to be the basis of civilization insofar as it both created and satisfied desire. Indeed, the wealthy performed their function just to the extent that their high standard of living encouraged an effective desire among the lower classes to imitate.

As early as 1830, however, statistics began to appear on the

7 Helen M. Lynd, *England in the Eighteen-Eighties* (New York: Oxford University Press, 1945).

relationship between occupations and health and on rural-urban differences in mortality, all of which helped to objectify the problematic aspects of the social revolution which had taken place. Sir Frederick Eden, the owner of an insurance company, had published a three-volume work in 1797 which focussed on the social conditions among the working classes throughout the country.[8] The findings, however depressing, were interpreted in the economic-liberal perspective: the lower relief scale and more frugal life of the northern counties, in contrast to the more lavish relief and wasteful living in the south, were cited as proof that improvidence rather than lower wages was the chief cause of working-class poverty.

Moreover, in 1851, Henry Mayhew, a journalist and one of the founders of *Punch,* had published a four-volume study subtitled, "A Cyclopedia of the Condition and Earnings of Those that Will Work, Those that Cannot Work, and Those that Will not Work."[9] He made his purpose explicit:

> My earnest hope is that the book may serve to give the rich a more intimate knowledge of the sufferings of the poor and cause those who are in "high places," and those of whom much is expected, to bestir themselves to improve the condition of a class of people whose misery, ignorance, and vice amidst all the immense wealth and great knowledge of "the finest city in the world," is, to say the very least, a national disgrace to us.[10]

8 Sir Frederick Eden, *The State of the Poor* (London, 1797). Eden's inquiry centered around a series of typical working-class family budgets and involved a questionnaire which was adapted from the work of an even earlier student, Sir John Sinclair. Cf. *The Statistical Account of Scotland. Drawn up from the Communications of the Ministers of the Different Parishes* (21 vols.; Edinburgh, 1791–99).

9 Henry Mayhew, *London Labour and the London Poor* (London: Griffin Bohn & Co., 1861). Each volume considered descriptively the typical life style of some segment of the urban lower classes. The first, for example, was a survey of London "street folk," comprising the street-sellers, -beggars, -finders, -performers, etc. In the final volume, however, Mayhew addressed himself to "the physics and economy of vice and crime," in an attempt to measure the comparative incidence of various forms of devience, on a county basis, for all of England.

10 *Ibid.*, II, *iv.*

Finally, some novels—e.g., Dickens' *Bleak House* and *Our Mutual Friend*—as well as official publications such as *The Report on the Sanitary Conditions of the City of London for the Years 1848–49*, also served to alarm thoughtful Londoners concerning the problems posed by the rapid increase in population and urbanization.[11]

For the dominant group, of course, there was no problem of "poverty." Rather, it was framed in terms of "the poor"—a matter of the character of a segment of the population rather than a condition of society. In the world view of economic liberalism, the individual was the given datum; society was artifical; profits were the primary consideration; and laissez faire was valued not only as an instrument of progress but also for its own sake. The middle classes universalized their perspective and reacted with moral indignation to personal failure or revolt against their standards.

In these terms, the problem became that of distinguishing between the "deserving" and the "undeserving" poor, in order that the former might be aided by private and public charity to maintain life, while the latter were denied aid to force them to work. The point of reference was "individual responsibility," and the problem posed was how to give aid without undermining self-reliance. As for the workers, they were conceived collectively as anonymous labor power—a tool to be purchased at the lowest possible price. Trade unions were despaired of as unnatural interferences in a natural economic order and process.

Lynd points out, however, that while neither "the poor" nor "the workers" posed any problem to the middle and upper classes, the concept of "the people" came to have more problematic and even fearful connotations as the century wore on. Increased communication, coupled with the extension of the franchise and a

11 London, for example, grew in population from less than one million in 1801 to almost four million in 1881. As early as 1851, 50 per cent of the population of England and Wales was classified as urban, and this percentage had increased to 72 by 1891. See Adna F. Weber, *The Growth of Cities in the Nineteenth Century* (New York: Columbia University Press, 1899).

correlative growing flow of public opinion, made the working class more conscious of its plight and more articulate and confident in its demands. The wealth that had piled up during the prosperity of the first half of the century had been disproportionately distributed in favor of the middle and upper strata. The people were becoming more frustrated in their attempts to identify themselves with middle-class values and perspectives, as well as more insecure economically.

As it happened, the ruling classes lost nerve. The depression, the land question, and the increasing health and housing problems fostered by the growing urban slums are cited by Lynd as directly connected with the growing recognition of the inadequacy of the established philosophy to solve the problems of the day. So, in the eighties exceptions to economic liberalism appeared and they were increasingly recognized as such. Further, there emerged the concept that the isolated individual was incapable of assuring his own welfare. Rather, the idea that the state had a function to perform in this sphere began to take root. Social legislation in the form of Factory and Housing Acts; state control of banking and postal services; a shift from international to domestic problems as the focus of political attention; and an ever increasing power and concern of municipal governments with respect to the welfare of their residents were some of the signs of changes that took place during this period.

The new collectivism postulated the organic nature of society. Many varieties of socialism appeared, all of which stressed the inequality of the existing economic organization and sought state responsibility and planning for the welfare of the citizens. By the end of the decade, economic liberalism was in a purely defensive position. Philosophers and economists were starting with the concept of human welfare rather than with unalterable natural forces. The obligations as well as the privileges of private ownership were more and more recognized.

In the face of the depression and the drift of the people from identification with middle-class values, a social revolution took place in the sense that the established philosophy was no longer taken for granted. New problems concerning the relationship between freedom and authority, individual rights and human welfare, were raised and framed in new terms:

> . . . the 'eighties was a period of education and preparation, of accustoming people to new ways of seeing England and of interpreting relations among men. It insisted on the urgency of questions of human well-being, enlarged the conception of welfare, and accustomed people to the possibility of social action to help create individual welfare.[12]

ORIGINS OF THE INQUIRY Charles Booth, by now a successful businessman equipped with "the personal power and free initiative due to a large income generously spent," was a part of all this.[13] Despite a constant journey to work as he integrated the affairs of the firm's offices in New York, London, and Liverpool, he renewed his concern with what had come to him to be "the problem of all problems"—the existence of chronic poverty in the midst of urban, industrial plenty.

Of course, as a businessman, much of his thinking remained in the vein of economic liberalism: facts were "scientific facts"; rational behavior was "economic behavior"; and religion was "Protestant morality." The first aroused in him a passionate desire to be objective, and he was constantly to reiterate his concern only to study "things as they are." The second convinced him of the futility of socialism, owing to, ". . . the absence of the judgement of the inexorable court of personal profit and loss, to which every . . . firm must submit, and by which it learns both prudence and wise daring."[14] And, it also made him discard communism as a possible solution: "Acting under false views of the constitution of our modern industry [communism] proposes to remove its directors, who form so essential a part of it."[15] The third was tempered by the new humanitarianism which, as Webb points out, resulted in "the transference of the emotion of self-sacrificing service from God to man."[16]

12 Lynd, *England in the Eighteen-Eighties*, p. 424.
13 Webb, *My Apprenticeship*, p. 219.
14 *Charles Booth: A Memoir*, pp. 94–95.
15 *Ibid.*, p. 95.
16 Webb, *My Apprenticeship*, p. 214.

The essential conflict and inconsistency between Booth the businessman and Booth the humanitarian are everywhere in evidence: his willingness to take the long-run view of the depression was certainly in the best economic-liberal tradition:

Looked at from nearby, these cycles of depression have a distinctly harmful and even cruel aspect; from a more distant view, "afar from the sphere of our sorrow," they seem less malignant. They might then perhaps, with a little effort of the imagination, be considered as the orderly beating of a heart causing the blood to circulate—each throb a cycle. . . . There are some victims, but those who are able and willing to provide in times of prosperity for the lean years which seem inevitable to follow, do not suffer at all.[17]

Regardless of his interest in and sympathy with the trade union movement, he warned of the increased costs of production brought about by strikes and stoppages and noted that such costs must be paid for. Moreover, "their cost does not normally come out of profits, for it is necessarily taken into account in planning."[18] Further, he advocated "engagement by the minute," on the ground that any contract was "an interference dangerous to the freedom of the working man."

Indeed, his individualism was everywhere in evidence, for he located all action as issuing from the individual and as unrelated to the social order: "To talent, even of a humble description, a career always opens, and energy and enterprise find nowhere a better market than at home."[19] And, individual motivation was explicitly viewed in economic terms: ". . . in the daily guidance of the greater part of the activities of life, it is not easy to see how [the court of personal profit and loss] can be dispensed with or adequately replaced."[20] More than this, Booth's own success was sufficient to convince him of the correctness of his views, and he became seriously concerned about the "slow but continuous retreat of individualist forces before the annual increments of

17 *Charles Booth: A Memoir*, pp. 97–98.
18 *Ibid.*, p. 166.
19 *Ibid.*, pp. 99–100.
20 *Ibid.*, p. 102.

socialistic legislation and administration."[21] At the same time, he had become convinced that "the simple, warmhearted, and thoughtless benevolence of former ages" was neither respectable nor productive in the face of the changed conditions.

In the meantime, he had made the acquaintance of numerous figures in the movement to bring about reforms: Octavia Hill and C. S. Loch of the Charity Organization Society, founded in 1869, which represented an essentially traditional approach to the problem of "the poor";[22] C. S. Hyndman of the more radical Social Democratic Federation; and Canon Barnett, who founded Toynbee Hall in 1884 and believed that unregulated capitalism and landlordism were greater evils than unqualified charity.[23] As Booth's wife noted, in addition, "among his friends at this time were several working men of Socialist opinions, and two of these were invited to spend three evenings a week at his house for a sort of symposium."[24] Finally, as the Simeys report, Booth had developed the habit of exploring the East End, mingling with the people and becoming familiar with their life styles; he became practiced in the arts of participant observation and reporting.[25]

In the context of these acquaintanceships and activities Booth became convinced that something had to be done with respect to the problem of poverty. But who was to do it? And how? The arguments were many, and each thesis seemed to have a mutually exclusive character relative to the other concerning both the

21 Webb, *My Apprenticeship*, p. 184.

22 The "C.O.S." approach was based on the following principles, according to Beatrice Webb: ". . . patient personal service on the part of the well-to-do; and acceptance of personal responsibility for the ulterior consequences . . . of charitable assistance; and finally . . . the application of the scientific method to each separate case of a damaged body or lost soul." Webb, *My Apprenticeship*, pp. 189–200.

23 Toynbee Hall was the prototype of the "University Settlement" and, along with Oxford House which was founded in the same year, was based on the desire to increase the personal contacts between the educated minority in English society and the masses of East London. Both engaged in detailed programs of educational and social work.

24 *Charles Booth: A Memoir*, p. 15.

25 Simey, *Charles Booth, Social Scientist*, p. 65.

causes and cure of the social and economic plight of London's masses. Private charity was felt by some to be the only possible answer; others saw the solution in state aid. Improvidence, ignorance, overproduction, free trade, biology—all were variously held responsible for the awful situation by different groups and individuals.

The moral responsibility of the poor was continually reaffirmed by the attitudes of the aristocracy, the new industrial middle class, the general public, the philanthropic agencies, and, in the operation of the Poor Laws themselves, the state:

> . . . the condition of the pauper ought to be on the whole, less eligible than that of the independent laborer. Help to the poor should, moreover, be administered in the poorhouse on the basis of the "workhouse test," rather than being made available in private homes . . . the policy of public relief was made as unpleasant as possible.[26]

At the same time, more and more people in England (and Booth was now among them) felt that "the laws of economic liberalism should operate; grown men should make their own bargains; the state should refrain from grandmotherly legislation—but people should not live like that."[27]

In 1883, a Congregational clergyman, the Reverend Andrew Mearns, published a vivid tract, "The Bitter Cry of Outcast London," in which he described the sufferings of the poverty-stricken masses of the city's infamous East End. Picked up and published by the editor of the *Pall Mall Gazette,* it was one of a number of broadsides which shocked the middle and upper classes by emphasizing the extent and depth of poverty that existed in the area.

Booth listened to the myriad of views on the causes and cure of urban poverty and was understandably struck by their extravagant and conflicting claims. His experience in business and his familiarity with positivism, however, converged to suggest a way of service. In the former he had developed the habit of rational inquiry, for the demands of a far-flung, complex, and constantly

26 Lynd, *England in the Eighteen-Eighties*, pp. 87–88.
27 *Ibid.*, p. 144.

shifting trade had, from the very beginning, necessitated the collection of data for predicting trends as the basis of commercial decisions. In the latter, although he had given up positivism in its religious and utopian aspects, like many others of his era, he remained convinced that only "science," in the sense of disinterested and methodical investigation, could light the way in the face of the social chaos that threatened. Parenthetically, in 1885 Booth became a member of the Royal Statistical Society, a step which reveals in a more explicit fashion the direction of his thinking, for at this point the connotations of "statistics" were far more substantive than methodological. As one member of the society observed:

I speak of "statistical" in its higher sense, as designating the science which treats of "the Structure of Human Society," and which, whatever may be the objection of applying it to the technical, and, as interpreted by many whose opinion I respect, the somewhat exclusive term "science," I hold to be the highest and practically the most important branch of human secular knowledge.[28]

In businesslike and positivist fashion, therefore, Booth became interested in the notion of getting at what he saw as "the basic facts." Only these, he felt, could provide a solid substratum for valid theories and productive programs for social reform. As his wife wrote, he had serious reservations:

. . . whether any of the proposed remedies would be of much avail, doubting not only the soundness of the reasoning on which they were based, but still more uncertain as to whether the facts on which all must depend had been accurately ascertained.[29]

And, as Booth himself was to observe at the conclusion of his classic inquiry, "The root idea with which I began . . . was that every fact I needed to know was known to some one and that the information had simply to be collected and put together."[30]

28 Sir Rawson W. Rawson, "International Statistics; Illustrated by Vital Statistics of Europe and Some of the United States of America," *Journal of the Royal Statistical Society*, 48 (June, 1885): 505–95.

29 *Charles Booth: A Memoir*, p. 16.

30 Booth, *Life and Labour*, Final Volume, p. 30.

The returns from the 1881 census had become available in 1883 and, at one of the most active periods in his business affairs, Booth set out to analyze the occupational censuses of England from 1801 to 1881. A member of his own staff was put to work on the myriad of calculations involved. Beyond ascertaining the total number of people supported by each branch of industry, he hoped that the discovery of trends might be helpful not only in understanding the present but also in planning for the future. As he observed in the paper which he delivered to the Royal Statistical Society on completion of the project in June, 1886:

> My business . . . is to state the facts as given in the census returns, and these show us that in the last thirty years England has changed from a population about half agriculture and half manufacturing, to one in which Manufacturing is double of Agriculture, and we have no reason to suppose that the process of change in this direction is yet ended.[31]

On these grounds he concluded that the denunciation of landowners for driving the agricultural population from the soil was mistaken, for he found that the shift in employment had been "accompanied by an enormous increase in the total population, so that, altogether, support has been found during this period, in other ways than tilling the soil, for a new population of 8½ million souls. In this immense figure, those who have failed to obtain subsistence from Agriculture are completely swallowed up."[32]

Needless to say, this effort proved an excellent apprenticeship for his later work, for it provided him with useful contacts in the Registrar General's office as well as with some notion of the limitations and ambiguities of census materials. Indeed, beyond the substantive findings, one section of the paper was devoted to suggestions for improving census returns! Booth emphasized especially the comparative possibilities and the usefulness of including inquiries on special matters which might be of occasional importance:

31 Booth, "Occupations of the People of the United Kingdom, 1801–81," *Journal of the Royal Statistical Society*, 49 (June, 1886): 327.
32 *Ibid.*

It must not be forgotten that all census statistics carry really a twofold value, first for the picture they give of the existing state of things, and second, for the indication of the march of events which can be obtained by comparison with similar returns taken previously, or to be taken later.

If inquiries are made again and again, the first value may be forgotten; but it is that main staple of all new inquiries, and therefore room should be allowed in the system adopted for the treatment of special subjects.

Inquiries into special subjects, undertaken once for all, and never intended to be repeated, can claim and receive, a special amount of attention and, once made, would give light and life to the figures of every succeeding census.[33]

At this point, however, Booth was not only unfamiliar with census materials but also relatively unschooled in statistical procedures. Many of his assumptions were questioned by his audience. But, more than this, Booth came to feel that his findings were far too general to be of value for the kinds of questions to which he ultimately sought answers: "Who are the people of England? How do they really live? What do they really want?"[34]

The first clue to Booth's intention and motivation to pursue a different line of attack is found in the autobiography of H. M. Hyndman of the Social Democratic Federation. In the fall of 1885 the federation made public the results of a sample study it had conducted of the economic condition of people living in London's working-class districts. Specifically, it aimed at determining the proportion of workers who earned insufficient wages. Hyndman reported:

We arrived at the conclusion that no fewer than 25 percent of the workers of the Metropolis were in receipt of weekly wages upon which it was quite impossible for them to live . . . in such a wise as to keep themselves and their wives and children from slow but sure physical deterioration.[35]

33 *Ibid.*, p. 347.

34 *Charles Booth: A Memoir*, p. 14.

35 H. M. Hyndman, *The Record of an Adventurous Life* (New York: Macmillan Co., 1911), p. 303.

This was too much for Booth's essentially conservative point of view; he felt that the publication of such a figure was incendiary, and he sought an audience with Hyndman to tell him so. The latter recollected:

Mr. Booth was quite frank . . . he told me plainly that in his opinion we had grossly overstated the case . . . [and] that he himself intended to make, at his own expense, an elaborate inquiry into the condition of the workers of London: the wages they received and the amount of subsistence they could obtain for the money remuneration they were paid, he being quite certain he would prove us to be in the wrong.[36]

Beyond Booth's understandable desire to prove the Socialists wrong in their estimate of the extent of poverty in London, the urgency of some kind of action was further motivated by the run of events. As the Simeys note, the *Pall Mall Gazette* supported the federation's findings and published the results of a house-to-house survey of its own. "Shortly afterwards, rioting again broke out in the West End, and it was commonly rumored that the unemployed had been incited to these extremities by Hyndman in person."[37]

In any event, even while at work on his analysis of occupational trends, Booth had begun to think of a different type of study. In the first place, he was critical of the sampling approach of the federation's inquiry; in the second place, he had become increasingly sensitive to the limitations of a sheerly abstract, statistical approach. On these grounds, he decided on a study which would combine at once the qualities of both extensive, quantitative inquiry and intensive, qualitative investigation. As he wrote to Beatrice Potter, whom he had met through his wife and who was to become his "industrious apprentice,"

As to methods of inquiry, I think I should say that the statistical method was needed to give bearings to the results of personal observation and personal observation to give life to statistics. . . . It is this relative character, or the proportion of facts to each other, to us, to others, to society at large, and to possible remedies, that must be introduced if they are to be of any value at all in social diagnosis. Both

36 *Ibid.*, p. 303.
37 Simey, *Charles Booth, Social Scientist*, p. 69.

single facts, and strings of statistics *may* be true, and demonstrably true, and yet entirely misleading in the way they are used.[38]

Now he set out to enlist the support of his friends for mounting a study which would focus on the relationship between employment and poverty among London's working classes. Two abortive attempts were made to set up a "Board of Statistical Inquiry" in the spring of 1886. His own cryptic outline of purpose read as follows:

General Aim. To connect poverty and wellbeing with conditions of employment. *Incidentally,* to describe the industrial peculiarities of London (and of modern towns generally) both as to character of work, character of workers, and of the influences which act upon both.[39]

And Beatrice Webb recollected in her autobiography the following aim: ". . . to get a fair picture of the whole of London society: that is the four miles by district and employment, the two methods to be based on census returns.[40]

Among those who participated in these early discussions were Beatrice Webb, Maurice Paul (a medical student and the son of the publisher), Benjamin Jones (an official of a workingmen's cooperative), and the secretary of a trade society. Significantly, with the exception of Beatrice Webb, none of this group played a part in the final endeavor. While C. S. Loch of the Charity Organization Society was enthusiastic about the project, many of Booth's associates, Canon Barnett, for example, felt that it would be impossible to obtain the information required.

Typically, Booth was daunted neither by the difficulties nor the magnitude of the task he had set for himself, although he had no inkling of either the length of time or scope the inquiry would ultimately involve—his original plans called for only a three-year effort! Despite expressions of doubt by many of those close to him

38 Cited in Simey, *Charles Booth, Social Scientist*, p. 78.

39 *Ibid.*, p. 79.

40 Webb, *My Apprenticeship*, p. 277. The Simeys note that in Mrs. Webb's original manuscript, the reference was to "the 4,000,000" rather than to "the four miles." Cf. Simey, *Charles Booth, Social Scientist*, p. 75, n.2.

as well as the dispiriting flagging of interest on the part of many on whom he counted, Booth persevered.

Parenthetically, while the effort was a collective one from its inception, Booth (and, increasingly, his wife) planned and directed every aspect of the research, including the special inquiries. Together, they also edited every sentence that was written. Some idea of Booth's own conception of his role as director of the project is provided by an excerpt from a letter he wrote to one of his research "secretaries": "I accept most, but do not like the changes you suggest on page 430. I like it as I had it, and so it must remain. You have stuck gallantly to your point."[41]

Not until Booth returned from one of his New York trips in mid-summer, 1886, however, did the plan for research begin to take specific form. Convinced of the necessity of organizing the work under a single director if it was to have any cohesion, in executive fashion Booth proceeded to map out the research steps, to train a research staff, and constantly to monitor the work of his associates. Characteristically, these tasks did not in any way impinge on the pursuit of those aspects of the study which he assigned to himself.

Booth chose to begin the inquiry in London's infamous East End as a result of his observations during his evening walks; because of the general consensus that "it is supposed to contain the most destitute population in England, and to be, as it were, the focus of the problem of poverty in the midst of wealth";[42] and because it also contained large numbers of the so-called "respectable poor," which gave the area a representative quality. A single school board division, Tower Hamlets, which comprised five census registration districts or unions, with a population of approximately 450,000, was the specific area selected.

By a happy chance, the School Board Visitors had been sug-

41 *Charles Booth: A Memoir*, pp. 138–39. In the final edition of the inquiry, a total of twenty-one different individuals are noted as contributors on the frontispieces of the various volumes. Six of these, incidentally, were women.

42 Booth, "The Inhabitants of Tower Hamlets (School Board Division), their Condition and Occupations," *Journal of the Royal Statistical Society*, 50 (June, 1887): 374.

gested as a source of data. These functionaries were obligated to keep detailed records, based on continuous home visits, of every family with children of school age. And Booth devised a plan for what Beatrice Webb later termed, "the method of wholesale interviewing,"[43] which the Simeys have described as follows:

The School Board Visitors responded nobly, each of the thirty-four submitting to some twenty hours of cross-examination on the information recorded in their routine notebooks. In order to assure uniformity, Booth interviewed the first of these in company with Paul and Argyle, then the only workers in the Inquiry. After this, each continued to work separately, Booth taking his fair share of the work. In these interviews they discussed with individual Visitors every inhabitant of every house in every street of the district, verifying the facts by reference to the Visitor's daily records. As the interviews proceeded, the information secured was entered into forty-six small notebooks, prepared on an identical plan so that any one of the entries could be compared with any other. The name of the street was given at the head of each page; every house in it was noted and the occupants of each room were enumerated; particulars were recorded of the occupation, and probable income, of every inhabitant, together with the number of children in each family.[44]

Booth's position was clear:

It is the sense of helplessness that ties everyone. . . . From the helpless feelings spring socialistic theories, passionate suggestions of ignorance, setting at naught the nature of man and neglecting all the fundamental facts of human existence. . . . To relieve this sense of helplessness, the problems of human life must be better stated. The a priori reasoning of political economy . . . fails from want of reality. At its base are a series of assumptions very imperfectly connected with the observed facts of modern life. We need to begin with a true picture of the modern industrial organism.[45]

And the fine hand of Auguste Comte can be seen in Booth's pronouncement that: "I have no foregone conclusions, and it is

43 Webb, *My Apprenticeship*, p. 220. Mrs. Webb termed Booth's detailed survey of the physical and social environment which complimented the statistics of poverty, "Social Topography."

44 Simey, *Charles Booth, Social Scientist*, p. 87.

45 Booth, "Inhabitants of Tower Hamlets," p. 376.

rather in the method here employed, than to the results yet shown, that I pin my hopes."[46]

His plans prepared, on September 10, 1886, the work began.

Fruition

Seventeen years were to pass and seventeen volumes were to be published before the inquiry, so modestly and ingenuously begun, was to be completed.[47] The constant demands of Booth's business, which involved long absences on trips to the Liverpool and New York offices, no more than the wearing journey to work occasioned by the purchase of a summer home in Leicestershire, were ever to reduce his interest in and commitment to the project. Moreover, despite the fact that the endeavor was to make him a person of both national and even international reknown and to engage his energies in a wide variety of important public services and positions, these matters involved only his leisure time and remained in the realm of avocations. Only the week ends and evening hours were available for the pursuit of a task which grew to momentous proportions with the passing of time. For example, while commuting by train between London and Leicestershire, "his children recollect[ed] that he was sometimes mistaken for a retired grocer . . . by reason of the fact that in order to put the time thus spent to good use, he would perch a row of candle-ends along the carriage window-sill by which to read."[48] Finally, it is indicative of the mark of the man that, regardless of his dual devotion to his business affairs and to his beloved inquiry, by presence of self

46 *Ibid.*, p. 375.

47 See Booth, *Life and Labour of the People in London* (17 vols.; London: Macmillan & Co., 1902–3), in series as follows:

1st Series: "Poverty" (4 vols.; 1902), hereafter cited as "Poverty."

2nd Series: "Industry" (5 vols.; 1903), hereafter cited as "Industry."

3rd Series: "Religious Influences" (7 vols.; 1902–3), hereafter cited as "Religious Influences."

Final Volume: "Notes on Social Influences and Conclusions" (1903), hereafter cited as "Final Volume."

48 Simey, *Charles Booth, Social Scientist*, p. 98, n. 1.

and by constant and lively correspondence during his absences from his family, Booth was able to develop and maintain an abiding intimacy with his wife. Indeed, she became a silent partner (in the Victorian tradition) in all his affairs and often had the responsibility for seeing volumes through the press when he was abroad on business.

Initially, the work proceeded in rapid fashion, and by May of 1887 Booth was ready to present the results of his first investigation to the Royal Statistical Society. Although some of his assumptions, his statistical operations, and his dependence on the opinions of the School Board Visitors rather than on objective budget data were questioned by his audience, the general reaction (including that of the press) was encouraging enough for him to proceed.[49] The inquiry was extended to cover the remaining registration Districts in East London and, a year later, a second paper, incorporating the findings of the first and embracing a population of almost one million, was read to the membership of the society.[50]

Together these two preliminary papers outlined most of what was to follow, in both method and substance. On the one hand, they involved statistical analyses based on the materials supplied by the School Board Visitors. These data were used to cross-classify each family according to the dual scheme Booth and his associates had worked out to indicate the conditions of "life" and the conditions of "labour." The former (which was to become the basis of the inquiry focussed on poverty) was concerned with the "apparent means" of each family. And, the population was distributed among eight different classes ranging from A—"the lowest class," consisting of "some (so-called) labourers, loafers, semi-criminals . . . etc.," to class H—the "Upper Middle Class," defined as "the serv-

49 E.g., only about one-half to two-thirds of the population of the area was estimated to have been brought directly into the study, by virtue of the Visitors' contacts only with families with children of school age. On the basis of some very questionable assumptions, Booth corrected his figures to represent the total population.

50 Booth, "Condition and Occupations of the People of East London and Hackney, 1887," *Journal of the Royal Statistical Society*, 51 (June, 1888): 276–331.

ant keeping class." The latter, which adumbrated the industrial inquiry, was concerned with classifying each family by the "character of employment of the heads," in thirty-nine "sections" ranging from "loafers and casual laborers" (who constituted the first two sections) through "sub-professionals and Professionals" as well as a number of sections dealing with female heads of families.

On the other hand, each paper also included qualitative descriptions of the physical, social, and institutional topography of each of the districts as well as brief reports on a variety of special subjects (e.g., "Employment at the docks," "The 'Sweating' system and middle men," etc.) related to the life and problems of the area's residents. These efforts, of course, were a function of Booth's abiding concern to bring life and meaning into his abstract statistics. Their more qualitative nature foreshadowed his interest in factors outside of income, life style, and employment that bore on the problem of poverty and that were to be the focus of his third and final project—the inquiry into organized efforts, especially those of religious institutions, to deal with the urban poor.

Parenthetically, the second paper paid considerable attention to the location of the data in space: the concepts of "inner" and "outer" rings of the city were introduced, and a large-scale map of East London, in which each street was colored according to the predominant social condition ("class") of residents, was presented. Both these devices were to figure prominently in the completed inquiry.

Finally, although in his first paper Booth made no pretense either of addressing himself to the question of the causes of poverty or of being concerned with the development of proposals for social action, based on his facts, to deal with the problem, both these matters were explicitly dealt with in his second paper. An analysis of a sample of 4,000 cases of poverty suggested that "circumstances of employment" (especially irregular employment) rather than matters of habit and character were the major causes of poverty. And, Booth observed:

. . . I think that someday the individualist community on which we build our faith, will find itself obliged for its own sake to take charge of the lives of those who, from whatever cause, are incapable of independent existence up to the required standard, and will be fully able to do so.[51]

Further, he concluded:

Industry will not work without some unemployed margin . . . but the margin in London today seems to be exaggerated in every department, and enormously so in the lowest class of labour. Some employers seem to think that this state of things is in their interest . . . but this view appears to me to be shortsighted.[52]

These intimations of inroads in Booth's traditional economic-liberal perspective were undoubtedly the direct result of the most salient and shocking finding of these preliminary researches: that 35 per cent of East London's population were in the four lowest classes (A through D), below "the line of poverty" which he had operationally defined as "a fairly regular though bare income, such as 18*s* and 21*s* per week for a moderate family."[53]

They were not enough to satisfy Beatrice Potter, however, who had moved further to the left, become more interested in collective action than in investigation, and who, for these and personal reasons, broke both her intimate and working relationship with Booth at this time.

Now completely invested in the project and encouraged by the reactions of both the press and the public, Booth announced his intention of publishing his results and turned his attention to gathering data on the rest of the city. To save both time and

51 *Ibid.*, p. 299.

52 *Ibid.*, pp. 297–98.

53 The classes were defined as: A—the lowest class of occasional laborers, loafers, and semi-criminals; B—casual earnings—together "the very poor"; C—intermittent earnings and D—small regular earnings—together, "the poor." Incidentally, the Simeys regard Booth's invention of the concept of the poverty line as "perhaps his most striking single contribution to the Social Sciences." Cf., Simey, *Charles Booth, Social Scientist*, p. 88.

money, however, he decided to make the street rather than the family the unit of analysis, and the classification by employment was dropped.

In 1889 the first volume of what was later to be termed the "first" or "Poverty" series, which dealt with East London, came off the press. In less than two years a second volume, covering the rest of London, together with an appendix volume containing basic data and two magnificent maps appeared, the three sharing the title: *Labour and Life of the People*.[54]

The final substantive result—that 30.7 per cent of London's population was below the line of poverty, "at all times more or less in want"—made crystal clear the scale of the problem. Moreover, Booth's thinking beyond the facts to the problem of social action had, by this time, progressed to the point of offering a general plan for dealing with Class B—"the very poor"—which he came to regard as the heart of the problem:

> . . . in Class B, we have the crux of the social problem. Every other class takes care of itself, or could do so if Class B were out of the way. These unfortunate people form a sort of quagmire underlying the social structure, and to remove this quagmire must be our principal aim.[55]

> To bring Class B under state regulation would be to control the springs of pauperism; hence what I have to propose may be considered an extension of the Poor Law. What is the Poor Law system? It is a limited form of Socialism—a Socialistic community (aided from the outside) living in the midst of an Individualist nation . . . My idea is to make the dual system, Socialism in the arms of Individualism,

54 *Labour and Life of the People*, ed. Charles Booth (2 vols.; London: Williams & Norgate, 1889–91). The "Descriptive Map of London Poverty 1889" was scaled at twenty-five inches to the mile and measured sixteen feet by thirty feet. Every street was colored according to the apparent means of the inhabitants in terms of a seven-point color system. A second map, "Shewing Degrees of Poverty in London in areas with about 30,000 inhabitants in each," was colored according to a seven-point scale of percentage poverty. The Simeys note that the title has been reversed from the publication of the first volume because of copyright difficulties. Cf. Simey, *Charles Booth, Social Scientist*, p. 115.

55 "Poverty," I, 176.

under which we already live, more efficient by extending somewhat the sphere of the former and making the division of function more distinct. Our Individualism fails because our Socialism is incomplete. In taking charge of the lives of the incapable, State Socialism finds its proper work, and by doing it completely would relieve us of a serious danger. The Individualist system breaks down as things are, and is invaded on every side by Socialistic innovations, but its hardy doctrines would have a far better chance in a society purged of those who cannot stand alone. Though interference on the part of the State with the lives of a small fraction of the population would make it possible, ultimately, to dispense with any socialistic interference in the lives of all the rest.[56]

The practical implications of his position were spelled out in a manner which revealed his basically conservative assumptions:

. . . my idea is that these people should be allowed to live as families in industrial groups, planted wherever land and building materials were cheap; being well housed, well fed, and well warmed; and taught, trained, and employed from morning to night on work, indoors or out, for themselves or on Government account; in the building of their own dwellings, in the cultivation of the land, in the making of clothes, or in the making of furniture. That in exchange for the work done the Government should supply materials and whatever else was needed . . .

It is not possible that action of this kind could be rapid. To open a little the portals of the Poor Law or its administration making within its courts a working guild under suitable discipline; to check charitable gifts, except to those who from age or infirmity are unfit for any work; to insist upon sanitation and to suppress overcrowding; to await and watch the results, ready to push forward as occasion served —this is all that could be done. Much would be learnt from an experiment. It might be tried in some selected district. . . . Such an experiment is what I venture to suggest.

The good results to be hoped for from such an extension of "limited Socialism" as I have suggested would be manifold. Class A, no longer confounded with "the unemployed," could be gradually harried out of existence. The present class B would be cared for, and its children given fair chances. The change would only come in a

56 *Ibid.*, pp. 166–67.

very gradual way; a part, sharing the improved chances of classes C and D, would be pushed upward into self-supporting habits, and another part, failing to keep itself even when helped by the State, would pass into the ranks of paupers, so that the total numbers to whom the proposed State organization would ultimately apply would be very much less than the present numbers of class B. Class C would then have more work, class D more pay, and both be able to build from the bottom, instead of floating, as now, on the top of their world. Great friendly societies might hope to include the mass of the population in their beneficient net. Improved *morale* of labour would go hand in hand with better organization of industry. The whole standard of life would rise, and with its rise the population difficulties, whether of internal increase or of immigration, would become more manageable.[57]

Even before the appearance of the first edition of the "Poverty" inquiry, work was begun on two new lines of investigation: in the first place, Booth was already planning his research into the conditions of work, which was to result in the second series on "Industry." And, in this connection, he served as a consultant to the Registrar General in the preparation of the schedules for the 1891 census. Indeed, he was able to prevail upon the authorities to include a special set of questions, on the number of persons per room and the number of servants employed, which became the basis of a new social classification of the people. Moreover, he personally instructed the 3,000 enumerators in order to maximize the validity and reliability of the results of these queries. In the second place, his data had suggested to him the special relationship that old age bore to the problem of poverty, and he turned the efforts of a part of his staff to a study of pauperism in two selected registration districts.

Booth reported the results of this latter investigation in a paper delivered to the Royal Statistical Society in December, 1891.[58] Significantly, apart from the factual demonstration that "sickness and old age are causes [of poverty] so overwhelming

57 *Ibid.*, pp. 168–69.

58 Booth, "Enumeration and Classification of Paupers and State Pensions for the Aged," *Journal of the Royal Statistical Society*, 54 (December, 1891): 600–643.

and obvious, as to draw a curtain over what has gone on before,"[59] his thinking had proceeded to the point of proposing non-contributory state pensions for the aged. As his wife noted in her *Memoir*, the opposition that greeted this suggestion was so general and so intense that a second meeting on the subject was held so that "all might have their say against it."[60] Later, Beatrice Webb was to observe in her autobiography:

It is surely significant that this wealthy captain of industry at this time Conservative in politics and strongly anti-socialist in temper and economic views, should have come out of his prolonged study with proposals the very reverse of the individualist.[61]

On the other hand, as his wife pointed out:

That the measure had a touch of socialism cannot be doubted . . . [but] . . . Charles Booth was not frightened by words. Labels and creeds meant little to him. He held aloof from political party and from any definite religious system, not from any contrariness, but because he found much to sympathize with in many forms of thought and methods of government, and too much to wish differently in nearly all to be willing to attach himself irrevocably to any.[62]

Armed with his new "facts," Booth characteristically plowed ahead with his proposal by taking time out from both his business affairs and the trades inquiry to write and publish a broadside, *Pauperism, a Picture, and the Endowment of Old Age, an Argument*, which appeared in 1892. His interest in the reform of the Poor Law and his commitment to the establishment of old-age pensions were to become lifelong and involved a paper on the statistics of pauperism among the aged in 1894, as well as two more volumes and three more broadsides addressed to the problem and the proposal between 1894 and 1911.[63]

59 *Ibid.*, p. 610.

60 *Charles Booth: A Memoir*, p. 23.

61 Webb., *My Apprenticeship*, p. 245.

62 *Charles Booth: A Memoir*, pp. 25–26.

63 Booth, "Statistics of Pauperism in Old Age," *Journal of the Royal Statistical Society*," 57 (June, 1894): 235–45; *The Aged Poor in England and Wales: Condition* (London: Macmillan & Co., 1894); *Old*

So successful was the first edition of the "Poverty" series that it was soon out of print. Public as well as professional recognition began to come Booth's way: his success as a researcher led to his election to the presidency of the Royal Statistical Society in 1892, and the society presented him with its Guy Medal for his statistical work. At the same time, his involvement in the problem of the aged poor resulted in his appointment as a member of a Royal Commission on the Aged Poor on which he served with distinction (despite its failure to agree) until 1895. During this period he was also elected a vice president of the Economic Section of the British Association and, in typical Booth style, "led a delegation to the President of the Board of Trade to press for the establishment of a permanent statistical organization and the taking of a quinquennial Census.[64]

Another portent of things to come was contained in his first presidential address to the Royal Statistical Society in 1892.[65] His topic was dock labour, a subject which had interested him from the very beginning of his East London experiences, and he chose to address himself primarily to the changes that had occurred since his 1887 investigation. It was the first time Booth explicitly extended his interest from "things as they are," to a comparative concern with "things as they tend." Indeed, as will be seen, many of the major qualities (as well as some of the major defects) of the inquiry stem from the fact that it covered a considerable span of time, with the result that questions concerning change and process were inevitably raised as the work progressed.

Between 1892 and 1893 a second edition of the "Poverty" study was published, in four volumes, and the established character of the research effort was confirmed by the removal of the

---

Age Pensions and the Aged Poor: A Proposal (London: Macmillan & Co., 1899); *Poor Law Reform* (1910); *Reform of the Poor Law by the Adaptation of the Existing Poor Law Areas, and Their Administration* (1910); and *Comments on Proposals for the Reform of the Poor Laws*, with note by Sir Arthur Downes (1911).

64 Simey, *Charles Booth, Social Scientist*, pp. 117–18.

65 Booth, "Dock and Wharf Labour," *Journal of the Royal Statistical Society*, 55 (December, 1892): 521–27.

operations from the London office of Booth's firm to the premises of the Royal Statistical Society.[66] Despite the energies expended in editing the new edition and in the study of the aged poor, work proceeded on the new inquiry into the conditions of labour. In November of 1893, Booth's second presidential address reported the results of his reclassification of the people in London based on the special questions which had been incorporated into the 1891 census.[67]

His paper included an ambitious but rather ingenuous attempt to interrelate poverty, crowding, early marriages, surplus of unmarried men, high birth rate, and high death rate by means of both a combined rank-order and a graphic representation based on data from London's thirty registration districts.[68] In addition, an intimation of what were to be the contents and modes of analysis in the "Industry" series was communicated by including a comparative analysis of two groups of trades—those connected with the manufacture of chemicals and those involved in the manufacture of soap, candles, glue, etc.

This preliminary report was remarkable, however, for the essential agreement of the results with those of his previous inquiry into the percentage of London's population found to be below the line of poverty. Based on the School Board Visitors' reports, the "Poverty" inquiry had discovered that 30.1 per cent of the population were "poor" or "very poor." His new research, which employed crowding and the number of servants as measures of social condition, showed that 31.5 per cent of the city's population was below the line of poverty.[69] As one of his listeners was moved to remark in the discussion that followed:

66 The second edition was also to include the five volumes of the second "Industry" series.

67 Booth, "Life and Labour of the People in London: First Results of an Inquiry Based on the 1891 Census," *Journal of the Royal Statistical Society*, 56 (December, 1893): 557–93.

68 Booth's growing methodological sophistication is indicated by his decision to combine three of the districts on the grounds of their small size and geographical contiguity. *Ibid.*, p. 572.

69 "The method which I have adopted for restating the facts . . . is as follows: So far as the population are living in less than five rooms

Mr. Booth had shown that certain census results, as regards the rooms, did in the main bear out his former conclusions, even more so than could have been expected. He had been, at first extremely sceptical as to Mr. Booth's line of inquiry, but he was now thoroughly convinced, and was gratified to find that Mr. Booth had succeeded so admirably.[70]

While Booth was aware of the limitations and ambiguities of his new measure of social condition, observing that "living in close quarters is no certain test of poverty, and we shall find accordingly that while some districts are more crowded than they are poor, others are more poor than they are crowded,"[71] his paper was also remarkable for his explicit recognition of the implications of his approach for the general study of human society and of the role of the census in such endeavors:

The plan of recording in connection with census enumeration some simple facts by which the position and manner of life of each family could be measured, seems to me to render possible comparisons of great social interest, and to open up a large field of inquiry into the actual structure of society. The facts which I have used to classify the inhabitants of London could be applied to any city—to Paris or Moscow, New York or Melbourne, Calcutta or Hong Kong; and for that matter would have served equally well in ancient Rome or Babylon. . . . I do not mean that the suggested method as now crudely laid before you could do all this. It would need to be improved and perfected by alterations and additions specially adapted to whatever object was in view.

The comparisons to be made will always be of a more general character as between country and country, and more minute as between different places in the same country or different sections of the

---

per family, the classification is based on the number of persons to each room; so far as they are employers of domestic servants, the classification rests on the number of persons served to each servant; while those who live in five or more rooms, but keep no servants, form a central class." *Ibid.*, p. 559.

70 *Ibid.*, p. 595. Unfortunately, Booth was ill and could not participate in the discussion. His paper was read by his private secretary, Jesse Argyle, who played an increasingly important role in the inquiry.

71 *Ibid.*, p. 566.

same town, but in all of them the intensive method of investigation should go hand in hand with the extensive. . . . For instance, only when we know the manner of life of the people employed in any particular trade, and the scale of earnings which in any selected district is usually connected with such a style of life, can we enjoy the full benefit of such work as that of Mons. *(sic)* Le Play and his followers. Without such general knowledge we cannot tell whether the example given is truly typical or in what respects it diverges from a true type.[72]

Between 1895 and 1897 Booth and his staff were engaged in the analysis of the materials which the "Industry" series comprised. Two volumes appeared in 1895, two more the following year, and the final volume, entitled *Comparisons, Survey, and Conclusions,* was published in 1897. Although Booth was clear in his own mind as to the general aim of the series: ". . . to review the people as they work, trade by trade, in their factories, warehouses, or shops, or pursue their avocations in the streets or on the railways, in the markets or on the quays; to consider their relations to those whom they serve, whether employer or customer, and the remuneration they receive; and finally, to examine the bearing which the money earned has on the life they lead";[73] and while the analysis of each of the seventeen general types of employment and of the eighty-nine specific occupations was carried out in terms of a standardized framework, the reception accorded the completed research hardly compared with that given to the "Poverty" series. In part, of course, the subject and the problems were less dramatic. More important, Booth's lack of formal training proved to be a formidable handicap when it came to dealing with the complexities of industrial life: the empirical forest was too strewn with thickets of facts for his primitive analytic tools to clear a path. Finally, the subject matter was such as to provide a maximum threat to Booth's own preconceptions. As a result, the Simeys note:

His intention had been to examine industry with a view to throwing light on the vexed question of the cause of poverty; what emerged was a testament of his faith in capitalist enterprise. The concluding volume

72 *Ibid.*, pp. 590–91.
73 "Industry," IX, 159.

constituted, in effect, a self-portrait of the Economic Man in terms of what he saw and how he saw it in the world about him. The steadfastness of his faith in competitive individualism extended over every page.[74]

Nevertheless, Booth remained true to his basic methodological prescription, providing objective statistical summaries based on census data, complemented by vivid qualitative descriptions based on detailed, special inquiries into the organization and processes, both human and material, of every London trade. Further, despite the defects of the effort, Booth was once more a generation ahead of his time: in fact, he and his associates had produced materials of a type not to be seen again until the rise of an academic interest in what was first to be known as "human relations in industry" and later, in more general terms, as "the sociology of industry."[75] Parenthetically, Booth received his first academic recognition in 1898, in the form of an honorary degree from Cambridge, where his volumes in the "Industry" series were being used as textbooks.

Having considered the conditions of life and work, however imperfectly he had connected the two, Booth pointed the way to his next endeavor in the final volume of the "Industry" series:

> Still this does not conclude the work, but what remains to be done is of a different character, being to estimate the forces for good or evil that are acting upon the condition of the population before we can arrive at that balancing of hopes and fear that will form our final judgment.[76]

For he had concluded, in considering the problem of poverty, which remained the focus of his concern:

> It is to other quite as much as to industrial remedies that we must look for the cure or relief of poverty. We have to consider what the State or private effort does or might do in London for the young and for the old, for the morally weak and for the sick, as well as for the

74 Simey, *Charles Booth, Social Scientist*, p. 131.

75 The first textbook in this area did not appear until 1951: See D. C. Miller and W. H. Form, *Industrial Sociology* (New York: Harper & Bros., 1951).

76 "Industry," V, *x*.

unemployed; and what religion and philanthropy are doing or might do to form public opinion, to supplement or modify the influence of legislation, and to disseminate wholesome views of human life; or what other action, public or private, may assist in eradicating the causes or softening the hardships of poverty.[77]

Booth turned immediately to planning what was to be the final series. And for the next six years his energies were engaged in carrying out the momentous tasks not only of collecting materials and writing up his analyses of the nature and impact of religious and other efforts to deal with the problem of the urban poor but also in completely revising "the Poverty Map of 1889." The latter task involved a systematic re-visiting of "every street, court, and alley." His general approach was explicitly noted in the "Introduction" to the new series:

Our plan of action may be likened to a voyage of discovery. We have moved our camp from centre to centre all over London, remaining for weeks or even months in each spot in order to see as well as to hear all we could. Spiritual influences do not lend themselves readily to statistical treatment, and we have not attempted it. The subject is one in which figures may be easily pressed too far, and if trusted too much are likely to be more than usually dangerous. Our object, rather, has been to obtain truthful and trustworthy impressions, which we might hope to be able to transmit to our readers, of whom, though many would know accurately some part, few can have surveyed the whole field.

In forming our impressions we have neglected no means open to us of giving them a sufficiently wide base. We have endeavored to see, and with comparatively few exceptions have seen, all the responsible heads of Churches of whatever denomination. The account of their work, its successes and failures, forming the basis and material of this work, is contained in written reports of nearly 1800 personal interviews, of which 1450 were with the direct representatives of religious work and nearly 350 with other authorities.[78]

Characteristically, none of these time-consuming tasks was sufficient to exhaust Booth's seemingly endless capacities: he con-

77 *Ibid.*, p. 318.
78 "Religious Influences," I, 7.

tinued to engage himself in the battle for state pensions for the aged; further, he developed a special interest in the problem of urban transportation, his studies having convinced him that in this direction lay at least a partial solution to the pressure of housing in the central city. In the very midst of his work on the final series of the inquiry, he not only published a third treatise on the subject of state pensions for the aged but became engaged in a more direct attempt to influence public opinion:

After its [*Old Age Pensions and the Aged Poor, A Proposal*] publication, Booth was invited to address a conference on the subject at Browning Hall. It is a tribute to the sincerity with which he stated his case that the outcome was a series of meetings in support of a universal pensions scheme, organized in seven provincial cities by local working-class organizations, at all of which he was the principal speaker.[79]

In addition, in 1901, he played an active role in the movement dealing with the problem of urban transportation by presenting his views at another Browning Hall conference, presiding over a second on the subject, and, as usual, detailing a member of his own staff to gather relevant data. In this instance, a large-scale map of all transportation facilities was drawn up to serve as an empirical basis for discussion. His position in the treatise he published at this time was, as the Simeys note, another example of the interaction of "the facts" with his own ideology, leading to a "limited socialistic" solution: while he was not in favor of public funds for housing, his proposal did involve such funds and authority for the creation and management of urban transportation facilities.[80]

Between 1902 and 1903 the inquiry came to an end, marked by the appearance of the seven volumes constituting the final series, including a "Summary" volume and a seventeenth, "Notes on Social Influences and Conclusion," which essayed the difficult

79 Simey, *Charles Booth, Social Scientist,* p. 168. "My proposal is . . . simply that all old people should receive an allowance of 5*s* a week after 65, and that the money should be raised year by year by suitable taxation." Draft letter to an editor, cited by Simey, p. 169.

80 *Ibid.*, p. 170.

task of summarizing the entire work. All were published as a final third edition that included revisions of the poverty materials as well as of the "Industry" series volumes.

In a very real sense, the third series was mistitled, for, despite the focus on "religious influences," Booth and his staff ranged far and wide on the assumption that,

> . . . just as life day by day is conditioned by the character of the home, the opportunities of education or recreation and the chances of employment, so there are other social influences which form part of the very structure of life, and some account of them is necessary to complete the picture of things as they are.[81]

Thus, as the religious communities were described (and especially their charitable and specifically religious efforts evaluated on the basis of the opinions of those engaged in the work), area by area and denomination by denomination, inquiries were also made into the influences of local government, the police, crime, health, housing, and drink, as well as of marriage and thrift. In fact, the series was shot through with the kind of sociological insights so characteristic of the "Poverty" series. Moreover, since these studies came at the end of the period of investigation, these volumes, especially, abounded with explicit references to changes observed and general processes revealed. Even Booth himself was moved to observe:

> I have reached the point at which my study of London began fifteen years ago, and in this final review am able to note the changes that have taken place under my own observations.[82]

As usual, Booth courageously went where his facts led, and his conclusions regarding both the style and efficacy of the efforts of the various religious groups to minister either to the religious or material needs of the poor were, for the most part, critical and negative. In regard to the first, and even more generally, he concluded:

> It is this, perhaps, normal condition of diffused religion that we have to reckon with in London. There are those who look for a great revival

81 "Religious Influences," I, 4.
82 *Ibid.*, II, 3.

. . . their faith demands it; and none can say from what quarter such a movement might come, or to what class it might appeal, or what shape it might take. But at present there is no sign of it. . . .[83]

As for the well-meaning attempts of the various religious bodies to serve London's poor:

There is, no doubt, a real difficulty in squaring the teaching we find in many passages in the Bible with the practical rules of action now laid down, not by the Charity Organization Society alone, but by all serious thinkers, including the leading representatives of every religious community in London, Jew or Christian, Roman Catholic or Protestant, Established or Non-conformist, Trinitarian or Unitarian. All practically admit the impossibility of acting upon the Gospel precepts, as does the whole of Christendom, with the possible exception of some sects in Russia. But by all the difficulty is evaded rather than met.[84]

Booth found himself hard put to write what his wife referred to as the "Star Volume," which would provide a cogent summary of the inquiry. To be sure, that the inquiry had a history was responsible for many of its qualities; on the other hand, its developmental character just as surely led to perhaps its greatest defect on completion—an aura of hodgepodge. As Ruth Glass has discerningly observed about the sometimes inconsistent and confusing quality of Booth's data:

Booth was so ardent an empiricist that in the pursuit of facts, his appetite grew with what it fed on, and the meal tended to become indigestible. . . . As one section of his inquiry came to an end, he saw the need for the next section, and then became so involved in it, that it grew much longer than he had anticipated. As he did not start his investigation in order to test any particular assumption or theory . . . he found it difficult to stop.[85]

Nevertheless, in the "Final Volume" Booth made a game attempt to review his early data by means of a statistical and graphic analysis of the interrelationships among poverty, crowd-

83 *Ibid.*, VII, 432.
84 *Ibid.*, p. 413.
85 Glass, "Urban Sociology in Great Britain," p. 46.

ing, birth rates, and death rates. However dated in comparison to modern methodologies, his "Index Map of London," which involved the coloring of fifty districts "according to their comparative Social Condition," provided dramatic evidence of the growth of his own analytic powers. Fully half of the book is a cryptic, detailed, small-print summary of the contents of each volume, while the remainder presents a series of brief but perceptive descriptive essays dealing with "Habits of the People." He hoped that these might "serve to reflect some light on the subjects treated in the preceding volumes."[86] He modestly admitted the many gaps in the inquiry—"that some subjects [e.g., "London Life of Art and Literature"] of extreme importance in connection with the life of London are hardly mentioned at all."[87] And his final conclusion was factual, candid, modest, and hopeful:

> The last word I would add is this: the object of the sixteen volumes has been to describe London as it appeared in the last decade of the nineteenth century. Beyond this I have sought, however imperfectly, to show what is being done to ameliorate its conditions, and have suggested some directions in which advance might be made; but this last was no part of the original design, which was, solely, to observe and chronicle the actual, leaving remedies to others. To this attitude I would now revert. For the treatment of disease, it is first necessary to establish the facts as to its character, extent and symptoms. Perhaps the qualities of mind which enable a man to make this inquiry are the least of all likely to give him that elevation of soul, sympathetic insight, and sublime confidence which must go to the making of a great regenerating teacher. I have made no attempt to teach; at the most I have ventured on an appeal to those whose part it is. Some individual views and convictions have been intentionally allowed to show themselves here and there in comments made, but no body of doctrine is submitted.
>
> The dry bones that lie scattered over the long valley that we have traversed together lie before my reader. May some great soul, master of a subtler and nobler alchemy than mine, disentangle the confused issues, reconcile the apparent contradictions in aim, melt and commingle the various influences for good into one divine uniformity of

86 "Final Volume," p. 41.
87 *Ibid.*, p. 214.

effort, and make these dry bones live, so that the streets of our Jerusalem may sing with joy.[88]

Final Chapter

Even as the last volumes dealing with religious influences were being prepared for publication, Booth's business obligations claimed his presence in America. And business problems in the face of an economic decline were his primary (and pleasant) concern after the final volume was edited. Indeed, nothing indicates more the fundamentally avocational nature of his social research efforts than the dispersal of his new well-trained staff at the conclusion of the inquiry.[89] Nevertheless, despite the continuing pressures of both his business affairs and his bouts with ill health, Booth continued to be active in his roles of public servant and commentator on public issues and, as was his due, he was the recipient of numerous public honors.

By far the greatest of the latter was a privy councillorship, which the Simeys note was accepted after "discreet approaches were made to discover his preference as between a knighthood and a privy councillorship."[90] This recognition was followed by another academic honorary degree, this time from Oxford, in 1904.

Between 1903 and 1908, service on numerous committees and commissions concerned with post office wages, the tariff, and the Poor Laws, consumed much of Booth's leisure time. The

88 *Ibid.*, pp. 215–16.

89 Significantly, leading members of his research staff were able to move on "to posts of responsibility in which several of them achieved considerable reputation." See Simey, *Charles Booth, Social Scientist*, p. 173, n. 1. Not the least of these was Sir Hubert Llewellyn-Smith, who, in addition to serving as Permanent Secretary of the Board of Trade and as chief economic adviser to the Government, directed the "New Survey of London Life and Labour" which was undertaken by the London School of Economics and Political Science in 1928.

90 *Ibid.*, n. 2. The choice, incidentally, recalled an earlier day when a friend, one of the younger Holts, had been gazetted a baronet against his will because his facetious refusal of the honor was interpreted as an acceptance. See Webb, *My Apprenticeship*, p. 211.

victory of the Liberal Party in 1906 saw the principle of state pensions for the aged, for which he had worked so long and hard, established. And it must have been with considerable satisfaction that he viewed the institution of such a program under law, in 1909. On the other hand, Booth probably felt a good deal of sorrow—the Simeys hint at bitterness—over events connected with his appointment to a second Royal Commission on the Poor Laws, on which he served with his old comrade in "social diagnosis," Beatrice Webb.

By now his formal political loyalties were Conservative, his "limited Socialism" approach was dated, and his devotion to individualism was ideological. The result was much dissension in the commission's deliberations. Although he resigned his appointment in 1908, Booth continued to take part in the public discussion of the issue: as president of a conference on the Poor Law in 1912, he presented three papers, previously published, which sought reforms only in terms of traditional economic-liberal assumptions.[91] His last publication, *Industrial Unrest and Trade Union Policy* (1913), while sympathetic to the cause of organized labor, castigated the trade unions for their narrow and unproductive economic concerns with wages and hours: "Their economic failure . . . has marred their political and social success."[92]

Booth died at his summer home—*Gracedieu*—in November, 1916. And it was not until after the war that he and his monumental inquiry received their final public recognition: a tablet to his memory in St. Paul's Cathedral, unveiled by Sir Austen Chamberlain at a Memorial Service; members of his family reconstructed a portion of the old University Settlement House, Toynbee Hall, renaming the unit "Charles Booth House"; and his friends and admirers established a Charles Booth Lectureship at the University of Liverpool, where his own firm endowed a Charles Booth chair of Social Science.[93]

However much Booth's liberal views were adulterated dur-

91 See n. 63 above.

92 Booth, *Industrial Unrest and Trade Union Policy* (London: Macmillan & Co., 1913), p. 5.

93 Simey, *Charles Booth, Social Scientist*, p. 177.

ing the last years of his life by his growing conservatism, his work was clearly a major influence on public opinion, preparing the way for what was to become "the welfare state" of the twentieth century. More relevant for present purposes, however, was the role of his inquiry in the development of empirical social science research, a question which will be considered after a brief survey of its scope, organization, and content.

2

SCOPE, ORGANIZATION, AND CONTENT OF THE INQUIRY

THE MOST STRIKING QUALITY of the inquiry is, of course, its amazing scope, which is uniquely accompanied by intensive analyses of a wide variety of specific aspects of city life and of the life of the poor. In spite of the difficulties of providing a bird's-eye view, the task is facilitated by the existence of two pervasive organizing principles: on the one hand, the analysis implicitly proceeded in terms of "class," "space," and "time" as basic points of reference; on the other hand, there were explicit substantive divisions of "poverty," "industry," and "religious influences."

As previously noted, Booth divided the population of London into a number of different classes on the basis of three separate investigations, each employing a different set of criteria and source of data. The first involved the reports of the School Board Visitors; the second was based on the judgments of school teachers; and the third was based on materials from the 1891 census. Regardless of the topic considered—style of life, occupation and earnings, or religion—the findings were related to these classifications of "social condition." In the second place, each aspect of the life of the people was invariably located in space on a reportorial basis; often, too, the distribution was spotted on a map of the city. Incidentally, the spatial dimension was generally responsible for the orders of presentation of the materials in both the "Poverty" and "Religious Influences" series. Apropos of this dimension, Booth marked off the city into various areas and considered them both separately and comparatively with respect to their institutional as well as their demographic characteristics. Finally, there was the temporal dimension of the survey, an unplanned but no less important by-product involving explicit reference to the changes which had taken place during the fifteen years of research: descriptive accounts of general processes, as well as hypotheses in regard to the forces at work.

Altogether, Booth presented a documented and detailed picture of the "life" and "labour" of fully 80 per cent of the people in London. While few data or descriptive materials referred to the wealthy "upper class" and "nobility," especially in regard to the more intimate aspects of their life styles, the picture on the demographic level was complete for the entire city of four million. Indeed, one of the abiding charms of the inquiry is the fact that it remains the *only* detailed empirical study of the social structure of a large city available to sociologists.

The Poverty Series

Even in the final edition, Booth did little to compensate for the *ad hoc* development of the materials contained in the "Poverty" series. Since it was the first, it understandably involved numerous partial and sometimes ultimately false starts which, while they served as admirable preparations for much of what was to come, make the task of portraying the plan and content of the four volumes a difficult one. Rather than essay a volume-by-volume presentation, the series will be treated as a whole.

UNITS OF ANALYSIS As previously noted, although Booth began his study in East London using *the family* as the unit of investigation, this was changed in the remainder of the inquiry to *the street.* This step, along with the decision to defer the classification by employment, was admittedly unfortunate, but necessary:

> Instead of noting the number of children going to school from each household with the employment and social position of its head, we have contented ourselves with stating the number of children street by street, dividing them as to class according to what is known of the parents, but giving only general particulars of the occupations. The result is that the division of the population according to the conditions under which they live has been maintained, but that according to employment has been dropped. It is no improvement, but . . . necessary.[1]

1 "Poverty Series," II, 1.

SOURCES OF DATA Given the pioneering nature of the task Booth defined for himself, two of the most modern aspects of the inquiry were the imagination employed in obtaining "the facts" and the magnitude of the efforts made in exploiting novel sources of information. The two major sources of data were, of course, the School Board Visitors and the 1881 census. As Booth observed concerning the former:

The School Board Visitors perform amongst them a house-to-house visitation; every house in every street is in their books, and details are given of every family with children of school age. They begin their scheduling two or three years before the children attain school age, and a record remains in their books of the children who have left school. The occupation of the head of the family is noted down. Most of the visitors have been working in the same district for several years, and thus have an extensive knowledge of the people. It is their business to re-schedule for the Board once a year, but intermediate revisions are made in addition, and it is their duty to make themselves acquainted so far as possible, with the newcomers into their districts. They are in daily contact with the people and have a very considerable knowledge of the parents of the school children, especially of the poorest among them, and of the conditions under which they live.[2]

Other sources included a variety of official functionaries—the school divisional committees, the relieving officers, the district superintendents, the police, the clergy, etc. In addition, a special inquiry was made into "London School Children" in which the school teachers were called upon to make judgments of the children taught in terms of Booth's lettered classes. Parenthetically, this effort provided Booth with his first comparative check on the amount of poverty in the city.

Finally, Booth and his staff also engaged in an increasing amount of participant observation as the work progressed. This method was employed with certain reservations at the beginning of the research:

At the outset we shut our eyes, fearing lest any prejudice of our own should colour the information we received. It was not until the books were finished that I or my associates ourselves visited the streets

2 *Ibid.*, I, 5.

amongst which we had been living in our imagination. But later we gained confidence and made it a rule to see each street ourselves at the time we received the visitors' account of it. With the insides of the houses and their inmates there was no attempt to meddle. To have done so would have been an unwarrantable impertinence.[3]

On the other hand, such inhibitions were later shelved in the interest of obtaining more relevant and intimate data on the ways of life of the working classes. And Booth remarked at the close of the series:

For three separate periods I have taken up quarters, each time for several weeks, where I was not known, and as a lodger have shared the lives of the people. . . . Being more or less boarded as well as lodged, I became intimately acquainted with some of those I met, and the lives and habits of many others came naturally under observation. My object, which I trust was a fair one, was never suspected, my position never questioned.[4]

CLASSIFICATION OF THE POPULATION The classification of the people in London according to "social condition" was, of course, the major axis about which the entire inquiry revolved. Since the ultimate aim was to distinguish between those living "in poverty" and those living "in comfort," the analytic categories were oriented primarily to economic considerations. At the same time, because the method employed was formally indirect, depending on the judgments of both the Visitors and Booth's staff, other

3 *Ibid.*, p. 25.

4 *Ibid.*, p. 158. The Simeys comment on the "striking picture of ease with which this wealthy stranger was able to slip into the ways of the various households in which he stayed, eating with genuine pleasure the coarse porridge and thick bread and butter set before him, enjoying the run of the house, and in the evenings sitting comfortably by the fire to write up his diary till the return of the family brought supper, the passing round of the common mug of beer, and general conversation. . . . Though he did not reveal his identity to the people with whom he thus came into contact, Booth made absolutely no attempt to disguise himself. 'If you want to conceal yourself, you must be yourself' was his policy, and the unquestioning ease with which his fellow lodgers accepted the fact that he went out to his place of work as they did to theirs is proof of its validity." Simey, *Charles Booth, Social Scientist*, pp. 104–5.

criteria entered in which allowed even Booth to speak of "social position" from time to time. Indeed, Booth made it clear not only that the lines between his classes were indistinct but also that the "classes" were not all homogeneous in the "social" sense, there being several "social grades" within a single class. These lettered classes were defined as follows:

A. the lowest class of occasional labourers, loafers, and semi-criminals
B. casual earnings—"very poor"
C. intermittent earnings } together the "poor"
D. small regular earnings }
E. regular standard earnings—above the line of poverty
F. higher class labour
G. lower middle class
H. upper middle class[5]

While these lettered divisions figured throughout the inquiry, Booth collapsed the descriptive categories when the study was extended to the rest of the city, as follows:

A. the lowest class—occasional labourers, loafers and semi-criminals
B. the very poor—casual labour, hand-to-mouth existence, chronic want
C. and D.—the Poor—including alike those whose earnings are small, because of irregularity of employment, and those whose work, though regular, is ill-paid
E. and F.—the regularly employed and fairly paid working class of all grades
G. and H.—lower and upper middle class and all above this level[6]

The division between the "poor" and the "very poor" was also necessarily arbitrary. The former were defined as all those having an income of from 18*s* to 21*s* per week "for a moderate family," and Booth noted:

My "poor" may be described as living under a struggle to obtain the necessaries of life and make both ends meet; while the "very poor" live in a state of chronic want . . . my first business is simply with the

5 *Ibid.*, I, 33.
6 *Ibid.*, II, 20.

numbers who, from whatever cause, do live under conditions of poverty or destitution.[7]

The final results of the analysis of the city's population according to social condition, in terms of Booth's lettered scheme of classes appears in Table 1.

TABLE 1. *Statistics of Poverty: Final Results of the Classification of the Population by Social Condition*

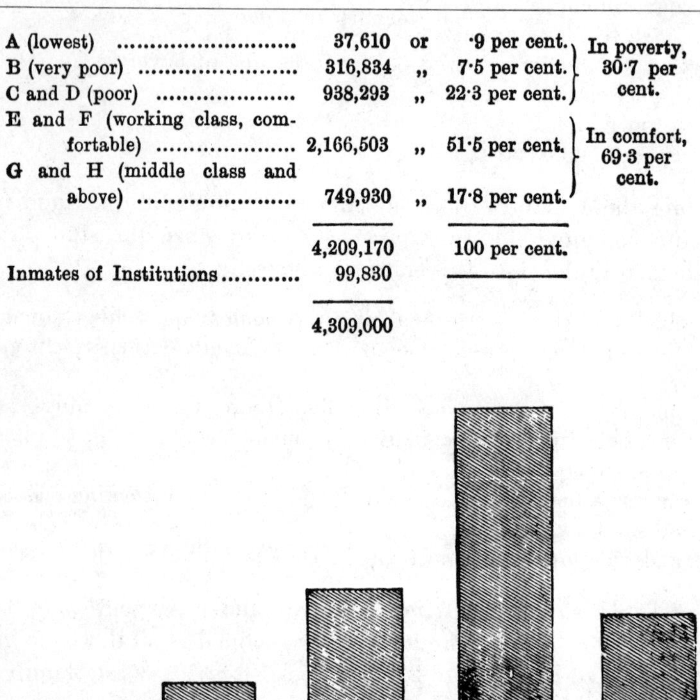

A (lowest)	**37,610**	**or**	**·9 per cent.**	**In poverty, 30·7 per cent.**
B (very poor)	**316,834**	**„**	**7·5 per cent.**	
C and D (poor)	**938,293**	**„**	**22·3 per cent.**	
E and F (working class, comfortable)	**2,166,503**	**„**	**51·5 per cent.**	**In comfort, 69·3 per cent.**
G and H (middle class and above)	**749,930**	**„**	**17·8 per cent.**	
	4,209,170		**100 per cent.**	
Inmates of Institutions	**99,830**			
	4,309,000			

SOURCE: "Poverty Series," II, 21.

7 *Ibid.*, I, 33. Sir Hubert Llewellyn-Smith was to remark forty years later: ". . . though Charles Booth arrived at his standards without

The analysis of the population by class was further complicated by the seven-color scheme used to classify the streets of the city "according to the general condition of the inhabitants." On the one hand, some of the colors were employed to represent a specific class; on the other hand, other colors were used to represent "mixed" streets, and at least one color referred to a mixture of four different classes. The class color scheme employed in Booth's "Descriptive Map of London Poverty" was as follows:

Black.—The lowest grade (corresponding to Class A), inhabited principally by occasional labourers, loafers, and semi-criminals — the elements of disorder.

Dark Blue.—Very poor (corresponding to Class B), inhabited principally by casual labourers and others living from hand to mouth.

Light Blue.—Standard poverty (corresponding to Classes C and D) inhabited principally by those whose earnings are small . . . whether they are so because of irregularity of work (C) or because of a low rate of pay (D).

Purple.—Mixed with poverty (usually C and D with E and F, but including Class B in many cases).

Pink.—Working class comfort. (Corresponding to Class E and F, but containing also a large proportion of the lower middle class of small tradesmen and Class G.) These people keep no servants.

Red.—Well-to-do; inhabited by middle-class families who keep one or two servants.

Yellow.—Wealthy; hardly found in East London and little found in South London; inhabited by families who keep three or more servants, and whose houses are rated at £100 or more.[8]

AREAL ANALYSIS The division of London into various spatial units for both the reporting and analysis of data constituted another major axis of and principle for organizing the materials

---

the aid of the modern scientific apparatus of calories and vitamins, he was guided by a sure instinct to conclusions not appreciably different from those which would have resulted from the use of the more objective methods now in use." Sir H. Llewellyn-Smith, "The New Survey of London Life and Labour," *Journal of the Royal Statistical Society*, 92, pt. 4 (1929): 536.

8 *Ibid.*, II, 40–41.

in the inquiry. The largest areal units employed were the traditional compass areas of the city: the work was begun in East London, then Central, West, and South London were considered in turn (see fig. 1).[9]

FIG. 1.—Sketch Map of London Showing Compass Quadrant Areas

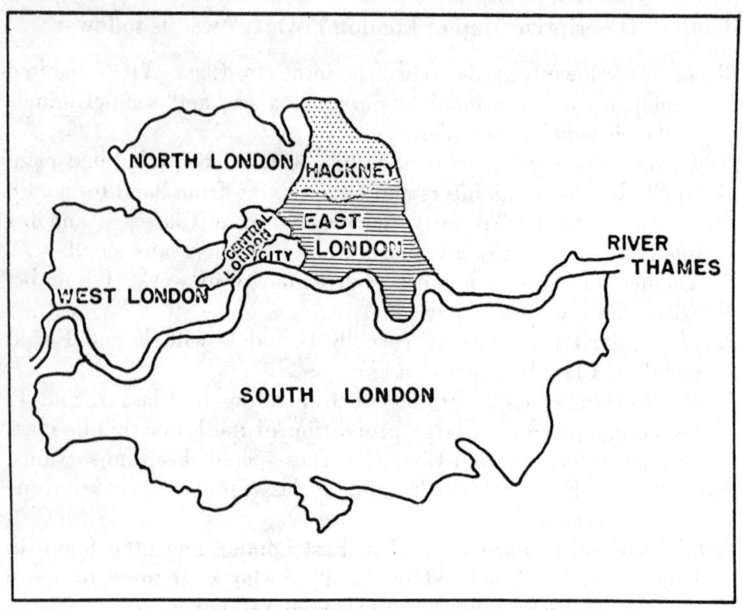

Adapted from "Poverty Series," I, 1.

Contained within these larger areas were the official "Registration Districts" and "Sub-districts" (numbering 30 and 127, respectively), which were the basis of census enumeration as well as the units of local government. As previously noted, Booth also introduced the concepts of "inner ring" and "outer ring" as another basis of spatial description and comparison: using the

9 These divisions did not include "The City," the non-residential area on the north bank of the Thames which contained the majority of the public buildings.

City as a center, two concentric circles were drawn, each with a radius of one and one-half miles.

While the data were tabulated in the East London inquiry in terms of the above units, another type of official territorial division was introduced in the study of the rest of the city: the school board divisions and blocks (numbering 11 and 500, respectively), which were the official administrative and enumeration districts of the London School Board. Booth was quick to recognize their limitations and noted:

These areas unfortunately bear no relation to either the registration sub-districts or to the ecclesiastical parishes, which again differ from each other. The street, even, is not a common unit, as long streets run through from block to block, from sub-district to sub-district. . . . Despite these difficulties it would, no doubt, be possible, if it were needed for any special purpose to group and subdivide the streets as given in our books as to yield fairly correct results for any area that might be required.[10]

Further, as the analysis progressed, Booth employed the school board blocks in combination to construct areal units of approximately 30,000 population, numbering 134. These, in turn, were combined into larger contiguous areas. Booth's compound block analysis is illustrated by the data in Table 2, and his final results in terms of both the subdivided traditional compass areas and the school board divisions are reproduced in Table 3.

Much of the "Poverty" series, especially Volume II, was given over to the presentation of basic data in a detailed picture of the occupants, "street by street."

SPECIAL SUBJECTS As a third major aspect of this series, there were separate inquires into a variety of special subjects related to povery and/or the areas under investigation. These studies, which are listed in the *Outline,* typically combined both detailed statistical data, vivid qualitative descriptive materials, and occasional interpretations of cause and effect, as well as proposals for social action.

10 *Ibid.*, II, 16.

TABLE 2. *Sample Block Analysis of Poverty Statistics*

No. on Map.	Position.	Population.	Percentage of Poverty.	—	
56	Bethnal Green (West)	28,701	58·7		
57	Bethnal Green (East)	27,003	44·2		
72	From Whitechapel to Bethnal Green......	33,973	49·1	89,677=51 per cent.	187,216 46 per cent.
73	St. George's-in-the-East	34,989	46·5		
74	St. Katherine's Docks	28,990	49·4	97,53942 per cent.	
71	Commercial Street to City	33,560	32·5		
61	Great Eastern Street	31,817	39·9		
62	Hoxton (West)	28,039	40·4	90,366=43 per cent.	179,841 41 per cent.
63	Hoxton (East)	30,510	48·4		
60	Haggerston	29,357	36·9		
59	Old Bethnal Green Road	29,628	37·6	89,475=38 per cent.	
58	Green Street	30,490	40·1		
	Central part of East London...............	367,057		44 per cent of poverty.	

SOURCE: "Poverty Series," II, 25.

The migration, the trades, and the public education studies are especially modern: the first involved detailed analyses of both the influx and efflux of migrants, the use of rate maps, and even a test of Ravenstein's law; the second was often less concerned with the nature and mechanics of price and wage rates than with the formal and informal organizations of the trades considered; and the third was notable not only because it provided a check on the School Board Visitors' data but also because it approached the nature and function of education from the perspective of class. The results of this investigation as they compared with the estimates of poverty from the visitors' reports are reproduced in Table 4.

THEORY In spite of Booth's avowed intention to confine his observations to things only as they are, an inquiry into such a problematic area inevitably involved a consideration of the

TABLE 3. *Statistics of Poverty: Final Results by Compass Areas and School Board Divisions*

Position:	Population.	Percentage of Poverty.	—
City	42,561	31	
Central part of East London......	367,057	44	
Eastern " "	328,361	32	
Northern " "	196,121	24	
Central " North London ...	225,330	43	
Northern " "	353,642	32	
Central " West London ...	371,091	21	
Western " "	483,298	25	
Northern " "	287,220	25	
Central " South London ...	387,248	47	
Eastern " "	362,333	32	
Southern " "	435,667	22	
Western " "	369,241	27	
	4,209,170	31	Average per cent. of poverty.

School Board Division.	In Poverty. A.	B.	C and D.	Total.	Per cent.	In Comfort. E and F.	G and H.	Total.	Per cent.	GRAND TOTAL.
City of London	574	2676	10,152	13,402	31·5	22,948	6211	29,159	68·5	42,561
Westminster ...	1314	15,998	33,395	50,707	24·5	115,151	41,323	156,474	75·5	207,181
Chelsea	3874	17,605	83,899	105,378	24·6	188,253	134,101	322,354	75·4	427,732
Marylebone ...	3762	27,996	116,816	148,574	25·8	300,049	126,487	426,536	74·2	575,110
Finsbury.........	6886	51,818	122,539	181,243	35·5	244,420	84,895	329,315	64·5	510,558
Hackney.........	4299	47,525	97,007	148,831	34·5	229,255	53,580	282,835	65·5	431,666
Tower Hamlets	6683	52,534	106,127	165,344	36·0	268,938	25,591	294,529	64·0	459,873
Southwark	4489	30,603	73,199	108,291	47·6	108,708	10,534	119,242	52·4	227,533
West Lambeth	1840	26,716	128,262	156,318	26·6	311,058	119,298	430,356	73·4	586,674
East Lambeth	3277	18,656	83,772	105,705	30·0	184,879	62,249	247,128	70·0	352,833
Greenwich	1047	24,711	82,882	108,640	28·0	193,467	85,342	278,809	72·0	387,449
Total...	87,545	316,838	938,050	1,292,433	30·7	2,167,126	749,611	2,916,737	69·3	4,209,170
								Inmates of Institutions		99,830
								All London		4,309,000

SOURCE: "Poverty Series," II, 31, 60–61.

causes of poverty and possible action programs to relieve the situation. In connection with such more "theoretical" interests, Booth tried to establish in a more precise fashion the empirical limits of some of his classifications. His drastic proposal to alleviate the problem by the semi-institutionalization of Class B, which he derived from a functional analysis of the relationships obtaining

TABLE 4. *Statistics of Poverty: Final Results Based on Visitors' and School Teachers' Reports*

Class	Estimates from S. B. Visitors' reports.		Estimates from School Teachers' reports.	
	No.	Per cent.	No.	Per cent.
A	37,610	0·9	53,107	1·3
B	316,834	7·5	440,833	10·5
C and D	938,293	22·3	1,399,196	33·2
E and F	2,166,503	51·5	1,566,104	37·2
	3,459,240	82·2	3,459,240	82·2
G and H	749,930	17·8		
	4,209,170	100·0		
Institutions	99,830			
	4,309,000			

SOURCE: "Poverty Series," III, 200.

among the classes in the economic system, as well as his analysis of the causes of poverty have been previously mentioned.

Worthy of special comment, however, was the attempt to delimit more sharply the concepts of poverty and standard of life. This involved a detailed analysis of a sample of family budgets, in the manner of Le Play, from representatives of all but Class A. For the purpose of comparison, the size of each family was reduced to adult male equivalents. Thirty budgets were analyzed in considerable detail relative to the proportions of total income spent for twenty-nine different budget items, the price range for each class, the number of trips to market, etc. As Booth noted, however:

The number of cases is too small to provide a perfectly safe basis . . . [for generalization]. . . . My object is attained if . . . I show exactly what I mean by the line of poverty with regard to which, as being below it, on it, or above it, I have attempted to classify the people[11]

11 *Ibid.*, I, 133–34. Booth explicitly pointed out that the concept, "standard of life," bore no relation to the "happiness" of the people in-

Finally, turning to the question of the "causes" of poverty, an analysis of a sample of 4,000 cases of Classes A though D was made in terms of three basic categories: (1) "questions of employment," (2) "questions of habit," and (3) "questions of circumstance." While Booth made explicit the fact that questions of "employment" rather than of "habit" or "circumstance" were the major cause of poverty, his devotion to individualistic principles once again prevented him from carrying through the implications of this finding, except in the case of "the lowest class" (see Table 5).

Beyond the basic and shocking "fact" that approximately 30 per cent of the city's four million residents were "poor," the "Poverty" series obviously raised more questions than it answered. Booth made no attempt to summarize or even to draw conclusions. Rather, he turned immediately to the most obvious gap in his study—an inquiry into the trades of London—in the hope that such an investigation would carry him further toward his original goal of "connecting poverty and well-being with conditions of employment."

Industry Series

Given the focus on the various general trades and on the specific occupations within each trade, the major axes of "class," "space," and "time," together with the new classification of the population according to social condition, the materials in the "Industry" series were presented in a much more organized form than in the "Poverty" series. The unit of inquiry again became the family, more especially, the family head, defined as anyone claiming to fill out an independent census return. As in the initial trades inquiry that figured in the previous series, a double enumeration

---

volved and he was more aware than many contemporary sociologists of the limits of relevance of purely objective criteria of status for imputing subjective states. Class A was omitted from the analysis because Booth did not consider it to be part of the problem of poverty but rather one of "heredity and disorder," a vestige of his economic-liberal ideological prejudices.

TABLE 5. *Statistics of Poverty: Causes by Degree of Poverty*

Analysis of Causes of "Great Poverty" (Classes A and B).

		Per Cent.		Per Cent.	
1. Loafers	—	—	60	4	
2. Casual work	697	43			
3. Irregular work, low pay	141	9	878	55	Questions of employment
4. Small profits	40	3			
5. Drink (husband, or both husband and wife)	152	9			
6. Drunken or thriftless wife	79	5	231	14	Questions of habit
7. Illness or infirmity	170	10			
8. Large family	124	8	441	27	Questions of circumstance
9. Illness or large family, combined with irregular work	147	9			
	—	—	1,610	100	

Analysis of Causes of "Poverty" (Classes C and D).

		Per Cent.		Per Cent.	
1. Loafers	—	—	—	—	
2. Low pay (regular earnings)	503	20			
3. Irregular earnings	1,052	43	1,668	68	Questions of employment
4. Small profits	113	5			
5. Drink (husband, or both husband and wife)	167	7			
6. Drunken or thriftless wife	155	6	322	13	Questions of habit
7. Illness or infirmity	123	5			
8. Large family	223	9	476	19	Questions of circumstance
9. Illness or large family, combined with irregular work	130	5			
	—	—	2,466	100	

SOURCE: "Poverty Series," I, 147.

was made (by individuals as well as by families) in order to calculate the total number of people supported by any trade or occupation.

SOURCES OF DATA As previously noted, the major source of data for the "Industry" series was the 1891 census, especially the "householder's schedule" which required reporting the number of rooms occupied, the number of servants kept, and data on occupational status. The latter was complemented by materials from the statistical department of the London Board of Trade. In addition, there were innumerable interviews with individuals—workers, employers, trade union officials, etc.; questionnaires were sent to a wide range of firms; and special studies were done by members of Booth's staff:

As regards employers in each trade, the plan adopted has been to approach as many as possible by circular asking from each an exact account of those employed, whether men, women, or boys, and the wages paid to each in an average, or better still, in a maximum and minimum week. This appeal brought in every case a fair proportion of replies. Those firms who were willing to give us further assistance were then personally waited upon and consulted as to other points of interest; for instance, as to usual hours and overtime; regularity and irregularity; seasons, methods of training, etc. Nothing could exceed the kindness with which our troublesome quest has in most cases been met. Factories have been opened to us, wage books have been shown, and particular and elaborate returns have been specially prepared for us setting forth in the most accurate way the hours worked as well as the pay received in busy and slack weeks, and the exact terms of piece and time employment.

Nor have the trades union officials been less ready to join in helping me to understand the relative positions of employer and employed in the trades with which they are connected.[12]

By now Booth was well aware of the many sources of error and bias in census data, and he observed:

So far from the data being accurate, they bear on their face the stamp of inaccuracy, as witness the concentration upon even figures . . . and the evidence and natural error in the ages returned by young women. . . . As to civil condition, marriage and widowhood are terms very

12 *Ibid.*, I, 27.

loosely used, and as to birthplace, what reliance can be placed on detailed accuracy?[13]

At the same time, he rightly insisted that information as to "number of rooms occupied" and "employment" had the advantage of being common knowledge and subject to objective check. He concluded:

On the whole . . . I am confident that any errors which may have crept in could not materially affect the general merits of the classification, and that the numbers counted in the census as occupying each tenement, and the number of rooms in each tenement . . . may, for all practical purposes, be taken as correct.[14]

TABLE 6. *Criteria of Social Classification in the "Poverty" and "Industry" Series, Compared*

Poverty Series	Industry Series	
Classes	Criteria	Classes
A and B	3 or more to a room to more than 1 to a room	Lower
C and D	1 to a room and occupants of common lodging houses	Lower
E, F and G	Less than 1 to a room More than 4 rooms Over 4 persons to 1 servant	Central
H	Less than 4 persons to 1 servant Inmates of hotels, clubs, etc.	Upper

Adapted from "Industry Series," V, 15.

CLASSIFICATION OF THE POPULATION The new measures of social condition and their relationship to the lettered classes are indicated in Table 6. Significantly, Booth compressed his social classification into a trichotomy in his analysis of the various trades ("lower," "central," and "upper" classes), which was suggestive of the complicated relativities involved in the study of social stratification. In general, "crowding" became the criterion of status for the poorer classes, whereas the number of servants kept was the criterion for the wealthy. As Booth pointed out, how-

13 *Ibid.*, pp. 12–13.
14 *Ibid.*, p. 14.

ever, while neither was a direct test of absolute wealth, they were "very fair tests of expenditure and an almost absolute test of the style of life."[15] Further, he observed:

In trying to find in the census a "common measure" of social condition, my object was the study of the terms on which life is lived in London in connection with the various industries and their enumeration. The same classification which has been applied to the whole population, and which can be applied to each district, I now propose to use in order to compare trade with trade.[16]

His results, which appear in Table 7, compared favorably with his previous investigations: thus, as he put it, "the total percentages 'crowded' and 'not crowded' agree very nearly with the

TABLE 7. *Statistics of Poverty: Final Results of the Classification of the Population by Crowding and Number of Servants*

		Per Cent.	Per Cent.	Per Cent.
(1 and 2.) 3 or more persons per room	**492,370 or**	**—**	**12·0**	**(Crowded) 31·5**
(3.) 2 and under 3 ,, ...	**781,615 ,,**	**19·0**	**19·5**	
Common lodging-houses, &c............	**20,087 ,,**	**0·5**		
(4.) 1 and under 2 persons per room...	**962,780 ,,**	**23·4**	**56·4**	**(Not crowded) 68·5**
(5.) Less than 1 person per room	**153,471 ,,**	**3·7**		
(6.) Occupying more than 4 rooms ...	**981,553 ,,**	**23·9**		
Servants	**205,858 ,,**	**5·0**		
Persons living in large shops, &c.......	**15,321 ,,**	**0·4**		
(*a*.) 4 or more persons to 1 servant ...	**227,832 ,,**	**5·5**	**12·1**	
(*b*.) to (*h*.) 3 or less persons to 1 servant	**248,493 ,,**	**6·0**		
Inmates of hotels and boarding-houses where servants are kept...	**25,726 ,,**	**0·6**		
	4,115,106			**100**
Institutions (excluding inmates of hotels, lodging-houses, large shops, and their servants)	**96,637**			
	4,211,743			

SOURCE: "Industry Series," I, 10.

15 *Ibid.*, p. 19.
16 *Ibid.*, p. 20.

totals of the previous classification 'in poverty' and 'in comfort.' "[17] But, he was explicit about the limitations of such an absolute comparison and noted that the agreement applied only to the "large average" provided by the "whole area of London."

The industrial classification of the city's population was oriented primarily to function and consisted of seventeen major trade groups (in addition to those in institutions and in other minor categories) which, in turn, comprised eighty-nine different "sections." Unfortunately, the major categories were far too socially heterogeneous to serve Booth's purposes when it came to relating them to social condition. Sample categories were as follows:

BUILDING TRADES:	1. Architects
	2. Builders
	3. Masons
	4. Bricklayers
	5. Carpenters
	6. Plasterers
	7. Painters
	8. Plumbers
	9. Gasfitters
WOOD WORKERS:	10. Cabinetmakers
	11. Carriage builders
	12. Coopers
	13. Shipwrights
PRINTING, etc.:	28. Printing
	29. Bookbinding
	30. Paper
	31. Stationery
	32. Bookselling
FOOD AND DRINK:	46. Millers
	47. Brewers
	48. Tobacconists
	49. Bakers, confectioners
	50. Dairymen
	51. Butchers
	52. Grocers
	53. Publicans
	54. Coffeehouse keepers[18]

17 *Ibid.*, p. 10.
18 *Ibid.*, pp. 21-22.

PLAN AND CONTENT With the exception of the last part of the fourth volume (in which the earlier study of pauperism is reprinted) and the final volume dealing with comparisons and summary matters, the "Industry" series is organized by the presentation of the materials trade by trade and, within each trade, section by section.

For the "Building Trades," for example, Booth began by presenting the objective facts concerning the entire group: age and sex, size of family, social condition (see Table 8), followed by comparative data on the constituent section (e.g., architects, builders, masons, bricklayers, etc.) in terms of poverty, crowding, numbers employed at intervals between 1861 and 1891, and numbers of employers versus employees. There followed a depiction of the nature of the trade relative to the relationships which obtained among the occupations included in it—how they acted together to perform the tasks for which they were hired.

Booth then turned to the particular sections and presented a more detailed but similar objective analysis: (1) from census data, an age and sex analysis of the occupational categories within each section; (2) from the family enumeration, the number of heads of families are considered in terms of place of birth (in or out of London), of employment status, the average size of family, and social condition; (3) a detailed analysis of the distribution in space in terms of inner and outer rings as well as by compass areas. These data are exemplified by the materials in Table 9 below. Also included for each section was an age-distribution diagram which compared those employed in the section with those in the entire trade, as well as with the total London work force.

Also included was a brief description of the function of each job category in the section. Finally, a detailed consideration was given to the portion of the inquiry entitled "Conditions of Employment." Here, such aspects of work were discussed as: training and job-getting, hours and wages, seasonal factors in the industry, trade organizations and abuses, health and social condition. In the inquiry into the building trades, for example, a sample of 124 interviews provided the data for the descriptive analysis in terms of these categories.

TABLE 8. *Social Condition of Families in the Building Trades*

Class	Condition	Number	Per cent	Group per cent	Crowding
Lower Class.	4 or more persons to a room ...	25,763 or	5·9 %	15·4 %	Crowded: 39·2 %
	3 and under 4 " " ...	41,237 "	9·5 %		
	2 and under 3 " " ...	102,944 "		23·8 %	
	1 and under 2 " " ...	109,679 "		25·4 %	Not Crowded: 60·8 %
Central Class.	Less than 1 " " ...	13,793 "	3·2 %	31·8 %	
	More than 4 rooms	111,154 "	25·7 %		
	4 or more persons to 1 servant ...	12,682 "	2·9 %		
Upper Class.	Less than 4 persons to 1 servant and 4 or more to 2 servants	5,933 "		1·4 %	
	All others with 2 or more servants	3,250 "		·7 %	
	Servants	6,470 "		1·5 %	
		432,905		100 %	

SOURCE: "Industry Series," I, 33.

COMPARISONS AND CONCLUSIONS Booth himself outlined the plan and content of the final volume of the "Industry" series in his "Introduction":

This volume, which concludes the present series, contains two parts. In the first, comparisons are made between the various trade sections as to apparent poverty, "crowding," earnings, proportion of

TABLE 9. *Sample Fact-Sheet on Industrial Sections—"Architects, Civil Engineers, etc."*

Census Enumeration.

Census Divisions, 1891.	Females. All Ages.	Males. —19*	Males. 20—54*	Males. 55—*	Total.
(1) Architect ..	12	154	1607	251	2024
(2) Civil Engineer	—	94	1823	412	2329
(3) Surveyor	—	61	1017	193	1271
(4) Rd. & Railway Contractor, Surveyor or Inspector ..	—	13	266	35	314
TOTAL	12	322	4713	891	5938

The number in these professions reaches its maximum at 25 to 35 years of age, and there is an unusually large proportion of men over 65. (*See* diagram.)

DISTRIBUTION.

E.	N.	W. & C.	S.	Total.
160	1598	1836	2344	5938

DETAILS OF OCCUPATIONS (FROM THE CENSUS DICTIONARY).

(2) Architectural, consulting, hydraulic, sanitary, mining, and submarine engineer.
(3) District surveyor, insurance surveyor, examiner of buildings, land measurer, quantity surveyor, wood surveyor.
(4) Railway stores contractor, railway signal, switch, and turntable maker; point and crossing-fitter.

Enumerated by Families.

Sex	Males		3673	Heads of Families, 3680.
	Females..............		7	
Birthplace	In London	40 %	1466	
	Out of London(*a*)	60 %	2214	
Industrial Status .. (*See* note.)	Employer	30 %	1088	
	Employed	49 %	1814	
	Neither	21 %	778	

(*a*) The large proportion born out of London is noticeable.

TOTAL POPULATION CONCERNED.

	Heads of Families.	Others Occupied.	Unoccupied.	Servants.	Total.
Total	3680	3064	9041	3461	19,246
Average in family ..	1·0	83	2·46	·94	5·23

CLASSIFICATION.

Numbers living in families.		%
3 or more to a room	249	1·3
2 & under 3 ,,	526	2·7
1 & under 2 ,,	1453	7·6
Less than 1 ,, / More than 4 rooms / 4 or more persons to a servant ..	8092	42·0
Less than 4 to 1 servant, and 4 or more to 2 servants	2916	15·2
All others with 2 or more servants ..	2549	13·2
Servants	3461	18·0
	19,246	100

	Inner.	Outer.	Together.
Crowded ..	12 %	3 %	4 %
Not ,, ..	88 %	97 %	96 %

DISTRIBUTION.

East ..	Inner 207	Outer 228	435
North	Inner 814	Outer 4126	4940
West ..	Inner 607	Outer 4025	4632
Central	Inner 649		649
South-East	Inner 122	Outer 3427	3549
South-West	Inner 452	Outer 4589	5041
			19,246

Inner 2851, or 15 %
Outer 16,395, or 85 %

NOTE.—*Industrial Status.*

In the sections which follow a Table is given showing "Status as to Employment." In this group, however, so few were returned either as "employer" or "employed," that the statement according to census enumeration is omitted as being misleading. But in the Enumeration by Families it was possible, by careful examination of the returns, and dealing only with heads of families, to allocate those returned to the class to which they probably belonged.

* The interpretation of the age symbols used in this and succeeding tables, is as under :—
"—19" indicates persons under 20 years of age.
"20—54" ,, ,, aged 20 to 54 years inclusive.
"55—" ,, ,, aged 55 years and upwards.

SOURCE: "Industry Series," I, 46.

Londoners, numbers in family, ages of workers, proportion of employers to employed, and increase or decrease . . . of numbers engaged. These chapters, though somewhat forbidding, contain matter of considerable interest, being in fact a distillation of all the statistics concerning the above-mentioned groups of fact.

The second part, drawing on the whole preceding accounts of London trades, treats of such subjects as irregularity of employment, trade unionism, methods and amount of remuneration, and industrial remedies for poverty. It deals mainly in generalizations, but any London reader can if he will shift the point of view from the general to the particular by taking as an example any trade or occupation, or the lot of any individual worker of which he has exact knowledge, in order to test the correctness of the conclusions to which we have come. He may classify himself or anyone whose circumstances are known to him, according to the trade at which he works, the wages earned and the character of the home in which he lives. There is no life that is led in London which may not serve as an illustration to this book, no individual who may not find his place in the schedules. In this way a definite value may be given to the gradations of my scale, and a test may be applied to the probability of the conclusions drawn.

The closing chapter touches upon the standard of life, actual or possible, and so steps into line with the first series of this work, thus completing the design originally laid down and expressed in the title of the book.

Still this does not conclude the work, but what remains to be done is of a different character, being to estimate the forces for good or evil that are acting upon the condition of the population before we can arrive at that balancing of hopes and fears that will form our final judgment.[19]

In discussing the relationship between crowding and "apparent poverty," Booth considered his definition of poverty more thoroughly and concluded that in spite of some exceptions,

. . . on the average, crowding does provide a reasonably fair measure of poverty; and some support is given to this assertion by the fact that the total percentage of poverty indicated by this test group agrees almost exactly with that reached in our previous inquiry by a different method. . . .[20]

The relative nature of such an index of poverty was apparent to Booth, however, and the point was made that a considerable dif-

19 *Ibid.*, V, *ix–x.*
20 *Ibid.*, V, 4.

ference resulted from applying it to the "inner" as against the "outer" rings of the city:

This difference, which we find in almost every trade, is largely due to the question of rent, but it also represents the broad circumstance that the poorer representatives in nearly every trade live nearest to, and the better off furthest from, the centre of London.[21]

Booth was also quite explicit about stating the nature of many of his assumptions when it came to the statistical data: for example, the use of crowding as the index of poverty assumed that the desire for housing accommodation was equal on the part of all classes; this, of course, was by no means the case.[22]

Having discussed the limitations of his indices, Booth went on to compare the percentage of crowding among the eighty-nine industrial "sections." The order ranged from 4 per cent for architects to 65 per cent for street sellers. A second group of comparisons dealt with the relationship between crowding and earnings. The difficulties of obtaining reliable data on the latter and of estimating the annual value of irregular employment (so much of which was in evidence at the time) led Booth to conclude:

Our attempt to connect the evidence as to poverty based on crowding with that obtained as to remuneration in each trade, has met with only partial success.[23]

And, when weekly earnings for the various sections were compared with the percentage of the poor, Booth's final judgment was that,

On the whole . . . it seems probable that the line of poverty in London, if we are to accept crowding as a test, lies a little above the figure formerly laid down. . . . It must be admitted, however, that the relationship between the statistics of remuneration and those of poverty as tested by crowding is not very close.[24]

21 *Ibid.*, p. 5.

22 See e.g., Maurice Halbwachs, *La Classe Ouvrière et Les Niveaux de Vie*, Book III: "Contribution to a Sociological Theory of Needs" (Paris: Felix Alcan, 1913).

23 *Ibid.*, p. 13.

24 *Ibid.*, p. 25.

Another set of comparisons analyzed the various sections with respect to: the proportion of heads of families born in or out of London, living in the inner or outer circle; place of birth and place of residence; size of family; and male heads of families. These comparisons were the basis for a number of empirical generalizations: (1) In regard to place of birth, the results ranged from 81 per cent born in London in the case of bookbinders to only 12 per cent of those in the army and navy. (2) As for living in the inner circle, the range was from 63 per cent of the leather dressers to 6 per cent of the gardeners. (3) With respect to place of birth and place of residence, "the greater proportion of born Londoners, the greater also the proportion of those living in the central district of London and the larger the number, too, of those whose houses are crowded."[25] (4) In regard to size of family and the percentage of males over twenty who were heads of households:

> Speaking generally, the families of laboring men vary from five to four and one-half members, and those of the professional classes from four and one-half to three and one-half members.[26]

And,

> This proportion [of adult males who are head of families] has an extraordinary range, varying from eighty-five per cent with shipwrights to thirty-four per cent with seamen and thirty per cent with army and navy.[27]

Significantly, the differences were interpreted not only as a function of age but also of economic position and class habits or styles of life.

The variation in age distributions among the different trades was also considered in an effort to show the manner in which work opportunities shifted with age. The status of employment (em-

25 *Ibid.*, p. 31. Booth also observed, "amongst Londoners there is a tendency to have crowded homes as well as to live in the inner circle and not at all necessarily the one because of the other." *Ibid.*, p. 34.
26 *Ibid.*, p. 37. Undoubtedly this difference would have been greater if Booth's classification of trades had been more consistent in nature.
27 *Ibid.*, p. 41.

ployer versus employee) was (incorrectly) used to indicate the size of business units and to conclude (falsely) that the tendency in modern industry was *not* to combine into larger units.

A final section was concerned with a temporal analysis—1861–91—in which increases in industries and professions located in London ran as high as 308 per cent for "undefined factory labor" and decreases as high as 72 per cent for "shipwrights."

The last portion of the series, entitled "Survey and Conclusions," was devoted to a series of related subjects in more general and theoretical terms. Among these were: rates and hours of labor; the training of London labor; large and small business units; and trades unions. Perhaps the most modern (and relevant for a sociological understanding of the city) were: London as a center of trade and industry; the localization and diffusion (*sic*) of trades; the choice of employments; and expenditures and standard of life.

While many of these latter subjects were investigated by Booth's major collaborator Ernest Aves, Booth was responsible for the discussion of the essential characteristics of modern industry.[28] Above all, he stressed its "organic" character and its basically "conflict" quality when it came to industrial relations. This was on his assumption that everywhere, always, "all life rests on a balance of forces." In his discussion of "Industrial Remedies," Booth saw education as the major basis for industrial reform, although he viewed irregularity of employment as more important than lack of work or low wages in producing urban poverty.

When it came to specific proposals for industrial reform, Booth turned again to his "limited Socialism": state aid was possible and permissible in the spheres of health and education but not in the areas of employment or savings. Reform of the individual by

28 Aves succeeded Beatrice Potter as Booth's closest collaborator and was responsible for much of both the "Industry" and "Religious Influences" series. The Simeys note that Aves first met Booth when he went from Cambridge to Toynbee Hall. Later, Aves became a government commissioner. Simey, *Charles Booth, Social Scientist*, p. 125.

the individual and the continued expansion of industry were set forth as the two remedial influences "already at work." He observed:

Looked at from the side of industry, life presents itself as full of chances, the best use of which demands free individuality. This is the main conclusion to which the study of London trades has tended. In this fact we find the only security for collective prosperity, and, through all do not share alike, I cannot doubt that it provides also the best hope for the diffusion of comfort and wealth.[29]

At the conclusion of this last volume of the "Industry" series, Booth pointed to his next task:

To the question of another critic, "What is the good of it all?" I shall still attempt no answer. I trust in the efficacy and utility of the scientific method in throwing light upon the social questions, and the work on which I am engaged is not yet finished. In spite of the length to which it has attained, I have to ask once more the patience of my readers. The circumstances which may lead to poverty are various. In my next volumes I hope to show the extent to which remedies of many kinds, wise and unwise, are now being applied; and in this way, before attempting to decide what further or other actions should be pursued, take stock of what is being done now, and try to trace the effects of the agencies and influences, actually at work, upon the existing state of things.

If I can accomplish this, and besides showing where poverty exists in London and in what degree, and something of its relation to industry, which has now been done, indicate also the manner in which the social condition of the people is affected for good or evil by social action of various kinds, it may become easier than it now is to avoid the wrong and choose the right path; and the question of my critic will have been answered.[30]

Religious Influence Series

Because of his own traditional commitment to religion and because organized religion was the major source of extra-official

29 *Ibid.*, p. 439.
30 *Ibid.*, pp. 338–39.

efforts to deal with the problem of poverty on the local level, Booth focused primarily on religious institutions in the third and final series. The research, as previously noted, ranged far more widely, and, as he stated in his "Introduction":

> . . . I have besides tried to appreciate other organized social and philanthropic influences, and also those that come under the heads of Local Government and Police, and in connection therewith have sought information on Housing and Health, on Drink, Prostitution and Crime, on Marriage and on Thrift; and though questions as to the extent and degree of Poverty do not enter directly, they will come constantly under my consideration.[31]

However, as the Simeys have noted, when it came to the analysis of the city's religious institutions, Booth was, in fact, engaged in two quite different but not unrelated tasks:

> The first, the more strictly social and scientific, was the path that has since led to the development of the sociology of religion; the second involved an excursion into territory that has usually been regarded as that belonging to the philosopher and the theologian rather than the social scientist. The first approach was based on the assumption that the institutional structure of each church can be described and appraised from the point of view of its connexions with the structure of the society of which it is deemed to be a part. . . . Booth carried this analysis a long way, and with great profit. At the same time, it tended to become confused in his work with the second line of analysis, that directed to the discovery of the extent to which the moral life of a society is influenced by religious teaching properly so called. This involved him in a critical examination of the teaching of individual churches, and in the appraisal of the religious life from its more personal aspects.[32]

PLAN AND CONTENT Booth sketched the plan of the series in his "Introduction" as follows:

31 "Religious Influences," I, 5.

32 Simey, *Charles Booth, Social Scientist*, p. 221. Also noted are the facts that not only did Booth write up the materials in the "Religious Influences" series without the aid of staff members but also that, unlike the other series, it was written entirely in the first person. Both these facts conspired to maximize the personal and subjective qualities in the analysis, a matter that did not go unnoticed by his critics.

The general scheme of the book is as follows: Beginning with London North of the Thames, in the far Eastern corner at the Isle of Dogs, we proceed along the metropolitan boundary by way of Poplar, Bromley, Bow and Hackney to Islington, St. Pancreas, Maida Vale and Hampstead. The whole of this outer ring has been built up within the memory of men still living. Within, between it and the City boundary, lies another ring, an "inner" ring," and to this our inquiry is next directed. Here old purposes and needs have given way to new, and destruction and rebuilding go on apace. Then the West Central district follows, after which the City and Westminster lead us to the true West End of wealth with its rapidly filling *hinterland* at Hammersmith and Fulham. Crossing the river to the South side, and beginning with the inner and riverside parts, we then trace the extension of London southward over outer and outermost rings of population, stretching from Roehampton on the extreme West to Eltham on the extreme East.

In connection with the part played by religious and other social influences, the physical peculiarities of each district and the housing and condition of the inhabitants are incidentally described, and the districts compared one with another. Six volumes are thus occupied and in the seventh these various threads are drawn together and the place of religion in the lives of the people is considered in a more general way.[33]

As can be seen from the *Outline*, Booth began with a very definite conception of the dimensions he wished to cover for each area of the city. As usual, the materials proved far too prolix; even before the conclusions of the initial volume, he was reduced simply to highlighting selected aspects of the original nine analytic categories in his consideration of each area.

Despite these problems, twenty-three "Sketch Maps" (see fig. 2) were made and a statistical fact sheet (see Table 10) was compiled for each major division. In addition, the original "Descriptive Map of London Poverty" was brought up to date and reprinted in twenty-one different, interleaved sections throughout the first six volumes of the series (see fig. 3). In regard to the areas delimited and the map revision, Booth commented:

33 "Religious Influences," I, 6.

Fig. 3.—Section of Revised "Descriptive Map of London Poverty—Westminster and Pimlico, 1900"

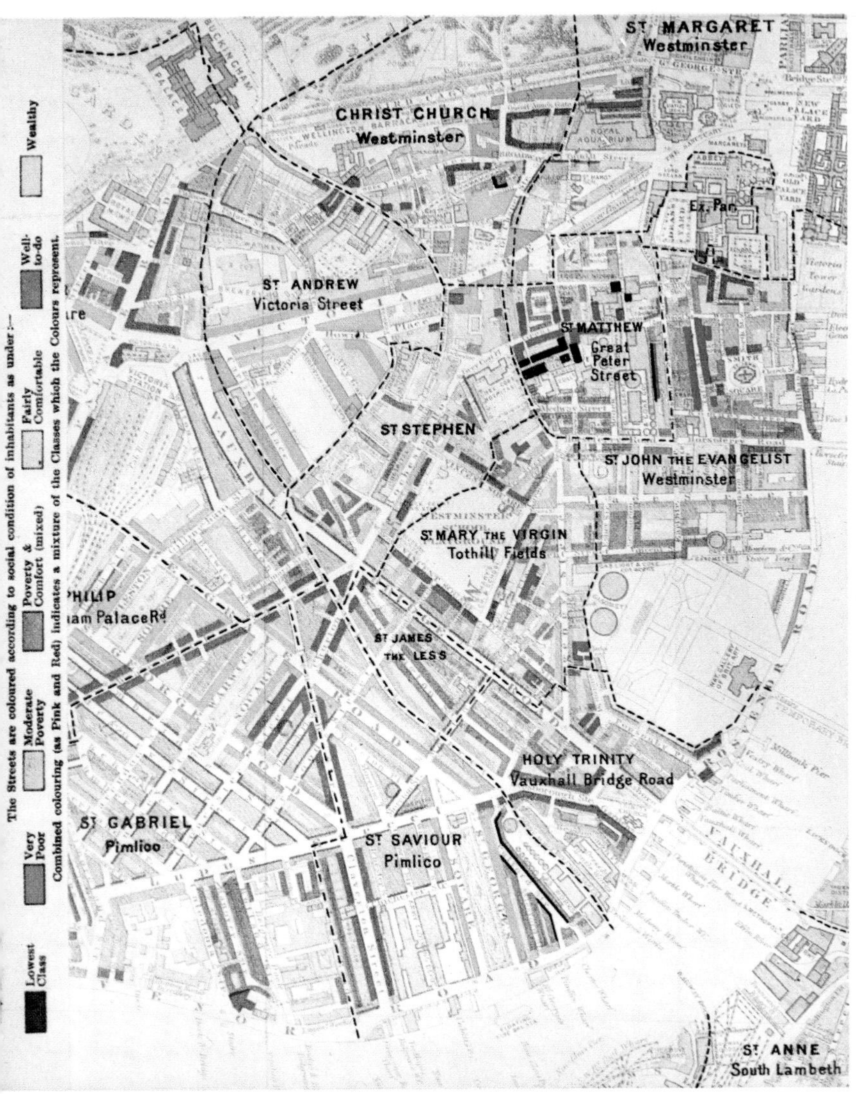

Source: "Religious Influences," III, 92 f.

In the grouping of parishes for each chapter, the larger recognized local areas have, so far as practicable, been adopted. When ignored, it has been in order to obtain sections presenting the greatest possible uniformity of condition; or in order to keep within the four corners of a rectangular map; a consideration which the actual boundaries—leaning on the past, and guided by the ancient limits of properties large and small, by farm and field, by rising meadow and meandering brook, by manor house and garden wall, churchyard and village green—entirely disregard.[34]

FIG. 2—Sample Sketch Map of a District: The West End

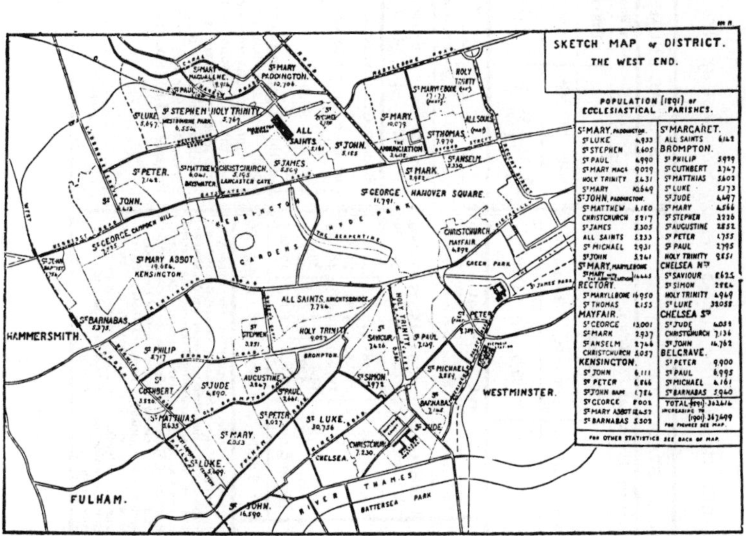

SOURCE: "Religious Influences," III, 95.

The "Poverty Map" of 1889 has been revised and much enlarged, and the revised map, cut into sections is bound up with the present volumes. The original map was based on information obtained from the School Board visitors, checked by local knowledge from various sources. The new map starts from the old one. There has been no attempt to obtain fresh information such as that on which the original

34 *Ibid.*, p. 9.

TABLE 10. *Sample Fact-Sheet on Sketch Map Area: The West End*

CENSUS STATISTICS.

Showing Increase or Decrease of Population.

Population in 1881.	1891.	1896.	1901.	Increase or Decrease 1881-1891.	1891-1901.
358,647	357,496	367,405	364,133	·29 %	1·86 %

Density of Population.

	1891.	1901.
Persons per Acre.	90·5	92·6
Inhabited Houses.	46,003	43,169
Persons per House.	7·8	8·4
Number of Acres.	3,948	

Age and Sex in 1891.

Age.	Males.	Females.	Together.
Under 5 years	15,236	15,373	30,609
5 & under 15 yrs	26,446	27,654	54,100
— 20 ,,	14,140	20,745	34,885
— 25 ,,	16,285	27,946	44,231
— 35 ,,	27,357	44,205	71,562
— 45 ,,	19,944	28,179	48,123
— 55 ,,	14,275	19,915	34,190
— 65 ,,	8,865	12,946	21,811
65 and over	6,812	11,173	17,985
Totals ...	149,360	208,136	357,496

NOTE.—The district includes Mayfair, and part of the Belgrave Registration sub-district of St. George, Hanover Square, Chelsea, Brompton, the southern part of Kensington Town, a detached portion of St. Margaret Westminster, St. John and St. Mary Paddington (except the Ecclesiastical parishes of St. Saviour and St. Peter), and the Rectory, Cavendish Square, and St. Mary sub-districts of Marylebone (except the ecclesiastical parishes of St. Mark and St. Luke). In these figures the whole of Belgrave is included as well as the four ecclesiastical parishes mentioned above. Cavendish Square (now combined with All Souls) is omitted, as well as the detached parts of St. Margaret and Kensington Town. Owing to these omissions it is probable that the whole area is less crowded than here indicated. For Special Family Enumeration see Appendix.

SPECIAL ENUMERATION FOR THIS INQUIRY (1891).

Sex, Birthplace and Industrial Status of Heads of Families.

Sex: Male.	Female.	Birthplace: In London.	Out of London.	Industrial Status: Employers	Employees	Neither.	Total Heads.
56,531 71 %	22,745 29 %	29,245 37 %	50,031 63 %	9,801 12 %	47,412 60 %	22,063 28 %	79,276 100 %

Constitution of Families.

Heads.	Others Occupied.	Unoccupied.	Servants.	Total in Families.
79,276 (1·0)	67,100 (·85)	139,879 (1·76)	52,395 (·66)	338,650 (4·27)

Social Classification according to *Rooms Occupied* or *Servants Kept.*

	Persons.	Per Cent.	
4 or more persons to a room	13,215	3·7	Crowded 25·3 %
3 & under 4 ,, ,,	22,734	6·4	
2 & ,, 3 ,, ,,	54·426	15·2	
1 & ,, 2 ,, ,,	70,168	19·6	Not Crowded 74·7 %
Less than 1 person to a room	12,881	3·6	
Occupying more than 4 rooms	44,132	12·3	
4 or more persons to 1 servant	18,739	5·3	
Less than 4 persons to 1 servant & 4 to 7 persons to 2 servants	16,945	4·7	
All others with 2 or more servants	33,015	9·2	
Servants in families	52,395	14·7	
Inmates of Institutions (including servants)	18,846	5·3	
Total	357,496	100	
Living in Poverty (as estimated in 1889)		17·4 %	100 %
,, in Comfort (,, ,,)		82·6 %	

Source: "Religious Influences," III, 96.

compilation was founded. On the other hand the revision has been very systematic. Every street, court and alley has been visited and when changes seemed necessary in the tint that had been given to it, these changes have been most carefully considered. Some of these alterations may be consequent on errors in the original map, but the bulk of them are simply the result of the natural alterations of ten years of demolitions, rebuilding and expansion involving changes in the character or distribution of the population. In our prolonged walks through London, when engaged in this revision—walks to be measured by hundreds, or even thousands, of miles—we had, by the kindness of Sir Edward Bradford, the company and cooperation of experienced members of the Police force, chosen for their local knowledge.[35]

Most of the volumes included a section entitled "Illustrations," which ranged from participant-observation reports on church services and mission operations to public houses, opium dens, funerals, and street life on Saturday night. The sixth volume, incidentally, included a special enumeration of the city's population by sex, birthplace, employment status of heads of families, and by social condition by registration districts and sub-districts, as well as a detailed index for the entire "Religious Influences" series.

RESULTS AND CONCLUSIONS In his final "Summary" volume of the series, Booth did not come forward with any proposals

35 *Ibid.*, pp. 6–7. Sir George H. Duckworth remarked forty years later on the occasion of Sir H. Llewellyn-Smith's paper to the Royal Statistical Society: ". . . for three years an ever-changing policeman who knew most about each little beat walked with Sir George through London, visiting every Court and Street. In the process full notes were taken and a color suggested for every street. Others were also engaged in this work, but Mr. Booth said there must be one among them who would make himself conversant with all the streets, so that those represented as dark blue in South London should be comparable with the dark blue in the North. It was for this reason that Sir George had the astounding chance, not only of working under Mr. Booth's supervision, but also of visiting every street in London, and writing down something about it—giving a description of the people who lived there—and so getting in a sense a standard that could with assistance of someone with specialized local knowledge be applicable to any part of London, and also to any town in England." Sir H. Llewellyn-Smith, "*New Survey*," p. 553.

for social action, and his generally skeptical conclusions concerning the efficacy of the efforts of organized religious communities to help the poor (or even to provide for their specifically religious needs) have already been noted.

Beyond a pointed analysis of each of the major religious communities—the Church of England, the Non-Conformist Protestant denominations, the Roman Catholic Church—as well as of the efforts of other religious bodies and such unique institutions as the mission, the settlement, etc., the relationship between religious institutions and the class structure of the community was highlighted and, indeed, pervaded the entire series. As early as the first volume Booth had remarked:

> The map seems to give the key to the situation, for the colours show in general outline the religious no less than the social, features of the district. Where the streets are red, we find a vigorous middle-class religious development combined with active social life. Where the streets are pink ["fairly comfortable"], there is, as regards religion, a comparative blank. Where the colour is blue ["very poor"] we have the missions, and step by step, as it deepens to black ["the lowest class"], the more hopeless becomes the task. From these broad conclusions there is no escape.[36]

And, by Volume III, he had concluded:

> In studying the influence of religion we have seen how limited are the possibilities it presents, and how closely everywhere it follows the line of class, similar conditions of life yielding similar results whatever the particular sect or whatever the special dogma preached may be.[37]

Finally, two other sociologically relevant contributions which figured prominently in this series should be noted: on the one hand, throughout his analysis of "special" (i.e., poverty) areas, Booth developed the general but implicit hypothesis that social isolation was a major factor in producing decay and disorganization on both the individual and community levels—an isolation that was more often than not physical in its inception:

36 *Ibid.*, I, 149.
37 *Ibid.*, III, 177–78.

The poorest and roughest part is the little group of streets already mentioned as going by the name of "Fenian Barracks." The area lies near the Limehouse Cut (a portion of the canal), and has a very bad name with the police for violence; sending, we are told, more police to the hospital than any other block in London. It can at present be approached only from Devons Road, and its seclusion is its bane.[38]

On the other hand, insofar as he departed from his traditional static approach, numerous postulates were presented concerning the change of population types through time against the background of the areal divisions of the city. For example, in regard to what (at a later date) would be referred to as "the ecology of social class," Booth concluded:

The drift of population from ring to ring can be clearly seen. . . . The greater part of the poverty patches are found near the center where site values are highest: the dark blue and black classes disperse only upon the demolition of their dwellings. The colour lightens with distance from the river. . . . The rebuilding by the railroad companies brings in a fairly comfortable class either from the outside or from the surrounding districts.[39]

Final Volume: Notes on Social Influences and Conclusion

The difficulties of summarizing his vast researches have already been mentioned. Indeed, Booth's own reservations were revealed in a comment to his chief collaborator, Ernest Aves:

I incline more and more to make less of and depend less upon the "Social Influences" volume. I do not think it will be wise to pin much upon it. We won't print any contents in advance, but merely refer to it as a winding up volume—a thin one, I hope.[40]

38 *Ibid.*, I, 47.

39 *Ibid.*, IV, 166.

40 Simey, *Charles Booth, Social Scientist*, pp. 157–58. A more objective indicator of the scale of Booth's researches is communicated by the Simeys' statement that the inquiry "had involved the expenditure of approximately £33,000." *Ibid.*, p. 157.

As indicated in the *Outline,* in its final form the volume was devoted to (1) a comparative analysis of the statistics of poverty and related matters; (2) a qualitative description of numerous dimensions of the life styles that Booth had observed among "the people"; (3) a series of "notes" on administrative problems connected with the life of the poor involving such matters as public houses and their licensing, crime and prostitution, housing, etc.; and (4) an almost poignantly brief "Conclusion" which the Simeys note, "amounted to no more than 16 pages." In fact, much of the book was devoted to a lengthy but cryptic "Abstract" of the total inquiry, volume by volume, page by page, which was prepared by one of Booth's staff members. Another magnificent map—of Inner and East London on which were spotted churches, elementary schools, and public houses—whose object was "to give the ordinary reader, at a glance, an impression of the ubiquitous and manifold character of the three most important social influences" was also included.[41]

POVERTY, CROWDING, AND VITAL RATES In a last attempt to deal with poverty in objective, statistical terms, Booth turned once more to his data on "apparent poverty" from the "Poverty" series and to his data on "crowding" from the "Industry" series. In what might almost be termed the culmination of his work and as striking evidence of the maturity his research efforts had attained, he compared and summarized his results in terms of a new and more meaningful set of areal units for the city as a whole:

> . . . the thirty registration districts were the areas [originally] selected, but some of these are inconveniently large and not sufficiently homogeneous for useful comparison. By a regrouping of the sub-districts, for all of which separate statistics are published by the Registrar-General, the irregularities have been to some extent obviated, and the whole metropolitan area divided into fifty districts fairly convenient for comparison.[42]

41 *Ibid.*, p. 119. According to Booth, the map was prepared for the social science section of the 1900 Paris Exhibition. It included an area of twenty-four square miles of the most densely populated and poorest sections of the city.

42 "Final Volume," p. 10.

The fifty districts were arranged in five rank orders relative to their *average per cent of poverty, per cent of crowding, birth rate, death rate,* and *rate of early marriage,* and the rank orders were graphically portrayed in a visual effort to discover the interrelationships among the variables. The social classification of the population was compressed into a trichotomy—lower classes, central classes, and upper classes—and related to the new fifty-district framework. The result was a clearer, although obviously less refined, demonstration of concomitant variation between class and the dependent variables.

As a final attempt at "scientific" comparison, an average "Social Index" for each of the fifty areas, based on the mean rank order of each district for the four characteristics, was computed. The result was a final "Index Map of London," colored according to "comparative Social Condition" (see fig. 4) in terms of four class intervals.[43] Although he launched into a considered and

FIG. 4.—Index Map of London in Fifty Districts, Colored According to Social Condition

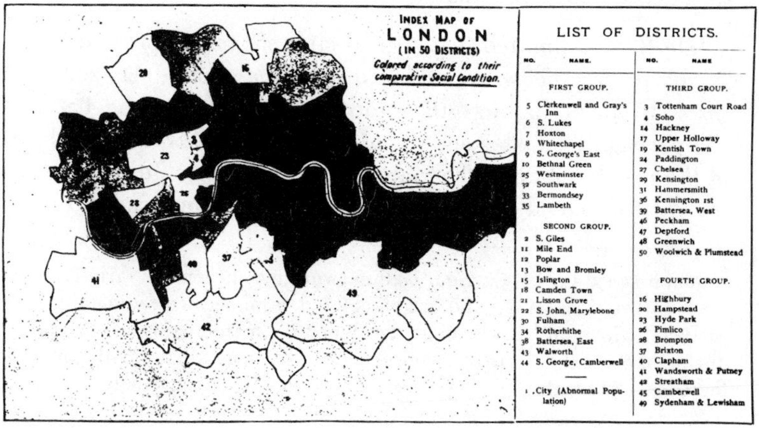

SOURCE: "Final Volume," pp. 18 ff. (Original map in color.)

43 Needless to say, Booth's command of statistical techniques was quite limited. Most of the measures he employed were either matters of

qualified exposition of the interrelationships, Booth still could conclude:

In both table and chart (as also in an accompanying map) the fifty districts into which London has been divided are arranged in the combined order of these four tests of social condition, and it will be seen how slightly these individual tests vary from their mean.[44]

At this point Booth briefly discussed "Poverty in Other Places" and remarked on the value of the "comparative method" with respect to such a universal phenomenon as urban poverty. He commented on the work of his contemporary Rowntree, who had completed a study of the problem in York and whose results (30 per cent in poverty) agreed with his own.[45]

Mr. Rowntree's researches at York have struck a note of comparison between town and town, and have thus helped to open up this great field, but that is not all; with great boldness he has attempted to introduce a new element. He has sought to show not only that a large portion of the population are ill-nourished to the point of being inefficient, but that for many of these it is impossible that it could be otherwise; the remuneration of unskilled labor, the coarse food, and the needs of the human body being what they are.[46]

While Booth admitted that special circumstances operated in different places, he was convinced that the more facts obtained through social inquiry, the more solid would be the basis of comparison, the better one would be able to penetrate to the heart of the problems, and "the more practical the uses" to which such information could be put. He was especially concerned to point

---

common sense or self-devised. Galton, working on genetic variation, had used correlation tables and graphically determined regression lines as early as 1875; and Karl Pearson developed the mathematics of correlation during the nineties. There is no evidence, however, that Booth knew of these developments; certainly he did not employ them in any of his researches.

44 *Ibid.*, p. 16.

45 Benjamin S. Rowntree, *Poverty: A Study of Town Life* (2d ed.; London: Macmillan & Co., 1902).

46 *Ibid.*, p. 30.

out the need for central and local government research bureaus as well as the opportunities for voluntary groups and private individuals in the field of social research.

CONCLUSION

Seventeen years and an equal number of volumes have been occupied with this inquiry . . . the subjects covered offer a wide range; being no less than life and industry as they exist in London at the end of the nineteenth century under the influences of education, religion, and administration.[47]

Thus Booth commented at the conclusion of his massive investigation. And while he saw much that was "black" in the picture of urban life, he nevertheless felt that the general tendency was in the direction of improvement.

The most pressing task, besides that of raising the general standard of living, was, in Booth's view, that of increasing the number of people "who know how to use aright the means that they have."[48] Once again he based his hopes on public education, its extension and reform:

Once more two tasks lie before us: to lift the whole level by recognizing the part which elementary education can really play, and then adapting it for that part; and also to increase the number and the opportunities of those who are capable of profiting more fully by that training they receive.[49]

He saw both religious and administrative bodies as having a part to play but expressed the belief that the trade unions generally had failed to perform their "expected" task in the organization of industry. Significantly, he saw the rise of a "new middle class" among the children of rural immigrants as the hope of the future:

Its advent seems to be the great social fact of today. Those who constitute this class are the especial product of the push of industry; within their circle religion and education find the greatest response; among

47 "Final Volume," p. 200.
48 *Ibid.*, p. 201.
49 *Ibid.*, p. 203.

them all popular movements take their rise, and from them draw their leaders. To them in proportion as they have ideas, political power will pass.[50]

Structural and administrative expansion coupled with a widening mental horizon—which implied the urbanization of the whole of England—were seen as further needs. In essence, Booth advocated a more vigorous expansion of life in all realms: social, political, educational, and industrial. The competition of town and country, each with something worthwhile to contribute, was set up as the *sine qua non* of progress.

At this point, however, his economic-liberal preconceptions became explicit; for, according to Booth, progress ultimately depended on "the deepening of the sentiment of individual responsibility." An aroused public opinion was seen as necessary to assure the existence and efficacious operation of this sentiment. The humanization of private corporations and associations, as well as the cooperation and balancing of the more-or-less mutually exclusive programs of the variety of political, philanthropic, and religious associations under the aegis of this same public opinion, was also viewed as a requirement. Further, the development of a sense of local responsibility on the part of local government boards was another prerequisite.

Characteristically, however, the greatest need remained the acquisition of more facts as the substratum for rational planning and reforms. Here, Booth hopefully and modestly concluded: "*the spirit of patient inquiry is abroad; my attempt is only one of its children.*"[51]

In this he was indeed correct. More than this, the ground of his own studies—the city as a physical and social fact—if not their field—poverty in the midst of plenty—was to become, at least in America, and hardly a decade later, the focus of both an empirical and an academic sociology.

50 *Ibid.*, p. 204.
51 *Ibid.*, p. 214.

3

THE CITY AS A PHYSICAL AND SOCIAL STRUCTURE

It is in the town and not in country, that "terra incognita" needs to be written on our social maps. In the country the machinery of human life is plainly to be seen and easily recognized; personal relations bind the whole together. The equipoise on which existing order rests, whether satisfactory or not, is palpable and evident. It is far otherwise with cities, where as to these questions we live in darkness, with doubting hearts and ignorant unnecessary fears . . . — Charles Booth

THE CRUX of urbanism seems to lie in the fact that over and above the concentration of population there develops a new way of life: when great numbers of people live their lives in close physical proximity and in the presence of an extreme division of labor, traditional modes of human association are transformed; there develop not only new forms of group life but also new perspectives and thought modes.[1] Even in the earliest empirical studies of the city—e.g., John Graunt's classic *Natural and Political Observations made upon the Bills of Mortality*, in seventeenth-century London—there was recognition of a relationship between the physical and social aspects of urbanism.

Not until the nineteenth century, however, did cities experience the kind of growth and expansion that was to make urban living the mode of Western man. And England's early start in the Industrial Revolution hung together with her early and rapid urbanization. As Weber demonstrated in his classic analysis of the rise of cities during this period, the forces basic to this development were primarily economic:

1 These postulates did not, of course, become explicit until the twentieth century in the work of such men as Spengler, Simmel, Weber, and, later, Park, Burgess, and Wirth.

. . . it was the opening of the railroads, with the concomitant development of the iron industry, and expansion of domestic and foreign commerce under free trade which occasioned the great concentration of population in the decade 1841–51, in the seaports and iron-producing districts.[2]

But however much the causal factors were economic in character, their social, cultural, and psychological consequences were of equal import and interest. As these dense concentrations of people grew within the matrix of the new technology and commerce, the problematic qualities of this distinctive form of group life forced itself on the consciousness of interested and intelligent men.

To be sure, Charles Booth never formally addressed himself to the task of formulating in general terms the relationship between the physical and the social structure of the city. Nor did he ever attempt in a self-conscious fashion to deal abstractly and systematically with "class" and "institution" as organizing concepts for the analysis of urban social structure. Neither of these omissions, however, detract from the fact that much of his inquiry dealt with these matters and that, consequently, much of the inquiry's special relevance for the development of an empirical sociology stems from its qualities in these respects.

It is doubtful if Booth ever heard of the term "ecology," much less that he viewed the spatial-distributive dimensions of his investigation as Park did, a generation later:

Insofar as social structure can be defined in terms of position, social changes may be described in terms of movement; and society exhibits, in one of its aspects, characters that can be measured and described in mathematical formulas. . . . It is because social relations are so frequently and so inevitably correlated with spatial relations; because physical distances are so frequently, or seem to be, the indexes of social distances, that statistics have any significance whatever for sociology.[3]

2 Weber, *Growth of Cities*, p. 56.

3 Robert E. Park, "The Urban Community as a Spatial Pattern and a Moral Order," in *The Urban Community*, ed. E. W. Burgess (Chicago: University of Chicago Press, 1926), pp. 166, 177.

Nor was Booth the first to use the spatial-distributive approach in the study of social phenomena: in the 1830's, for example, a number of investigations were made which considered the spatial patterns of such phenomena as crime, prostitution, and vital rates.[4]

Previous investigators, however, either confined themselves to the study of the spatial distribution of a single phenomenon or concerned themselves with such patterns on a nationwide rather than on a community basis. Booth's innovation was to consider the distributive aspect of a wide range of related social phenomena and to focus on a single community. Moreover, the phenomena studied were often treated in conjunction with one another in the context of a single area. Finally, as a result of the predominance of the spatial dimension in Booth's work, a conception of urban areas as analytic tools underwent significant development on both the theoretical and methodological levels. Implicit was an assumption which Park and his students were later to make explicit:

> . . . the underlying notion was that if we could explain the distribution of social problems which varied according to different areas in the community, we could go far in understanding the underlying forces and background causes of urban problems such as crime, delinqency, boys' gangs, homeless men, suicide, divorce, poverty, and so forth.
>
> The emphasis on the distributive aspects of these problems, their concentration, or varying incidence in certain areas of the city was conceived as a new ecological approach in sociology.[5]

When it came to the concepts of "class" and "institution," the situation was much the same. Concerning "class," while Booth was, of course, familiar with the popular conception of communism, it is doubtful if, in fact, he ever read Marx.[6] At the same time his general view of the class structure as well as his interpre-

4 See M. C. Elmer, "Century-old Ecological Studies in France," *American Journal of Sociology*, 39 (July, 1933): 63–70.

5 Walter C. Reckless, *Vice in Chicago* (Chicago: University of Chicago Press, 1933), pp. *viii–ix*.

6 The Simeys cite a letter written to his wife in 1878 in which Booth wrote: ". . . Karl Marks (*sic*)—is that the name? . . ." Simey, *Charles Booth, Social Scientist*, p. 58.

tation of his results for the theory of class conflict stemmed directly from his own economic-liberal prejudices. In regard to the first, in his *Final Volume* Booth viewed class from the accommodative perspective of traditional economic functions:

The settled rich are the holders and trustees of wealth, but, as with the working classes, their true function is to spend wisely rather than to save. . . . With the working classes the object is to render irregularity of income equal to the calls of a regular expenditure; with the rich it is reversed, and the aim is rather to make a comparatively fixed income meet the claims of varying expenditure. . . . It is on the class between that the real task of accumulation devolves. Excluding a section of the professional men whose savings (like those of the working classes), are mainly a matter of insurance, the main object of the lives of the members of this class is money making, and in doing so, even when they are narrowly self-seeking and indifferent to the welfare of others, they must, to a great extent, serve the public.[7]

And in regard to the second, Booth's position was even more patently ideological:

The popular and superficial division of the industrial world into camps of employers and employed is not infrequently accompanied by the assumption that the occupants of each camp represent forces united by the presence of a common enemy. But it would appear that this view is not only superficial but harmful, since the analysis of almost any trade shows us the number and variety of its divergent interests; while a broader view reveals the strength of the forces that, in spite of conspicuous forms of conflict and unrest, make for solidarity among all sections concerned.

For the almost unbroken continuity in the gradations of conditions which is presented to us, not only by society at large, but by the component sections of many individual trades, is among the best-known and healthy characteristics of the national life, while a complete change of individual status is far from uncommon. The discussion therefore of the industrial relationships of employer and employed, as if, on the one side there were a body of rich men with assured incomes, and, on the other, a miserable proletariat, involves a caricature of modern industrial society in this country, for which, in spite of the extremes of poverty and wealth that it presents, there is happily no

7 Booth, "Final Volume," pp. 94–95.

justification. There is neither fixity nor finality in industrial relations, and there are no sharply dividing lines.

But, though this complete gradation is true of the aggregate, analysis shows us a hundred sub-divisions, some by status, but most by occupation. If we take colours for occupations and different shades for the number employed, we can see, in imagination, for every great centre of population presented to us as with a patchwork surface. Sometimes the colour by which an occupation is represented is uniform throughout, but more often it is divided by the clearly defined shades of differing status. . . . The demarcation whether between different colours or between different shades of the same colours, are not lines of severance; the great fabric holds together, albeit with ragged edges and some thin places.[8]

Beyond these matters, however, what is relevant in Booth's analysis of the social structure of London is the implicit but nonetheless pervasive conception of class as "style of life" and, correlatively, as a force in the community. And the latter postulate was immeasurably enhanced by Booth's common-sense and naturalistic approach to social institutions: on the one hand they were implicitly viewed as any formally organized collective function; on the other hand, none was too minor or too sacred to be considered—the catmeat shop, the brothel, and the Church of England all came into Booth's purview. Indeed, it was the fruitful articulation of the notion of class with that of institution which communicated so well the force of class differences in the lives of the people and in the functioning of the community—a theme, incidentally, that was not to be revived either theoretically or empirically in sociology until the work of W. Lloyd Warner and his students in America, in the thirties.

In both these general areas—the spatial-distributive aspects of the urban community and the force of class in its social organization and processes—the contributions of the inquiry will be seen to lie in the objective manner and spirit with which the research was pursued, in the wide range of facts considered relevant, and,

8 "Industry Series," V, 140–41. Later studies, especially those of Warner and his students in America, were to be less self-consciously, though no less functionally, ideological.

beyond the facts uncovered on the descriptive level, the numerous postulates and propositions developed not only to account for things as they "were" but also things as they "become."

The City as a Spatial Order

Probably no other type of study contributed so directly to the development of an empirical social science than that which aimed simply at the location of social phenomena in space. Beyond Booth's focus on the city as a spatial entity and his resulting concern with differential patterns of distribution which led to an increasingly sophisticated concept of areas as units for social analysis, the introduction of the time dimension raised questions concerning typical sequences which, in turn, led to the explicit formulation of hypotheses concerning the forces which governed the processes observed. The explication of Booth's contributions in these respects will consider (1) patterns of distribution of urban population types and functions in both their static and dynamic aspects; (2) conceptions of areas—administrative, natural, and analytic; and (3) urban growth and planning.

PATTERNS OF DISTRIBUTION Booth's social classification of the city's population and graphic spatial summaries of his results by means of his "Descriptive Map of London Poverty" and "Map Shewing Degrees of Poverty in London," as well as his final "Index Map of London," colored according to the social condition of the districts drawn, have already been noted. A detailed perusal of the first, which was often referred to as the "social map of London," leads to the following conclusive observations with respect to the *residential patterns of the various classes:* (1) *The wealthy or upper classes* were almost confined to the West End; their homes surrounded the two great intra-city open spaces —Regent's Park and Hyde Park; and their only other appearances on the map were in South London, a good distance from the river, and as they worked their way towards the suburbs in the northwest. (2) In the case of the *well-to-do middle classes,* the most striking fact was their tendency to settle along the main thoroughfares which led into the center of the city, often cutting through relatively poor areas.[9] Their greatest concentrations were on the west side of the city between the wealthy and the poor and on the outskirts on the north and south. (3) *The poor or working classes* were to be found in the east, on both sides of the river but especially in the "East End," abutting the City. Given the color scheme employed, in which the darker colors were associated with the lowest status and income, the color of the streets become noticeably darker whenever the river, railroad tracks, or terminals were approached. As Booth generalized, conversely, "the color lightens with distance from the river."[10] (4) While the majority of the *lowest class* lived in the east and south, there was also observable a random character to their distribution, accounted for by the operation of special distorting factors (largely isolation), which will be discussed in the consideration of areas. Booth's succinct (and somewhat prophetic conclusions in the light of later developments in human ecology) was that, ". . . residential London tends to be arranged by class in rings with the most uniform poverty at the centre."[11]

In addition to the distribution by class of London's residents, the "Industry Series" provided Booth with the data for tracing their *distribution by occupation.* Here, as previously noted, the methods employed to summarize the data were the conceptual devices of "rings" and "compass areas" (e.g., North London, East London, etc.), rather than maps. The concepts of "inner" and "outer" rings became especially handy instruments for obtaining rough measures of relative concentration or dispersion of the residential patterns of various types of workers. Needless to say, the contrasts were often striking: whereas among those employed in "education" 16 per cent lived in the inner ring in contrast to 84 per cent in the outer ring, the respective figures for dock laborers

9 A similar pattern existed in large American cities before the advent of the motor car and other rapid, convenient, and inexpensive forms of transportation which opened up the periphery of the city to residential settlement.

10 "Religious Influences," IV, 166.

11 "Final Volume," p. 205.

were 65 per cent and 35 per cent. Booth summarized his findings as follows:

> . . . we find for all London 38 per cent of families living in the inner and 62 per cent in the outer districts. The mean position in this case is occupied by bakers, butchers, and fishmongers, who, as they cater to local wants, are found fairly evenly distributed throughout London. The same is true for general laborers, probably for a similar reason. The extreme instances of centralization are docklaborers . . . tailors, leather-dressers, fur-pullers, etc., and costermongers, all of whom have 63 to 65 per cent of their number dwelling in the inner circle. At the other end of the scale . . . we find professional men and commercial clerks with only 15 to 20 per cent living inside, and 80 to 85 per cent living in the outer districts.[12]

In the special inquiry into the "Influx of the Population" in the "Poverty Series," the pattern of residence of yet another urban type, *the migrant to the city,* was investigated. Typical was the manner in which the study was posed:

> . . . amid these vague surmises nothing definite is known [as to the extent and significance of rural-urban migration]. When do the immigrants come? Why do they come? What industries do they engage in? What social classes do they recruit? How do they affect the volume of metropolitan crime, pauperism, and distress? What, in short, is the contribution which they furnish to the common life of London?[13]

After considering the sources by region and distance from the city, age, and causes in terms of "push" and "pull" factors, the distribution of the influx was analyzed by source and residence within the city. A series of excellent rate maps was constructed to portray the results (see fig. 5).

The proportion of provincial migrants was observed generally to increase with distance from the center of London, with the exception of the City area: "As a general rule [provincial migrants] settle most in the newer and more sparsely peopled outlying parts,

12 "Industry Series," V, 31. The small shopkeepers invariably "lived in," which accounted for their mean position.

13 "Poverty Series," III, 59. H. Lewellyn-Smith was given credit for this investigation in the index to the volume.

FIG. 5.—Proportion of Population of East London and Hackney Born in Other Parts of the United Kingdom, by Registration Sub-districts.

SOURCE: *Labour and Life*, I, 545 ff. (Original map in color.)

especially those which have been rapidly built over."[14] The intra-city distribution of provincial migrants was also calculated relative to the traditional compass areas of the city, the north and west having the largest proportions.

Foreign immigrants to the city showed exactly the reverse pattern of residence: they tended to locate near the center, their proportions decreasing as distance from the center increased. Moreover, they were observed to be segregated into small colonies, with the exception of the Germans, but especially in the case of the Russian and Polish Jews and the Italians.[15]

Nor did Booth neglect the dynamic aspect of these distributive patterns. The most documented general observation in this respect was what Booth referred to as the "centrifugal tendency" of the classes to move outward from the center of the city: "The dominant social fact observable is the steady movement northward of the people. Throughout London movement from the centre outwards is noticeable."[16]

Indeed, this empirical finding was conceptualized at one point as the *general law of successive migration* in which there was a decided drift from ring to ring, those coming into an area tending to be poorer than those who left. For example, in the southwest:

> The red and yellow classes ["well-to-do" and "wealthy"] are leaving, and the streets which they occupied are becoming pink and pink-barred; whilst the streets which were formerly pink turn to purple and purple to light blue.[17]

This orderly process of class residential succession was seen

14 *Ibid.*, p. 12. This exception was accounted for by the "peculiar composition of the resident population of the City, which is largely made up of caretakers and shop assistants living on business premises—two classes which seem to number more than the average proportion of countrymen, perhaps because of the responsibility and steadiness required." *Ibid.*

15 This situation was viewed in large measure to be due to the power of the pennypost: one member of an immigrant family having come to London and made good, a letter home would bring other relatives and friends.

16 "Religious Influences," I, 15.

17 *Ibid.*, V, 194.

again and again. With respect to Hackney in the northeast, Booth commented:

No district . . . shows so well the general law of successive migration. The tip of the tail of wealth may be seen disappearing out of the nourthern edge of the map. The wealthy outgoers move . . . their place being taken by a comfortable servant keeping middle class as shown in the North. . . . Further South on the Western edge of the map when compared with that of ten years ago, shows the change from "red" to "pink-barred-with-red," denoting generally the incoming of lodgers and notices of "apartments" in the house windows. South again the "pink-barred" becomes the "pink" of the artisan.[18]

Moreover, while Booth never used the term, the following quotation can be seen to be an almost perfect "natural history" of neighborhood change and decay in the context of the general centrifugal movement. Especially notable are the implications of both generality and inevitability:

Now the difference between a red street which might almost be yellow and a yellow street that is suffering from decay is enormous, and hardly to be indicated by any scheme of colour. . . . In the [latter] pretence in some form reigns supreme. Great sacrifices are made to maintain appearances. . . . Houses are now occupied, now empty; tenants come and go. The house, a home no longer, is made a source of income. There are guests who pay, or the drawing room floor is let, or boarders are taken, or at length the fatal word 'Apartments" appears in the fanlight over the door. Against its downfall each street struggles in vain. Those who can afford to do so leave the stricken district, and those who come or those who do not go are alike in seeking to grasp an elusive advantage, desiring to trade on that vanishing quality—the fashionable character of the neighborhood.[19]

Booth was not content, however, merely to describe the typical patterns of residential segregation of various types of people and the operation of the general process of succession. He went on to consider the forces underlying such patterns and processes. And the most potent force which gave rise to the observed patterns of

18 *Ibid.*, I, 111.
19 *Ibid.*, III, 108–9.

residence was seen as the pressure which existed at the center and which, in turn, was transmitted from ring to ring.

Four primary factors were hypothesized to underlie the development of this central pressure: (1) the natural increase of the population; (2) the excess of migration from rural areas and abroad; (3) the demand for space for other than residential purposes; and (4) the requirements of a higher personal and official standard of living. Parenthetically, Booth regarded the centrifugal tendency as the natural result of, and method for alleviating the central pressure: he reasoned that insofar as the general freedom of movement of the metropolitan population was restricted by such obstacles as the lack of adequate transportation facilities, municipal ordinances as to crowding, and so forth, congestion inevitably resulted and became a characteristic feature of urban life.

The increase in population owing to the influence of both natural increase and an excess of immigration was fully documented. The third factor, the expansion of the central business district, deserves further comment in the light of later developments in theories of urban growth and patterns of residence. In the first place, according to the evidence, a considerable amount of construction was going on at this time in London by both the municipality and private concerns, calculated to catch up the city, so-to-speak, with the service demands of a population which had been growing by leaps and bounds for a century. The new concerns for public welfare and new concepts of municipal services and local administrative responsibilities in this respect were just becoming operative. As a result, a great deal of demolition was taking place in the inner portions of the city to make room for expanding business premises, warehouses, low-cost model dwellings, as well as railroad terminals and trackage. This, of course, resulted first in the displacement of the poorer classes which, as we have seen, were concentrated in the "inner ring" of the city. In turn, an "invasion" of the middle-class districts, farther out, took place. An example of the operation of such a process in the east central and west central areas of the city may be seen from the following:

The greatest change during the last ten years has been the displacement of dwelling houses by warehouses, the last to leave the more central parts being the poor or the inhabitants of the model dwellings . . . the poor, displaced by demolition, having first tried to crowd the neighboring streets and only partially succeeding, have been forced to go further afield.[20]

The rich and fashionable, who once dwelt in Soho and Bloomsbury, have left . . . their places have been taken by business houses, offices, hotels and boarding houses. . . . Generally speaking, the poor have been driven out by demolition and by rebuilding for the middle classes, and the middle classes by the encroachment of business houses and the multiplication of boarding houses and hotels.[21]

In nineteenth-century London, even the middle classes were not immune from the forces of urban expansion.

Once the development of the central pressure had been accounted for, the factors operating to produce the differential sifting of the various classes and the direction which the general movement took were considered. Among others, Booth regarded the available means of transportation as a primary factor in determining the direction of movement:

More generally the movement takes place gradually from ring to ring accompanied by a slow change of class. But the advance on new ground shows a noticeable tendency to shoot out tongues, like the Sun's corona; the intervals between being filled up later. These tongues follow the "lie of the land" and the facilities offered for speculation in building; but the more important cause and the key to the explanation is always to be found in the available means of communication. . . .[22]

The result of this factor was further illustrated by noting its double function: whereas the intra-urban railway functioned to bring residents from the outer ring into the center of the city, it also operated just as surely to "carry them off." And Booth documented this latter function and its results time and again:

20 "Religious Influences," II, 166.
21 *Ibid.*, p. 206.
22 "Final Volume," p. 183.

Part of the deterioration of the middle class streets in the West . . . is due to the carrying off of their people to Western suburbs by the Tube Railway and the electric tramways.[23]

Moreover, not only did transportation facilities operate to produce social decay by facilitating the exodus of the well-to-do, but also, on occasion, it acted to prevent degeneration of an area. For example:

In Shepherd's Bush and Hammersmith [in the Outer West] . . . there was fear of decay until the electric railway gave new life to the whole district by connecting it with inner London.[24]

Besides transportation facilities which governed accessibility in terms of time-cost considerations, the physical "lie of the land" was also seen to affect the distribution of population types within the city. According to Booth, the general rule seemed to hold that, the higher the ground, the greater the value, and, correlatively, the greater the tendency for it to be inhabited by the wealthy and for the lower classes, conversely, to be relegated to the lower ground. For example, Booth noted: "As the land rises toward Putney Heath, so the inhabitants rise in the social scale."[25]

The Parish of St. Thomas extends to the higher ground . . . and thus contains an admixture of rich and poor . . . but Holy Trinity parish lies entirely on the lower level, both socially and physically.[26]

The character of the houses and of the people . . . changes with the ground . . . on the higher ground, marked improvement is at once apparent.[27]

While both transportation facilities and the lie of the land had monetary values and were thus ultimately operative in terms of their cost in the determination of residential location, Booth noted the operation of a different type of force if this factor was held constant.

23 "Religious Influences," III, 132.
24 *Ibid.*, p. 160.
25 *Ibid.*, V, 207.
26 *Ibid.*, p. 82.
27 *Ibid.*, VI, 106–7.

The decision . . . [to move out to the suburbs] depends not so much on class or on amount of income—over a certain minimum—as on the constitution of the family. The father of young children finds it best to establish their home as far from the crowded parts of London as he can afford to travel to and from his work . . . but later on, when employment is sought by the younger generation, or better opportunities of education for them, or of pleasure for all, the balance may turn in favor of more central quarters.[28]

In other words, the position of the family in terms of its growth cycle was hypothesized as another factor in the determination of residential location.

In conclusion, Booth indicated that in any individual case or within any single district, many of these factors operated in a complex. Thus, while a general tendency (such as the correlation between high ground and high status) might hold, other forces might operate to negate the force of a single factor. For example, if an area was predominantly industrial, the poor were sometimes observed "to make the crests and the sides of the hill their own."

The city, of course, has been traditionally characterized not only by the size of its population and the heterogeneity of its inhabitants but also by the complexity of its division of labor. The latter also expressed itself on the purely spatial level. And, especially in the "Industry Series," Booth documented in great detail the centralization of urban functions—he typically employed the term "localization"—ranging from the various trades and professions to the different types of service institutions indigeneous to the urban scene.[29] For example:

London, as the head of English journalism, has for its center the locality of Fleet Street. Within a half-mile radius of this thoroughfare

28 "Final Volume," p. 205. Booth also mentioned the *type of housing* and *reputation of the area* as other factors determining the spatial sifting of population types.

29 Earnest Aves was given credit for writing most of the summary materials, Part II, of the "Industry Series," the most relevant of which in the present instance were: "London as a Centre of Trade and Industry" and "The Localization and Diffusion of Trades in London." "Industry Series," V, *vi.*

are produced the great bulk of the two thousand periodicals which are issued from London printing offices.[30]

Again: "Bermondsey is the center of the London leather trade. Here is the leather market, and here round the market are tan yards—in which the raw hides are treated."[31]

Moreover, the division of labor in a single manufacturing process was also reflected in space:

The manufacture of silk hats is concentrated to a great extent in the neighborhood of Blackfriar's Road. No less then seventeen factories, or about half the whole number in London, are in this district.[32]

Caps . . . are chiefly made in the Jewish workshops of East London . . .[33]

The economic advantages that accrued from the centralization of industrial functions were held by Booth to be the major factor in its development. On the most general level, he recognized that localization resulted in the development of an organic entity whose size and complexity were directly a function of the size of the market. There resulted, ". . . in a given area the same interdependence of parts that national or even international industries illustrate in other aspects, on a larger and grander scale."[34]

And, for many different types of industry, there was observed:

. . . the grouping around the main processes of those allied and sub-

30 *Ibid.*, IV, 150.
31 *Ibid.*, II, 126.
32 *Ibid.*, III, 26.
33 *Ibid.*, p. 36.
34 *Ibid.*, V, 97. On the highest level, Booth observed: "The recognized characteristics of modern industry are an extreme division of labor, a continuously expanding use of machinery, and a general complexity of organization [which], are closely associated with its organic character. . . . The result is an interdependent and very complicated machine, bound together by the ligaments of credit, in the action of which the productive impulse is gradually removed from immediate requirements of the actual consumer, and becomes dependent on speculation and the forestalling of demand." *Ibid.*, pp. 69–75.

sidiary trades and processes, which, combined with adequate means of distribution, go to secure the maximum of aggregate efficiency.[35]

Such centralization had the further result of developing a trade "atmosphere and environment" which operated further to increase the advantages of the locale.

As examples of such industrial and commercial centralization, Booth pointed to the Fleet Street area (already mentioned) and the East London furniture trade, among others. In regard to the former, all the functions connected with printed intelligence were found in the area: newspaper offices, printing firms, and further, " . . . nearly every branch of allied service . . . the whole affording a conspicuous instance of centralization and development."[36]

Significantly, the explanation of trade concentration was sought originally in irrational factors, the locales being a matter of chance rather than rational planning or relevant inherent qualities of the *site qua* site: "The precise localization [of any trade] finds an explanation not in any inherent advantages possessed by the particular areas in which they flourish, but rather in chance."[37] Beyond this, however, centralization itself became a self-reinforcing process:

A favorable start has been followed by a gradual development, adding to the strength of the trade and securing in an increasing degree, the advantages of connection and efficiency that concentration tends to ensure. In the absence of any particular unfitness, the locality gradually acquires a special suitability: a great market is established; a tradition formed, and the associations of a trade dominate and give character to the whole district.[38]

Incidentally, Booth was especially appreciative of "the City" as the "centre and core of London," which was the locus of functions whose inuuences spread far beyond the local complex:

The Stock Exchange and Lloyds; the great produce centers of Mark and Mincing Lanes; and Paternoster Row are among the many impor-

35 *Ibid.*, p. 97.
36 *Ibid.*, p. 98.
37 *Ibid.*
38 *Ibid.*

tant examples, all with their appropriate settings of offices, warehouses, and showrooms within the City. But the greatest instance of all is found in the localization within its borders of the banking system of the Empire . . . in this we have an instance of concentration so profoundly important in its effects that even the chances of employment of the poorest seamstress or casual laborer of East London are connected, by a chain of sequence that would be easy to trace, with the stability of a few associations established within a stone's throw of the Bank of England.[39]

Once more, numerous hypotheses were presented concerning the factors determining the localization of various urban industries: the localization of the packing-case workers in the City, the carriage builders near the West End, and the heavy-van builders mainly in the east and southeast was to be explained by "the wish to secure the advantages of nearness to an appropriate market."[40] On the other hand, the light-van makers, insofar as the demand for their product was more general, were cited as an instance of a complete lack of centralization.

The manufacturers of envelopes, while forced to move because of an increase in ground rents, were, in their new location, "still near to the center of business correspondence and exports.[41] Yet again, certain trades (e.g., brush-making and watch-making) clung for traditional reasons to their original sites. Especially interesting was Booth's recognition of the grouping of the heavy industries on the periphery of the outer ring of the city because,

. . . they required, relative to the numbers employed, large premises [in addition to conformity with municipal ordinances] and it . . . is likely to be explained by the double necessity of avoiding high rentals, and of securing the easy command of cheap means of transport.[42]

The box-making factories, for instance, were noted to locate near the canals, which provided an excellent and inexpensive means of transportation for their products.

39 *Ibid.*, pp. 100–101. Shades of Darwin's "cats and clover"!
40 *Ibid.*, p. 99.
41 *Ibid.*
42 *Ibid.*

The character of a trade itself in terms of the time factor in distribution was proposed as another element governing the need for central location or lack of it:

Book-work proper, as distinguished from periodicals, is leaving London . . . with Magazines it is different, their position approaches that of newspapers which must be printed where they are published . . . Weekly and Monthly Journals fall into the same category as magazines and other periodicals, but the Daily Papers form a distinct group . . . rapidity of production is the most important point . . . rapid distribution is as essential as fast machinery.[43]

Finally, the purely physical features of an area might account for the location of some types of industries: e.g., the riverside trades. Indeed, Booth often pointed to the importance of the Thames in the life of London, not popularly, as a source of pride, but in terms of its great and pervasive influence on the city's industrial and social processes.

As in the matter of residential location, in the final analysis a complex of typical factors operated in particular instances to determine the locus and degree of centralization. These were summarized as follows:

1. Presence of a supply of labor
2. Proximity to an appropriate market
3. Accessibility to suitable means of transportation
4. Variations of rent in different parts of the city
5. Physical necessity
6. Municipal ordinances
7. Tradition

Not only were the industries of the city seen to display a variety of patterns with respect to their location and centralization, but the professions were marked as subject to similar forces. In these instances, the presence of an appropriate market, together with tradition, were viewed as the major factors in the determination of their location:

In the West End . . . the representatives of medicine and dentistry are found in their greatest number in the neighborhood of Harley Street

43 *Ibid.*, II, 196.

and Hanover Square. Over the remaining districts they are scattered fairly evenly, though the dentists have a traditional home in St. Martin's Lane and Ludgate Hill, and all seem to give preference to houses situated in a square, or at the corner of a street. In a square the light is better and there is greater quiet, while a corner has the counterbalancing advantages of greater prominence and the convenience of a side door to the surgery.[44]

Further:

London seems the natural home of barristers, solicitors and law clerks, and the majority are London born. Their headquarters are in the Inns of Court and Chancery Lane, at the junction of the City and the East End, with the Courts of Justice in their midst, and a large proportion of the legal business of the whole country . . . is here transacted . . . the Barristers' chambers are to be found in the quiet backwaters formed by the courts and gardens of Grey's Inn, Lincoln's Inn, and the Temple. . . . Solicitors are more scattered. A number of large firms have their offices in the City and there are a good many also in the West End proper, some of high repute and active in "family business," and others, especially in the streets off Bond Street and Regent's Street, who do business for tradesmen and money-lenders and choose this position in order to be near their clients.[45]

By their nature, service institutions such as retail shops, churches, amusement places, etc., were found to be relatively dispersed throughout the city—insofar as they catered to local needs—in contrast to the comparative centralization of the larger wholesale and manufacturing establishments. Booth commented especially on the retail distributor who must be "ubiquitous and suited in every case to his immediate surroundings."[46]

The conception of the "suitability" of institutions relative to their environment and clientele was one of the most discerning hypotheses presented in this area of the inquiry. Even a typology of retail shops based on the character of its environment and patrons was developed on the assumption that:

44 *Ibid.*, IV, 80.
45 *Ibid.*, p. 72.
46 *Ibid.*, V, 101.

Determination of the character of the shop by the character of its neighborhood illustrated in every branch of distribution . . . and the same relationship is found when many branches are combined in a single undertaking, as in large stores.[47]

There were, thus: (1) the small "general" shop in the poor, back streets near the center of the city; (2) the prosperous glitter and exuberant shows of the main thoroughfares of industrial or suburban districts; (3) the substantial establishments of the City; and (4) the more delicate catering of Regent Street and Piccadilly.

While retail shops were found to be relatively dispersed, on the basis of the above typology, differential concentrations appeared, for example:

It is noticeable how indigeneous is the general shop to the more central poor districts of London. Although the "inner" ring" has only a little over a third of the total population of the metropolis, it contains 58 per cent of the general shopkeepers.[48]

Again, the exceptional and unique nature of "the City" was demonstrated:

. . . its retail shops . . . reflect the demands, not of its residents, but of its immense day population. Certain streets and particular firms that have established a special reputation are, in somewhat analogous way, exceptional to the extent that they are able to attract a demand from those living in other parts.[49]

As previously noted, Booth turned to the "spot map" as a device for summarizing his findings with respect to the localization in space of such institutions as the church, missions, schools, and public houses. Moreover, different symbols were employed to denote denominational differences in the case of the churches, "board" as over against "voluntary" schools, and different types of licenses in the case of public houses.

In general, the public houses were concentrated at busy centers, along the main thoroughfares, and in the poor districts. In-

47 *Ibid.*

48 *Ibid.*, III, 251 n.

49 *Ibid.*, V, 101 n.

deed, Booth proposed that "poor and old districts can be traced by the number of beer houses in them."[50] On the other hand, he noted that "in the new areas, "jug" licenses replace beer houses as the mark of the poor or working class areas, and grocer's licenses mark the shopping streets of the well-to-do."[51]

Although unmapped, the localization of places of amusement, public markets, transportation and communication facilities was also noted in Booth's descriptions of the various areas of the city. Implicit, at least, was the hypothesis that there was a basic complement of institutions which must exist and locate so as to serve the needs of the neighborhood or local community.

Nor did Booth employ maps in portraying the distribution of other social phenomena such as crime, prostitution, etc.; nevertheless, their spatial aspects were fully documented. For example, the concentration of crime in East London was noted:

Hoxton is the leading criminal quarter of London, and indeed of all England; and it is easy to see how pleasantly central and suitable a position it occupies for nefarious projects. . . .[52]

The prevalence of prostitution was observed wherever family life was relatively absent and the population tended to be mobile: Booth generalized on the relationship between the presence of railway terminals and the incidence of prostitution, regarding the former as a "stimulus" to the latter.

Finally, in his inquiries into the city as a spatial order, Booth was led to a very modern insight into the problematic separation between place of residence and place of work. For even at this point, the dissociation between the two, although not present in the degree to which it exists today, was generally marked and becoming increasingly so with the development of convenient, rapid, and inexpensive forms of intra-urban transit facilities. As he remarked:

. . . the localization of a trade does not involve a corresponding localization of the homes of those engaged in it. On the contrary, place of

50 "Religious Influences," IV, p. 159.
51 "Industry Series," I, 193.
52 "Religious Influences," II, 111.

residence and place of work are steadily becoming increasingly independent of, and even remote from, each other.[53]

Further, the difference between the day and night populations of the City was cited as evidence of the degree to which such a separation had taken place:

. . . it is clear that in this remarkable divergence, [301,384 as compared with 37,964, the day and night populations of the City] we have only a conspicuous illustration of a widespread modern tendency. The probability that the City banker or merchant will live in Kent or Kensington, and the City clerk in Camberwell or Crouch End, finds its counterpart in the influences and facilities that are inducing many operatives of every class to live in the outer ring of London, with the certainty of lower rents and the hope of better hygienic conditions.[54]

Thus, it was pointed out that while the workers tended to disperse to the various quarters of the city according to their class and means, the trend in industry was toward centralization and segregation. This separation, coupled with the increase in intracity transportation facilities, was suggested to result in an increase in the mobility of the urban resident:

It may, indeed, be argued that in large centers of population, it will become a more conspicuous feature, for while the migration of the family remains necessarily difficult and costly, the movement of the individual to and fro, is constantly becoming cheaper and simpler. The advantages of localization are thus secured by an increasing number of trades, the members of which may play and sleep many miles distant from the area in which they work, and the individual worker becomes, to an increasing extent, the relatively mobile element in modern industrial life.[55]

Understandably, the prominence of the spatial dimension in the life and labour of the people inevitably led Booth, sometimes implicitly, sometimes explicitly, to deal with the problem of "areas"—as bases for reporting data, as units of analysis, and

53 "Industry Series," V, 96.

54 *Ibid.*, p. 189. No indication is given concerning the source of these data.

55 *Ibid.*, p. 97.

even as theoretical factors in the understanding and explanation of the social phenomena at stake in the inquiry. And it is to this aspect of his research that we now turn.

CONCEPTIONS OF AREAS Nowhere is the developmental character of the inquiry more clearly illustrated than in Booth's changing conception of and use of areal units. Nevertheless, despite elements of confusion and inconsistency (which stemmed in part from the time span the research involved), one of its most modern aspects was the development of an increasingly explicit, precise, and thoughtful appreciation of the qualities and defects of various types of areal units for social research. In addition, Booth had something to say about the determinants of areal character, as well as about the functional significance of different types of areas in the life of the city.

At least four different types of areas can be identified in the course of the inquiry: (1) administrative areas, (2) presentational areal constructs, (3) "natural" areas, and (4) analytic areal constructs. The first type—*administrative areas*—involved those territorial divisions of the city delineated by various official bodies for their own purposes. Examples of such areas employed by Booth were the previously mentioned School Board divisions and blocks which were the basis of reporting the data in the "Poverty" series, and the Registrar General's registration districts and sub-districts which were the basis of reporting the crowding data in the "Industry" series. A third example was the ecclesiastical parishes of the Church of England which played a role in the "Religious Influences" series.

Unfortunately, where their boundaries were not completely arbitrary, they were drawn with an eye to particular administrative rather than "social" concerns. As a result, these areas were found by Booth to be typically heterogeneous with respect to location, size of population, and social characteristics. The parishes, for example, numbered over 600 but varied in population size from a few hundred to over 30,000. Nor did the boundaries of a single area known as "Hackney" drawn by the Registrar General completely coincide with those drawn by the London School Board.[56]

The *presentational areal constructs* were employed by Booth primarily to organize the presentation of his data rather than to serve an analytic function. This type was exemplified by the previously mentioned traditional compass areas of the city (e.g., East London) and the twenty-three "Districts" that figured in the "Religious Influences" series. The former illustrate perfectly the kind of inconsistency encountered throughout the inquiry: though their designation remained fairly constant, that of their subdivisions varied considerably. Similar to administrative areas, they varied as to size and degree of homogeneity; their boundaries were not always functional for sociological purposes; and Booth tended to be rather impressionistic in his treatment of them.

The "Districts" simply represented relatively small and convenient areas for presenting the results of the investigation into religious and other influences on the problem of poverty. Some were homogeneous enough to give them an element of sociological meaning; others, such as "North London," were just the reverse:

> [The North London District] does not lend itself very well to treatment as a whole, nor does it fall readily into component parts having a unit of their own. . . . The district is cut up by great thoroughfares and by several railway lines, and by the artificial channel of the New River; but the divisions thus formed carry no social significance. . . . There is no symmetry of convenience or natural order of any kind in these arrangements . . . [it] . . . reflects the absence of well-defined subdivisions, either physical or social.[57]

The third type—*natural areas*—refers to those areas which were the unplanned product of physical, technological, and sociocultural forces through time, in the urban situation. While Booth never employed this terminology, his recognition of the existence of such areas as unit entities within the metropolitan spatial pat-

56 In order to compare his data on "apparent means" and "crowding" as measures of poverty, Booth was forced to develop methods for adjusting his data. "Labour and Life of the People in London," p. 567.

57 "Religious Influences," I, 115–18.

tern, as well as his understanding of the forces underlying their development and of their functional significance, constitutes yet another major insight. Under this category are included "the City," the previously mentioned "trades areas," together with such concepts as "neighborhood," "foreign colony" (the Jews of Whitechaple), and, especially, the "poverty area."

All of these were viewed as having an existence as real units. While the concepts of "neighborhood" and "foreign colony" were essentially employed in a common-sense fashion, that of "poverty area" represented one of the most developed and sophisticated areal concepts in the inquiry. Specifically, it denoted the little groups of "black and blue" streets which, it will be remembered, had a more or less random pattern of distribution on the "social map" of London.

Analytic areal constructs constituted the fourth type and were exemplified by the "compound blocks" that Booth employed in the construction of the rate map "Shewing Degrees of Poverty in London," and by the fifty "Districts" colored according to social condition and used in the final "Index Map of London." Both these territorial divisions were self-consciously conceived and constructed with specific analytic purposes in mind. Along with the concept of natural area, they represent the most solid ecological insights and contributions to a physical view of the city contained in the inquiry.

Apropos of the concept of areas, Booth also made explicit their unit qualities as environments as well as the factors which gave rise to their characters as environments, both generally and in specific areas of London. Of course, many administrative areas did have distinct qualities of their own, a fact which was often observed:

> Each district has its character—its peculiar flavour. One seems to be conscious of it in the streets. It may be in the faces of the people or what they carry—perhaps a reflexion is thrown in this way from the prevailing trades—or it may be in the sounds one hears, or in the character of the buildings.[58]

58 "Poverty Series," I, 66.

On the other hand, Booth was soon made aware that many such areas did not always express the spatial dimension of his own interest in any valid fashion. For example:

Midway between Whitechapel and Stepney, in character as well as geographically, comes St. George's in-the-West. Doubtless a line might be drawn which would fairly divide the population of St. George's into two portions, the one falling naturally (*sic*) with Stepney and the docks, the other side with Whitechapel and the Jewish quarters.[59]

Needless to say, the question of areal character and analytic function led inevitably to the matter of boundaries. In the first place, the irrelevance to the purposes for which they were drawn of the boundaries of even some administrative areas (especially the ecclesiastical parishes) was often noted:

From a religious point of view it is reasonable to treat this . . . group of parishes as a whole, for with those who attend church, parochial boundaries have no practical existence.[60]

Again:

As regards their congregations, parish boundaries do not exist, and as regards work among the poor these boundaries are as a matter of course broken into and overlapped and ignored by the numerous missionary enterprises.[61]

But Booth soon learned that boundaries were often more than merely a line drawn on a map or even a street, and the function of physical barriers as boundaries (whether natural or technological) was often emphasized: "Docks and railways make a distinct break between Rotherhithe and Deptford; the creek and Ravensbourne [valley] sever Deptford from Greenwich. . . ."[62] And again, "The hospital and park, with Blackheath in the rear, separate East from West Greenwich."[63]

59 *Ibid.*, pp. 63–64.
60 "Religious Influences," VI, 81.
61 *Ibid.*, II, 184.
62 *Ibid.*, V, 3–4.
63 *Ibid.*, p. 41.

Such barriers occasionally functioned in the delineation of administrative districts and also played a part in Booth's own presentational areal constructs. The best example of the latter was, of course, the river Thames, which divided North from South London. In more inclusive terms, Booth observed:

South London is different from North London . . . the differences lying deep. They are historical and physical (*sic*) in origin, but are industrial, social and moral in result. . . .[64]

Railroads and topographical elevation, as well as open spaces, were also observed to make for more functional and realistic dividing lines between areas. Concerning the "Districts" employed in ordering the materials in the "Religious Influences" series, this point was often made:

Crossing the barrier formed by the Great Eastern Railway, we pass into another world. We leave behind the floating population of common lodging houses and night shelters the low women of the "furnished rooms," and the foul but thriving poverty of the Jews. We are no longer struck by the foreign appearance of the streets; we are conscious of a different moral atmosphere.[65]

. . . the ridge of hills . . . is broken . . . by the valley . . . and the rising ground is continued to its highest point. This ground forms a natural boundary dividing the district from the rest of London.[66]

. . . the most notable feature of this district are its open spaces . . . this chain of grass and trees divides the district and in what follows we shall adopt this division.[67]

On the other hand, such barriers were often observed within delineated administrative areas, detracting from their meaningfulness as units of analysis:

Old Deptford itself may be said to be divided into two parts by the railway, that on the river side . . . still retaining the picturesque charm . . . which is lacking altogether in the depressing district to the South.[68]

64 *Ibid.*, IV, 5.
65 *Ibid.*, II, 67.
66 *Ibid.*, VI, 57.
67 *Ibid.*, I, 169.
68 *Ibid.*, V, 7.

Finally, physical barriers were observed also to have a more general, disorganizing function on occasion:

The number of railway lines carried on arches and embankments act as barriers and make local communication unnecessarily difficult.[69] The Common is like a sea . . . in winter it is a barrier rarely to be crossed.[70]

Indeed, while Booth was not always consistent and explicit about the functional nature of physical and technological barriers as areal boundaries in his own constructs, his "poverty areas" typically involved physical boundaries which acted to isolate both the area and its inhabitants from the mainstream of urban life and activities:

Another dark spot of long-standing poverty and extremely low life . . . is wedged in between the Regent's Canal and the gas works.[71]

In Battersea poverty is caught and held in successive railway loops . . . beginning with the dark blue and black area lying between the gas works and the railway. . . . One area with only two exits . . . [another] with only two footpaths across the railway . . . [another] with only a nothern exit. . . . This is one of the best object-lessons in "poverty traps" in London.[72]

Boundaries and barriers, however, did not in themselves exhaust the concept of area for Booth. Rather, areas were defined relative to their social character. And in view of the primary focus of the inquiry, the *class of the resident population* was typically viewed as a determining factor.[73] Often even administrative areas were relatively homogeneous in this respect, and Booth generalized accordingly:

69 *Ibid.*, p. 78.
70 *Ibid.*, V, 189.
71 *Ibid.*, I, 51.
72 *Ibid.*, 192.
73 Because of his primary interest in the problematic aspects of the relationship between poverty and industry, Booth never explicitly developed a "functional classification" of urban areas, although he often referred to districts as "residential" or "industrial," and the City implied the existence of a "commercial" area.

In East London the working class and in North London the middle class dominates . . .[74]

Hyde Park and Kensington Gardens . . . is the home of fashion and wealth.[75]

On the other hand, some were quite heterogeneous:

As we pass from East to West along the Northern boundary of London, the problems of life become at each remove more complicated by class. We begin with the working men . . . as the dominant class . . . so far we have only two classes: skilled and unskilled. . . . It is not until we reach Victoria Park that the presence of another class is felt . . . this is the lower middle class. Further north and West the lower middle gives way to or is mingled with upper middle and middle.[76]

In Deptford there is unfortunately a complete class division as between North and South, the line separating them being the New Cross Road.[77]

The obvious force of "population type" as a general factor in the determination of areal character could best be seen where it was observed to be the dominant factor as, for example, in the case of the Jewish community in Whitechapel:

In the midst of the chaotic elements of East London, the Jewish settlement stands out as possessing a distinct religious and social life and a definite history of its own.[78]

Physical site was a second factor noted by Booth to play a role in determining the character of an urban area. He observed that a number of districts "were under the influence of the river," the best example of which was the registration district of Rotherhithe, virtually a seaport:

Glimpses are caught of large ships . . . men in jerseys with clean shaven upper lips and goatee beards; the names of ship chandlers, or notices

74 *Ibid.*, I, 166.
75 *Ibid.*, III, 93.
76 *Ibid.*, I, 165.
77 *Ibid.*, V, 38.
78 "Poverty Series," III, 166.

of mast and oar, pump and block makers . . . all proclaim that shipping or seafaring is . . . the main business of the people.[79]

It should be noted that the influence of the river changed as one progressed along its banks to the west, and Booth observed that "the river begins to be a place of amusement." In other words, physical site was interpreted as a limiting rather than completely determining factor, contingent on the operation of other factors for its ultimate impact. And the force of elevation in determining the differential patterns of residence of the classes of population has already been noted. As Booth observed at one point:

The land rises and falls and the contour lines can almost be exactly traced by the colors showing social condition; "blue" and "purple" marking the low ground . . . while the hill tops . . . stand out in "red" and "yellow" with "pink" and "pink-barred" about their base.[80]

Correlatively, a third factor explicitly observed to play a role in determining the nature and function of an area was the presence of various *types of institutions*. Whether economic, social, or cultural, their function in this respect was documented time and again:

As we pass South and West the industrial element which is never absent increases and becomes dominant.[81]

In no district . . . can the prevailing industries be so readily detected by their smells. . . . In one street strawberry jam is borne in on you in whiffs hot and strong; in another, raw hides and tanning; in another, glue; while in some streets the nose encounters an unhappy combination of all three.[82]

The relation of . . . factories . . . to the neighborhood in which they are situated is probably one of mutual reaction. They tend to perpetuate the low conditions of home life upon which their supply of cheap labor depends.[83]

79 "Religious Influences," IV, 140.
80 *Ibid.*, V, 75.
81 *Ibid.*, IV, 10.
82 *Ibid.*, pp. 120–21.
83 *Ibid.*, p. 120.

The place is dominated by the barracks and the military. At garrison Church of St. George, the worship of God goes forth by bugle call and tuck of drum. . . . The presence of soldier affects every form of social life. . . . Woolwich as a great national workshop spreads its influence wherever its employees reside.[84]

The Strand focusses the theatrical life of England.[85]

A fourth factor especially decisive in determining the class of residents as well as institutional complement might be termed *situation*, in contrast to site. Here Booth took special note of the accessibility of areas to one another, particularly areas of living to areas of work:

[The condition of the area] is greatly affected by propinquity to Fleet Street, the Strand and West Central London generally; as well as to Westminister and the Public Offices.[86]

The whole district . . . is within easy access of the West End and the City, and is largely tenanted by clerks and managers and West End shop assistants.[87]

This part of London is characterized by its extreme accessibility to the City and West End. . . . Its advantages of position in this respect will also be the salvation of the locality. . . . People to whom accessibility is important tend to come from all parts . . . of London.[88]

Booth was particularly conscious of the importance of available means of transportation. He considered the increase in these facilities "from the twopenny omnibus to pennytram and again from the horse traction to electric railway" as having played a great part in both determining and changing the character of many areas of the city:

Kensal New Town, owing to its distance from inner London, was not a popular district for artisans, but the opening up of the Central London

84 *Ibid.*, V, 92–94.
85 *Ibid.*, II, 205.
86 *Ibid.*, IV, 28.
87 *Ibid.*, VI, 27.
88 *Ibid.*, V, 192.

Railway and the advent of electric trams have completely altered its outlook as a place of residence for the "pink" class.[89]

The railway crossing makes Loborough Junction remarkable and nowhere have the possibilities of locomotion a greater effect on the character of the population than here. There is an all night train service and the tired compositor . . . returning to his home encounters the meat salesman as he goes forth to work. The district never sleeps. . . . Social condition may fall in, but in a district such as this cannot fall far, accessibility being so convenient to the great centres of employment.[90]

In all of this, of course, there was the implicit assumption that population types and functions had been distributed in space by orderly, natural processes; and Booth often spoke of people to whom accessibility was important of "naturally seeking their homes" in such districts as those mentioned above or of the poor as "naturally gravitating" to the undersirable parts of the city. In the final analysis, however, it was the complex and confluence of a number of factors—site, situation, population type, institutions—which determined the character of any particular area of the city. And Booth himself recognized this, as the following examples suggest:

The character of the locality is affected by its nearness to the city and to the river, by the oldness of its houses, and by the presence of a large and extending colony of Jews. . . .[91]

In this district there is a tendency almost unknown elsewhere for the purple streets to become pink instead of the opposite. . . . This is attributed to the improved access to the city afforded by the opening of the Tower Bridge; the general convenience of the train service; to the realization of the value of great open spaces . . . to the abundance of houses having gardens at comparatively low rents; and last, but not least, to the fact that the houses have actually been built for the class that occupies them.[92]

89 *Ibid.*, III, 158.
90 *Ibid.*, VI, 50.
91 *Ibid.*, II, 104.
92 *Ibid.*, IV, 155.

As usual, Booth did not neglect the dynamic aspect of these spatial phenomena. The succession of population types owing to the development of central pressure and the availability of transportation facilities have already been mentioned. Basic, of course, was a competition for space on an ability-to-pay basis, not only between residential and commercial interests but also between different residential types:

There is [no district] to be found so accessible to the centre of London that is less crowded. . . . In each of these great thoroughfares [present in the district] there have been changes in recent years which indicate that they will not long retain their residential character. . . . Such wide roads in the immediate suburbs have seldom escaped the commercial taint. Shops extending over the roadway are here or there built out over the garden . . . let but one house advance its front, seeking some small immediate advantage and all is lost.[93]

Market porters and other laborers of rough class are likely to be driven out . . . partly by the provision of better accommodation, which will inevitably be occupied by those whose work ties them closely to the neighborhood of the greatest shopping streets and who can afford to pay the higher rent. They compete among themselves and are again overbidden by those whose occupations, still more definitely localized, will not bear investigation. Very high rents can be afforded by those who traffic in vice. . . .[94]

Equally modern was Booth's consideration of the relationships between land values, crowding, and the growth of the slums: implicit again is the assumption of the operation of natural processes and order in the production of a ubiquitous urban social phenomenon:

The result [of population pressure] has been to raise site values and of late there has been little or no fresh building. Extravagant claims are made by the owners of slum property, and every scheme of improvement is hampered. . . . The immediate return is the only thing considered. There is no responsible owner; the houses are rack-rented and ruined. Finally the last string of leaseholders who may be the actual occupier, or may be merely a speculator in leasehold property,

93 *Ibid.*, VI, 38–39.
94 *Ibid.*, I, 107.

finds his account in farming out the rooms. They readily find occupants but only in this way can the high rents, which are promised, be actually collected. When a lease nears its termination, no money will be spent that can possibly be avoided, and when it is anticipated that a site will shortly be wanted, coming events cast their shadow before them. It may be for the extension of business premises . . . or for the widening of a street, but though in themselves good objects, their shadow is the shadow of death. In Somers Town one infant in five dies within the year. Except for these conditions the place would be healthy.[95]

At the same time Booth noted that the invasion of an area by a lower class of people did not always result in a financial loss to the owners of property, just as, on occasion, despite the general drift outwards of the better class, the process was occasionally reversed. In the first instance, for example:

It does not follow, necessarily, that the degradation of property affects its money value. Lower rents are matched by less formidable initial expenses, and uncertainty in their collection by smaller outgoings for maintenance. In a similar way the complete change of a district from middle to working-class occupation does not necessarily in the end involve financial loss. . . . Two or three families occupying one house floor by floor pay as much rent as was previously obtained by one tenant; and gardens or other spaces can be made use of for trade or other purposes which could not have been entertained while it was necessary to maintain a high residential character. Values may not rise with such a movement, but neither need they fall.[96]

And, in regard to the latter:

On the Eastern side we have spoken of the inward drift of the poor and of the growth of a new district of the pink on the high ground in Clapton; both come from the inner London; the fairly comfortable coming in greater numbers than the poor. There is also an onward migration of working classes from the district to Tottenham on the

95 *Ibid.*, I, 188–89. Booth described the practice of "house-farming" as follows: "Speculators take a number of houses, perhaps whole streets, and make what they can by sub-letting . . . it is the house-farmer's interest to spend as little as possible on repairs, so the property falls into worse and worse condition. . . ." *Ibid.*, II, 101-2.

96 *Ibid.*, I, 107.

North and Walthamstow on the East. . . . To Dalton there is some return of the people of the "red" class owing to its accessibility and to the excellence of its houses which have been allowed to stand.[97]

Parenthetically, not the least of Booth's relevance for the development of an empirical sociology lay in the advances made during the course of the inquiry in the use of areal concepts. In the early part of his investigations, Booth more or less confined himself to the use of pre-existing administrative areas, primarily for descriptive purposes. At the conclusion of his research, he not only constructed his own areal units, comparable in size and area, for research purposes and for measuring the concomitant variation among specific social phenomena such as crowding, poverty, and vital rates; he also reached the point of using areas in an explanatory capacity. Thus as previously noted, the "poverty areas" tended to be literally walled off from the rest of the city by barrier-like boundaries that isolated their inhabitants, minimizing their normal participation in the life of the city about them. Significantly, Booth not only considered the purely physical character of these areas but also its implications for another order of data: personal and social disorganization. First, the general observation as to the physical isolation:

Nearly all . . . have more or less the cul-de-sac character, shut off by railway, river, or canal and needing above all to be opened up by the building of bridges and carrying through of streets.[98]

Then, the insight into the functional significance of such isolation for the area and its inhabitants:

. . . the line of poverty which follows the Grand Junction Canal leaves between itself and the railway another isolated district shaped like an old shoe and just as full of children and poverty as was the old woman's dwelling in the nursery rhyme.[99]

In the middle of this area is a strange group of streets, hemmed in on one side by the railway and entered only here and there on the other

97 *Ibid.*, I, 111.
98 *Ibid.*, I, 64.
99 *Ibid.*, III, 137.

three sides like a fortress through its gates. . . [There are no other places] whereon the word "outcast" is so deeply branded.[100]

The parishes . . . which complete the district are alike in being surrounded and cut off by railways, docks, from the rest of the world, and the population seems to suffer in vitality.[101]

The canal on the North, the City on the West, and the river on the South hem the population in on three sides and the whole area tends to become uniformly poor.[102]

Finally, the general proposition as to the relationship:

It is . . . a very general rule that groups of poor streets, when cut off from communication with the surrounding districts and lacking the guarantee which through traffic provides, tend to become disreputable.[103]

There is no doubt that Booth's concern with the spatial aspects of London, however much a by-product of the focus of his research, made him sensitive to the city as a dynamic phenomenon. Indeed, at one point he referred to his inquiry as "this study of a city in motion." At the same time, his abiding concern with the problematic aspects of city life inevitably led to an interest in the need to bring about changes in both its structure and functioning.

URBAN GROWTH AND PLANNING The most obviously dynamic qualities of London at this point were, of course, its rapid increase in population and its correlative expansion in space. Both these processes were the subject of empirical documentation and theoretical consideration on Booth's part. Significantly, in H. Llewellyn-Smith's inquiry into population "influx and efflux", population increase was shown to be greater for the districts in the outer ring and in the immediately contiguous suburban areas than for other parts of the city: ". . . the most rapid growth has taken place in districts . . . which industrially are a

100 *Ibid.*, VI, 15.
101 *Ibid.*, IV, 159.
102 *Ibid.*, II, 104.
103 *Ibid.*, III, 119–20.

part of London, but are not included in the metropolitan area."[104] With respect to immigration, this "fringe of urban districts" was demonstrated to receive two-thirds of the total influx: "The exact gain by migration of the outer ring in 10 years previous to 1887 was 198,887 and of the whole area of greater London for the same period, 306,663."[105] The central districts, on the other hand, were shown in many cases to have incurred actual deficits in spite of positive rates of natural increase. This was particularly true of the East London area.

The more rapid rate of growth in the outer ring was attributed to the dual nature of the source of the influx: the movement of urban residents outward from the center of the city and the drift of countrymen to the city. The thesis was advanced that the country literally "nourished" the city by providing it with an excess of young adults whose presence maintained a continuing excess of births over deaths. Speaking of the central districts of East London, it was pointed out that:

> It is however, likely that the interchange of population has indirectly stimulated population in the town. Had London been left to itself, the birth and death rate would probably both have been different, . . . the structural change which is continually going on in London in consequence of the admixture of outside elements is powerfully operating to keep up the excess of births over deaths which might even conceivably change into an excess of deaths over births. . . .[106]

It was in connection with the interpretation of these statistics, however, that one of the most modern insights of the inquiry was produced—the concept of "Greater London." It was only implicit in the early stages of the research and indexed by such *ad hoc* observations as the fact that the working-class district of West Ham "lies beyond the metropolitan boundary but is otherwise an integral portion of London,"[107] or that the line separating the

104 "Poverty Series," III, 64.
105 *Ibid.*, p. 124 n.
106 *Ibid.*, p. 65.
107 *Ibid.*, I, 254.

"London of the Registrar-General" and that of greater London was "imaginary." In the final volume, the proposition was explicitly made:

It would be rash to assume that the population of London must continue to multiply at the rate shown for many decades, and even centuries past; but it would be still more rash to say that it could not or would not do so. It seems, at any rate, certain that if our national prosperity is maintained, London will share in it, and her growth continue. Whether this be within the present county boundary is immaterial in proportion as that boundary is unreal. In recent years the increase of the outside population has disguised the facts of growth, but it will not be long before a "Greater London" will have to be reckoned with for administrative purposes. Fresh links of brick and mortar are being constantly made; the intervening spaces tend to fill up; and suddenly we shall become aware that the centre of our spider's web of streets plays its part not to four or five but to seven or eight, or more millions of people, who will, in reality, if not in name, be citizens of London: coming and going, pressing in and pressing out, serving and being served by the same large centers of industrial and social life.[108]

Finally, Booth's original position that the first office of scientific social research was to provide a sound factual basis for future reforms is nowhere more clearly implied than in his approach to urban planning and reorganization. Significant was his recognition of the essentially "unplanned" nature of city growth and development on the one hand, and of the operation of forces inherent in the urban situation that must be dealt with as limiting factors, on the other hand. In regard to the first, he observed:

Let anyone now design a place of residence for our four or five million inhabitants, and how greatly it would differ in plan and structure from London. . . . At every point we have much to learn . . . but great possibilities clearly lie before us in the reorganization of urban life within itself, as well as in its relations with the surrounding country and with the [still] wider world beyond.[109]

108 "Final Volume," p. 179.
109 *Ibid.*, p. 180.

And, with respect to the second, he proposed:

> We do not have to create, or even to arouse the forces which tend to expansion; we only have to give them play and to make use of them; guiding them toward the desired ends and averting so far as may be, current evils.[110]

Moreover, it was not the London of the Registrar General that Booth considered in his approach to planning, for he announced his intention to "ignore local divisions and treat London and the immediately surrounding districts as a unit."[111]

Booth saw the solution to the problems engendered by the expansion and growth of the city in terms of two major factors: transportation and housing. He discussed the former in terms of time-cost considerations and outlined a detailed plan for a unified system of transportation. Interesting in this connection was Booth's agreement with and citation of H. G. Wells concerning the effects of increased communication possibilities on city life:

> . . . about an hour is the outside limit of time that any man will be content to spend daily in travelling to and from his work; and that consequently the distance that may be covered in about that time from the centre to the circumference, sets bounds to every city's satisfactory growth.[112]

While not in any sense a final answer, the charm of Booth's approach lay in his naturalistic and realistic formulation of the problem and in his concern that urban planning be framed in terms of human values—the "welfare and comfort of the inhabitants of London"—rather than with respect to abstract aesthetic and architectural values, which were to play so prominent a role in the city planning movement at a later time.

110 *Ibid.*, p. 186.

111 *Ibid.* On the problem of London's functional expansion beyond its legal boundaries, he observed elsewhere: "On the serious character of this problem I have laid stress. Nowhere is it adequately grasped. The immediate evil of the crowded inner portion naturally and inevitably presses more than does that which lies in the womb of the future." "Religious Influences," VI, 155.

112 "Final Volume," p. 188.

As for housing, it was seen in terms of rent and a novel tax plan that stemmed from the theories of Henry George and that would tax city land purely on the basis of "site value," in order to encourage building. Moreover, in the course of this analysis, a number of other pertinent generalizations were made, based on his research findings, as to the presence and limiting function of other factors in the urban complex: for example, the trend toward the absorption of space by industry at the center was observed to be decreasing along with a correlative tendency for factories to move to the suburbs, where more ground at lower rents was available; the spatial requirements for non-residential purposes, which tended to increase pressure at the center of the city, was also observed to have increased as a result of the demand for transit and retail distribution facilities. As to the obstacle of abnormally high land values at the center to future reconstruction, Booth felt that this would become less important as the city grew: "Not only does the expense needed for alterations at the centre bear a smaller proportion to the whole, but bolder engineering expedients can be adopted."[113]

Moreover, at various points Booth took his findings and theories into account in making specific recommendations for urban reforms. This was especially true in considering the development and maintenance of slum districts, the desirability of securing open spaces, and the beneficial effects of opening up hemmed-in poverty areas:

> . . . the district is not badly provided with open spaces, but it would be well if the island loops . . . could be secured for public playgrounds for the inhabitants . . . if built upon, their situation would fit them for dangerous slums.[114]

> A small group of courts which were equally bad have been improved. They were entered under an archway and formed a *cul-de-sac*, but have been opened up, and although still low, no longer deserve or retain the sobriquet of "little Hell" which they formerly had.[115]

113 *Ibid.*, p. 182.
114 "Religious Influences," V, 77.
115 *Ibid.*, pp. 162–63.

It is perhaps mainly to the bad service of trains and the failure to extend tramways across Blackheath that we owe today the extent of these fields and woods; and it is very clear that we cannot prudently advance in one direction without considering what will be spoiled as well as what is brought into use; and without safeguarding, for extending London, as much grass and trees and air as possible.[116]

In no neighborhood would [low-income block dwellings] be more likely to be successful. For no other purpose is a considerable portion of the district equally suitable. It is not so subject as are the parts of London which surround the City, to enhancement of values from competition of business premises . . . nor is much of it so suitable or so likely to be used for rich men's houses as Upper Chelsea.[117]

While Booth admitted the possibilities of increasing centralization as a result of his concern for expediting communication and transportation facilities within the city, the trend toward the development of local centers was predicted to increase in any case, and he concluded:

Such centres are to be found now all around London, with brilliant shops, streets full of people, churches and chapels, perhaps a Town Hall, and probably a theatre. The growth of such local life in London during the past decade is very noticeable. . . . I would emphasize once more the point to which [these remarks] lead: the crying necessity for forethought and plan in the arrangement of our great metropolis.[118]

The City as a Social Structure

While the importance of "the study of the community as a physical fact for the understanding of it as a social phenomenon and as a state of mind" was only a latent assumption in the inquiry, the significance of the class structure was happily made more manifest. [119] And because Booth's study represents the only

116 *Ibid.*, p. 131.

117 *Ibid.*, III, 78.

118 "Final Volume," p. 199.

119 See Louis Wirth, "Human Ecology," *American Journal of Sociology*, 40 (May, 1945): 483–88.

empirical attempt, at once both extensive and intensive, to view the social organization and functioning of a large, industrial-commercial metropolis from the perspectives of class and institution, as well as because later efforts proceeded along essentially similar lines, this dimension of the investigation is also singularly relevant for an appreciation of the rise of an empirical sociology in the context of the problematic aspects of the city as a social phenomenon.[120] To be sure, these were not the questions Booth and his associates asked but, in many respects, they were the ones they answered, into which they gained considerable insight, or about which they raised leading questions.

In this connection, the charm of Booth's study will be seen to lie, first of all, in the empirical evidence that was uncovered to demonstrate the existence of class lines in the community. In the second place, despite the lack of conceptual sophistication (especially the abiding confusion between what has since been technically differentiated as "economic" [power] classes versus "social" [status] classes) and the presence of correlatively confusing versions of the shape and span of London's class structure, the concept of class as "style of life," involving a multiplicity of criteria, was central, however implicit. The concept of class ultimately took on a communal character in that each stratum was observed to have its own culture. Finally, the force of class in the community was dramatically portrayed by Booth's observations concerning its impact on various types of social institutions: on the one hand, certain institutions were shown to be class-specific in their membership and function; on the other hand, class differences were demonstrated to operate within particular institutional forms.

Status considerations were, of course, secondary throughout the inquiry, and the understandable focus of interest as well as the majority of data referred to the lower and working classes.

120 Cf., e.g., R. S. and H. M. Lynd, *Middletown* (New York: Harcourt-Brace & Co., 1929); T. H. Marshall, "Social Class," *Sociological Review*, 26 (January, 1934): 55–76; R. S. and H. M. Lynd, *Middletown in Transition* (New York: Harcourt-Brace & Co., 1937); and W. L. Warner and P. S. Lunt, *The Social Life of a Modern Community* (New Haven: Yale University Press, 1941).

Many of the data on life style came from interviews and participant observations that were not always completely objective and representative. In spite of these limitations, however, the broad outlines of the nature and force of social stratification in the organization and functioning of the community were clarified. The details were missing here and there; the problem of social mobility was never objectified, as such; but, for sociologists, the whole remains uniquely informative and suggestive.

THE CLASS HIERARCHIES Given Booth's focus on the problem of poverty, the concept of class served a pragmatic rather than a theoretic function and was employed primarily to make operative distinctions among different degrees of poverty and well-being. Indeed, just to the extent that no concerted effort was made to rationalize the concept of class, certain empirical and theoretical insights into the nature and function of urban social stratification resulted which might not have developed within the limiting confines of a more rigorous approach.

The complex relativities indigenous to social stratification are suggested not only by the variety of structures formulated in the course of the inquiry and the explicit inconstancy of the number of levels denoted, but also by the implicit fluctuation of the criteria of differentiation and analytic functions. Retrospectively and from a conceptual point of view, two essentially different types of class hierarchies figured in the inquiry: the "letter" classes that generally informed the "Poverty" and "Industry" series, involving what has been termed by Weber, class position in the market; and the specifically "social" classes that received the greatest attention in the "Religious Influences" series, primarily involving position in a system of status-honor.[121]

Since Booth addressed himself primarily to the manner in which the city's population was divided into various degrees of

121 Cf. H. H. Gerth and C. Wright Mills, *From Max Weber: Essays in Sociology* (New York: Oxford University Press, 1946), pp. 180–95. Needless to say, such concepts were not employed by Booth and his associates and have been introduced by the editor to order and clarify the discussion.

poverty and wealth, the letter classes were, in the first place, simply convenient categories constructed for this purpose. From the perspective of the conceptual apparatus of modern social stratification theory, they were "income" classes: as previously noted, Booth referred to them as a "hierarchy of means"; the "poverty line" was defined in terms of income; the lower classes were denoted by terms which connoted progressive amounts of income (e.g., "very poor," "poor," "regular standard earnings"); and, furthermore, Class H was often employed as a residual category for all the "social" classes above the "lower middle" (see Table 11).

In contrast, Booth's social classes (see Table 12) represented the status system of the community from the upper-middle-class perspective of Booth and his associates. No evidence was presented as to their numbers and proportions in the population of London and, relative to the focus on the lower classes, little information was presented on their other relevant characteristics. The criteria of differentiation implied by their definitions in Table 14 varied among family status, occupation, and income.

The notion of social class first appeared in the discussion of education in the "Poverty Series," where a distinction was made among the professional, middle, and working classes, at which time the limitations of occupation as a criterion of status position were pointed out:

> . . . it is . . . very difficult in many cases to draw the line accurately between professional, middle, and working class . . . many occupations do not correspond closely to a particular social class. The majority of the professional class who attend such schools are the sons of clergymen, doctors, accountants and school masters; while licensed victuallers are prominent among the parents of the middle class, besides, of course, clerks, shop-keepers, managers, agents, and officials.[122]

Nor was the absolute amount of income considered to be a reliable index of status differences. This was shown to be especially true of the division between the lower middle class and the upper working class:

122 "Poverty Series," III, 260.

TABLE 11. *Booth's Conceptions of the Letter Class Hierarchy*

Hierarchy	Designation	Description
I[a]	A	Lowest class; semi-criminals
	B	Casual earnings; very poor
	C	Intermittent earnings; the poor
	D	Regular small earnings
	E	Regular standard earnings
	F	Higher class labour
	G	Lower middle class
	H	Upper middle class and above
II[b]	A	Lowest class
	B	Very poor
	CD	The poor
	EF	Regular working class comfort
	GH	Well-to-do; lower middle and upper middle
III[c]	A	Lowest class
	B	Very poor
	CD	Standard poverty
	EF	Working class comfort
	G	Well-to-do
	H	Wealthy
IV[d]	AB	Very poor
	CD	The poor
	EF	Comfortable
	GH	Well-to-do
V[e]	AB CD	Lower classes
	EF G	Central classes
	H	Upper classes
VI[f]	AB	Very poor
	CD	The poor
	EF	Comfortable
	G	Lower middle
	H	Middle and upper classes
VII[g]	AB	Very poor
	CD	The poor
	EF	Comfortable working class including servants
	GH	Lower middle, middle, and upper middle classes

[a] "Poverty Series," I, 33.
[b] *Ibid.*, II, 20.
[c] *Ibid.*, pp. 40–41.
[d] *Ibid.*, p. 272.
[e] "Industry Series," I, 13.
[f] *Ibid.*, p. 15.
[g] "Final Volume," p. 9.

TABLE 12. *Booth's Conceptions of the Social Class Hierarchy*

Hierarchy	Description
I[a]	Professional class
	Middle class
	Working class
II[b]	Wealth (with fashion)
	Upper middle class (without fashion)
	Lower middle class
	Regular wage earners
	The poor
III[c]	The Oldest English families—those of rank and station
	Those who fill the principal places in the Civil Service, officer the Army and Navy, plead in our courts of law, supply the Church of England with many of her clergy. The borders of this class have been extended by the increase of wealth.
	Legal and other professional men, some civil servants, men of business, wholesale traders, and large retailers.
	Those of inferior rank in the same professions, men of business in both wholesale and retail trade, with "lower division" civil servants, and an enormous variety of salaried people. "The new middle class."
	Lower middle class—clerks.
	Upper working class—foremen and skilled artisans.
	Working class
	The poor

Here the primary emphasis is on status, and the upper reaches of the social scale are more fully developed and refined than in the letter classes. And Booth also pointed out that various "social grades" are represented by people whose "rank is the stamp of Education or the seal of Art."

a "Poverty Series," III, 260.
b "Religious Influences," VII, 44.
c *Ibid.*, pp. 396–99.

The organization of modern industry finds room for much cheap clerk work for which the elementary schools ensure a copious supply, and requires also, on the practical side of the work, men of skill and character, who earn higher wages than these clerks. Thus the financial distinction between clerk and working men tends to break down. . . .[123]

And in more pointed fashion Booth observed:

The line of class is not always poverty. There are many clerks who,

123 "Religious Influences," VII, 399.

though perhaps not poor from a subsistence point of view, are pinched owing to the increased requirements of life, and some even in great poverty who do not lose class.[124]

Booth's approach did not provide him with data on the general pattern of income distribution as a perspective on the city's social structure. And while he was able to indicate something of the status differences among the various trades and occupations, the latter were never employed as indexes of class status to depict London's stratification system. Relative to income, the nearest approximation to an over-all picture appeared in the "Industry Series":

The results of our inquiries make it reasonably sure that one-third of the population are on or about the line of poverty or below it, having at the most an income which one time with another averages 21*s* or 22*s* for a small family (or up to 25*s* or 26*s* for one of larger size), and in many cases falling much below this level. There may be another third who have perhaps 10*s* more, or taking the year round from 25*s* to 35*s* a week, among whom would be computed in addition to wage-earners, may retail tradesmen and small pasters; and the last third would include all those who are better off. The first group, who are practically those who are living two or more persons to each room occupied, contain our classes A, B, C, and D. The next, with the average nearly one room to each person consists of class E, with portions of F and G; while the final group includes the rest of F and G and all of class H—that is, all those who employ servants as well as some of those who do not. Of the first, many are pinched by want and all live in poverty, if poverty be defined as having no surplus. The second enjoy solid working class comfort, and of the third group, the worst off live in plenty and the best off in luxury.[125]

Moreover, the data in Tables 4 and 7, which were based on the reports of the School Board Visitors, the school teachers, and the census materials on crowding and the number of servants, provide a basis for suggesting the form of the city's social structure: briefly, given the cutting points among the classes employed in

124 Ibid., I, 150.
125 "Industry Series," V, 324.

the inquiry, it took the form of a pyramid, prophetically, at least, bulging at the midsection.[126] But Booth, of course, never looked at his data in these terms.

In fact, income was never even the sole criterion of the letter class schemes portrayed in Table 13. Despite the major objective of the research, Booth was often patently concerned with more than a simple division of the population into the "poor" and the "non-poor," a task that logically would require only two categories. According to the purpose in view, the letter class hierarchy was quite elastic: at times each category stood alone; at other times a level was combined with others to compose a single stratum. Moreover, class A, "the lowest class"—traditionally defined as the "undeserving poor"—constituted almost a characterological segment of the population—a "status group" rather than a class.[127]

Despite the focus on economic status, Booth's letter class distinctions were admittedly not entirely devoid of status considerations and were often suggestive of a scale of social position as well as of means. Status differences, for example, were often observed and commented on:

I watched with interest the relations existing between classes E and D in the person of my landlady and her other tenants. *Mutatis mutandis*, they were not very different from those which exist in the country between hall and village. There was the presence of a dress altered to suit the hard-worked, ill-dressed child . . . the rebuke dignified, well-timed, and, as it appeared, efficacious, of the father's drunken ways; amounting in the end to "mend your ways or go"; and the word in season to the little girl whose "tongue was too long and must have a bite off" . . . the women met over their washing in the yard, and the children allowed to play together . . . but if there were sweets to be eaten, it was my landlady's little girl who paid for them. In short, there was evinced a keen sense of social responsibility, not unaccompanied by a sense of social superiority.[128]

126 See Table 4, p. 58, and Table 7, p. 63, above.

127 The summit of the social class hierarchy—"England's Oldest Families"—was another "status group" in contrast to a "class" in the terminology of modern stratification theory.

128 "Poverty Series," I, 159.

In the final analysis, however, neither income, character, nor status served, in itself, as the test of either Booth's letter or social classes. Rather, it was what Booth termed "the standard of life," which incorporated all these criteria in addition to others. Thus, classes C and D could be lumped together as "the poor" when the paramount interest was simply in designating the percentage of the city's population "in poverty." On the other hand, although both classes received the same annual income, class D's was based on small regular earnings whereas that of class C came from irregular income and employment. Insofar as an appreciation of the force of class in the community was at stake, this difference was crucial and necessitated a division between the two strata, for it led to significant objective as well as subjective consequences in the life of the people:

It would not be impossible for the family of a man who earned on the year's average 21*s* a week, to live regularly at that rate, although he might make 35*s* in some weeks and not more than 7*s* in others. But such self-control is not to be expected, and consequently as a rule there is a great difference between the ways of life in class C, where work though fairly well-paid is irregular, and uncertain, and the habits of class D, where the wages, though not high, are the same . . . all the year round. . . . The people of class C, though on the whole worse off than those of class D, have in a certain sense a higher standard. For this class demands and aims at more than it can achieve, except when times are good.[129]

Even Booth's methodology suggested the primacy of the concept of standard or style of life in his approach to the class system of the community, for all three empirical attempts to categorize the population of London according to class assumed it as the operative criterion: the School Board Visitors and the school teachers had no other basis on which to judge the class of their clients than gross indications of life style; and the use of numbers per room and number of servants was explicitly noted by Booth to be "an almost absolute test of the style of life."[130]

129 "Industry Series," V, 327.

130 *Ibid.*, I, 14. Booth further observed in this connection: "As to wealth, the new classification has every advantage; indeed the previous one

THE CONCEPT OF THE STANDARD OR STYLE OF LIFE The importance of Booth's view of class in terms of life style or culture stems from data and hypotheses in the inquiry which made it clear that class limited and sometimes determined the individual's "life-chances" (to borrow a term from Weber); that there was a determinant relationship between the objective and subjective dimensions of a class's culture; and that the differences involved had significant implications for the organization and functioning of the social institutions of the community.

Referring to life chances, another of the dramatically "modern" aspects of the inquiry was Booth's concern with the implications of class differences for educational and, correlatively, economic opportunities. Despite occasional lapses from his usually objective perspective with respect to the "appropriate" type of education that should be accorded each class, empirical evidence was found for distinctive and significant class differences in this respect.

That education beyond the elementary school was directly a function of the class of the individual concerned was indicated by an analysis of the occupations of parents of secondary school boys on the basis of several samples from different schools.[131] Booth concluded:

> . . . the great majority of the boys attending the secondary schools of London are of the middle and lower middle classes, with a fringe of sons of professional men, and in endowed schools [i.e., no fee] a sprinkling of the children of working men.[132]

Further, even the scholarship children, who were enabled to con-

---

made no attempt in this direction but lumped together all the servant-keeping classes, and even some of the lower middle classes, who, though keeping no servants, live in middle class streets, and send their children to middle class schools." *Ibid.*

131 It should be noted that elementary education, although on a fee basis, was available to all, and provisions were made for the remission of the fee to families that could demonstrate their inability to pay. There was, however, no general organization and availability of secondary education under the supervision of a public authority.

132 "Poverty Series," III, 261.

tinue their education beyond the age of thirteen, at which point the elementary school ended, were noted to come, not from the lower and working classes (as might be expected and which was the avowed purpose of the grants), but rather from the middle classes.

TABLE 13. *Occupations of Parents of Scholarship Pupils in Three East London Secondary Schools for Boys*

Occupation	Number
Middle class and professional	
Architects	1
Retail tradesmen	43
Licensed victuallers	6
Clerks	4
Commercial travellers	3
Warehousemen	2
Managers and foremen	11
Total	70
Working class	
Artisans	26
Policemen	1
Street-sellers	1
Labourers	2
Total	30

Adapted from "Poverty Series," III, 277.

And Booth concluded:

Thus the social class of the majority of boys selected by scholarship does not differ very greatly from that of the other pupils of secondary schools. . . . This fact . . . shows plainly that it has yet failed to reach more than the upper fringe of the working class.[133]

A similar situation was found with respect to the education of girls; on the basis of a number of small sample studies, overwhelming evidence showed not only that in general it was the middle- and upper-class girls who continued their education but also that such girls received the scholarships and were able to profit by their education by securing professional positions, in contrast to working-class girls:

133 *Ibid.*, p. 277.

. . . from these facts it is evident that our middle schools afford a secondary education to girls of the middle and lower classes only . . . and that the girls who obtain scholarships and spend some time in the higher grade schools are not welcome in elementary schools . . .[134]

Booth went on to note that these facts were related not only to the objective aspects of the class situation of those concerned but also to the attitudes of the different classes toward the education of their children. The importance of children's earnings in the budgets of lower-class families was held to be a major factor in the curtailment of their education and the general failure of the scholarship system:

The experience of "junior scholarships" open to penny schools . . . shows conclusively that the offer of free education fails to "catch capacity" from among the children of the poor, where loss of a boy's earnings is a serious pinch to the family. . . . Boys who are successful in the competition . . . come from richer homes, for by the age of 11 and 12 the influence of the home atmosphere has had time to tell to such a degree as to handicap severely the boys from the rougher homes where there is little appreciation of education and little opportunity for quiet study. Thus we get an undesirable social selection.[135]

Needless to say, Booth considered education an excellent test of class and remarked on the differences in attitudes which obtained among the different strata in this respect:

At the very bottom education is disregarded, and every effort made to avoid or abbreviate school life; in the next class the children are hurried through their "standards" in order to go to work as soon as possible; above this, the period is voluntarily extended from 13 to 14 . . . and so on, till, with those who go to the university, the educational period lasts till twenty-three or twenty-four years of age.[136]

Moreover, Booth explicitly emphasized the status-giving quality of education by observing that many lower-working-class boys who did manage to go on to secondary school continued for only a semester or, at the most, a year, "in order to get a finish":

134 *Ibid.*, p. 305. The latter observation was based on a sample study of the occupations of girls after leaving "middle school."

135 *Ibid.*, p. 279.

136 "Industry Series," V, 332.

They derive little or no good educationally from the higher school, but they get not only a certain social prestige but some commercial advantage when seeking a post from being able to say that they have been at secondary school.[137]

Finally, another insight was gained into the force of class position in this area by the recognition of a tendency for sons to follow their fathers in their occupations, as well as of the existence of certain "traditional" occupations for girls, especially in the lower classes:

. . . each class follows its own course, guided as to the boys mainly by the necessity for immediate earnings, and as to the girls by the relative gentility of this or that kind of work. In these respects the shortening or prolonging of education is closely connected with the choice made, and here again we recognize a distinction which holds good throughout society.[138]

And the point was also made that in the "upper working classes" the children were inclined to be more mobile both occupationally and (hence) socially:

Their sons take places as clerks and their daughters get employment in first-class shops or places of business; if their wives work at all, they either keep a shop, or employ girls at laundry work or at dressmaking.[139]

Of course, as previously noted, Booth documented the relationship between "poverty" and other phenomena relating to the matter of life chances such as vital rates and rates of early marriage. But these were not considered in the context of "class." Also contained in the inquiry, however, were observations and data that either demonstrated or suggested class differences in attitudes and perspective, highlighted status considerations in the life of the people, and drew attention to class-based variations in folkways and mores. The last, especially, served to emphasize the conception of class as style of life.

Status differences were most obvious, seemingly, where women

137 "Poverty Series," III, 278.
138 "Industry Series," V, 332.
139 "Poverty Series," I, 53.

were concerned. The phenomenon of "home work," which pervaded every grade of working-class society and included the lower middle class as well, was a good example. It was not merely that the force of status played a role in keeping down the wages for such labor (for both adults and children), but that significant differences in class attitudes toward this type of employment were made explicit:

In the lower middle class especially will be found many girls and single women who do not care to enter into competition openly with a class of labourers whom they consider beneath them and hence prefer the privacy of home work. This class is not of necessity pecuniarly better off than the artisan class below it, but the wholesome theory that the man should be the breadwinner of the house pervades it. It is keenly sensitive to social distinctions, is fairly educated, and its anxiety to keep up appearances demands an increasing expenditure . . . which is more than commensurate with its income. The daughters as they grow up make themselves useful at home either in housework or by assisting in the shop, and are to a certain extent to be distinguished from the class below them by the fact that they do not go out to work. In this class there is a tendency among girls to exaggerate the income of their fathers and to imitate the habits and living of girls of the upper middle class. They are sometimes inclined to imagine that to work for a living is a thing to be ashamed of, and frequently hard-working girls will libel themselves by representing or allowing people to imagine that they have no occupation beyond their share of domestic duties. As an actual fact, if they are to dress as they think suitable to their superior position, they must work for money. . . . The majority of skilled artisans and shopkeeping class, however, are not ashamed of working, or of working for money, but they are most anxious to make it clear that they are only earning pocket-money—pursuing a trade of their own free choice, not because they are obliged.[140]

Thus, whereas the lower-class wife might work outside the home in a laundry or factory without losting status, the lower-middle-class

140 *Ibid.*, IV, 296–97. Booth also noted, ". . . the more sensitive the parents are as to their social position, the lower the rate at which they will allow their children to work 'for a friend at her house.'" *Ibid.*, p. 267. Further, he pointed out that the comfort of the classes which earned low or irregular wages, "depended above all on a good wife." *Ibid.*, I, 161.

wife was forced to resort to the subterfuge of "needlework" at home, although the motives were the same. In this connection, the phenomenon of "middle-class poverty" was noted, and Booth spoke of "the pinched and pathetic lives of some of the lower middle class, who are struggling to maintain a social position they cannot afford."[141]

Beyond the type of house and area of residence, which were definitely correlated with class, various other aspects of home life were noted to be class-linked.[142] This involved more than the number of rooms or servants but, rather, included the division of labor and specialization of function among the rooms, the type and arrangement of furniture—indeed, the whole gamut of "housekeeping ways." For example, the typical class B home was described as follows:

> The furniture, whether much or little in quantity, consists of things barely worth pawning, or they would have been pawned; things not only shabby and broken but foul . . . the same room serves for living, sleeping, cooking and washing, for the children of all ages as well as for man and wife. . . . Remains of food are always about—there is perhaps no cupboard. . . . The window, broken, patched and dirty, indicates more perhaps than anything else that no housewifely pride is taken.[143]

On the other hand, an entirely different level was reached in class D:

> The window is bright, shrouded with clean cotton-lace curtains, and often filled with plants; or a little table holding some treasured ornaments is pushed forward between the curtains, that passers-by may see it. . . . The condition of the window is typical of all the rest.[144]

141 "Religious Influences," I, 79.

142 Booth had little to say about the style of life of class A, owing to the absence of any significant amount of family life among its members. As he put it: "The common lodging house caters for their necessities and the public house for their superfluities." "Industry Series," V, 325.

143 *Ibid.*, p. 326.

144 *Ibid.*, p. 328.

In class E, Booth observed a greater degree of "housewifely pride," but his own class bias led to a judgment of "a deplorable lack of taste" in the matter of furniture style and arrangement. The kitchens in the homes of this class, interestingly enough, were noted generally to be the most attractive rooms. And still another level was represented by class F, "the summit of the working class," in the matter of the character of the home:

> . . . there is a wide distinction both in the character of the accommodation and in the use made of it. Class E may have a parlour as well as a kitchen, but it is not used except on Sunday; or if regular use is made of it, it is as a bedroom for overflowing children. Class F not only has a parlour, but uses it as such.[145]

Such differences led, in turn, to others that made for status differences within the working class. Thus, in the matter of habits of washing and dressing Booth observed:

> In class E . . . ablutions are usually performed at the sink in the back kitchen, or sometimes in warm weather a tap in the yard may be resorted to. This rule applies to both sexes. Little children, on the other hand are generally washed before the kitchen fire. Men going early to their work do not wash in the morning, and when they come home commonly eat before doing so. But, hunger satisfied, they wash and dress "for street" before going out. . . . In class F the back kitchen as a place of ablutions is superseded by the bedroom, and not infrequently in new houses by the bathroom. . . .[146]

Parenthetically, Booth also noted that where people in different status levels of the working class resided in the same place, a vertical differentiation took place: "Poverty . . . seems to go by floors; the poorest people, often extremely poor, are to be found at the top of the houses, and as you descend floor by floor, the position mends."[147]

Other differences in domestic life ways linked to class were discovered in the analysis of a small sample of family budgets

145 *Ibid.*, p. 330.
146 *Ibid.*
147 *Ibid.*, I, 297.

which suggested class-specific trends not only with respect to the necessaries of life but also relative to class-defined "necessaries." Concerning the former, the absolute number of items as well as the variety in any single category of expenditure was seen to vary directly with the increase in income from class to class. In regard to the latter, the presence of "insurance and club money" as well as "beer money" as constant charges on income provided insight into the importance of these practices in the lives of the people as well as into the class-defined aspects of expenditure:

On the whole, the evident fact is that the three classes [B, C, D, and E] live much the same way, only with increasing liberality, especially as to meat, green vegetables and cheese. . . . With class F . . . a marked change occurs. Fish comes in, not as a substitute, but in addition to meat, and eggs are a considerable item; while the amount for fruit, jam and such things as rice is five times that for class D and ten times that for class B. The housekeeping is altogether different in character.[148]

Bread was observed to be the staple food in classes B, C, and D, giving way to meat in classes E and F. Incidentally, the status difference between the lower-working-class housewife who bought "a piece of meat at the market street," and the upper-working-class *hausfrau* who purchased "a joint at the butchers" was viewed as a wide and unbreachable social gulf. Even the time of purchase served to discriminate among status levels where the place of purchase was the same:

. . . the poorest are the last to make their purchases. They are latest on Saturday night, and those who do not buy till Sunday morning seem poorer still. Prices are lower, the best of everything has been sold. . . .[149]

148 "Poverty Series," I, 134–35. Needless to say, such differences were related to class differentials in vital rates, especially infant mortality. Referring to the budget study, Booth noted specifically: "The number of articles of food . . . varies on the whole from 10 to 35; by classes it rises from 19 in B to 27 in E. . . . The . . . number of other items of expense vary from 8 to 36, and rise according to class from 14 to 22." *Ibid.*, p. 140.

149 *Ibid.*, I, 184.

Although the generalizations were impressionistic and often indicated Booth's own middle-class preferences, the matter of clothing was also emphasized as an aspect of class differences in standard of life. The lower classes were distinguished by the wearing of secondhand clothes which were bought and sold among them as well as given. Booth noted that class B, in particular, "may almost be distinguished by its deplorable boots." The general appearance was, of course, one of mild incongruity:

> . . . cast-off clothes of the wealthy . . . carry with them a faded smartness even as regards men's clothes, while the outer garments of the women show much tawdriness of trimmings and the relics of past fashion, in shapes which have lost what meaning they may have ever possessed.[150]

As classes higher in the social scale were encountered, the use of secondhand garments gave way to the ready-made attire of the lower working class. Of this class (D), it was observed that:

> More generally . . . these people buy new things of common though often sterling quality at cheap shops, and both men and women look credibly dressed. It is on the children that the passion for finery spends itself. . . . Children . . . being at once the plague and pride of their parents' lives.[151]

The factory girl, daughter of the parent of lower-working-class status, was typically described on her evening out as wearing,

> . . . a gorgeous plush hat with as many large ostrich feathers to match as her funds will run to—bright ruby or scarlet preferred. Like all the women in the East End she wears good tidy boots on all occasions, perhaps with high heels, but suitable for walking, although a little higher always than those adopted by the National Dress Society.[152]

And in the upper strata of the working class, where middle-class values with respect to dress were more firmly rooted, Booth noted that the people were practically indistinguishable from those above them as far as "outward appearance" was concerned:

150 "Industry Series," V, 328.
151 *Ibid.*, p. 330.
152 "Poverty Series," IV, 323.

. . . the true working classes . . . can and do dress well. . . . As to their wives and still more their daughters . . . it needs a fine eye for class distinctions to pick them out amongst the other prettily dressed women. . . .[153]

The subjective consequences of class differences in the objective dimensions of life style were made especially clear in Booth's appreciation of the contrast between "the factory girl" and the working girl of middle-class social background. In the first place, this involved a general hypothesis:

There are a great many steps between the warehouse work girl [of the lower middle class] . . . and the girl who has been accepted as the type of the factory girl. . . . There must be a difference in the thoughts and habits of the family who live in a cottage and of the family who herd together in one or at the most two rooms.[154]

In the second place, insofar as the middle-class girl's style of life bore no relationship to her actual earnings (it will be recalled that she worked only for what she and her parents were pleased to call "pocket-money"), an anxiety was hypothesized to exist concerning the day when she must inevitably live on the basis of her real wages:

The workgirl of the lower middle class, when she begins to reflect on the future, does dread it. There is hardly one thing . . . [the factory girl] requires in the way of food, clothing or lodging, which is not equally desired by the City workwoman in this rank [i.e., the middle class]. Of the two the . . . [factory girl] . . . can resign herself the more easily to shabby dresses and hats, has no fear of losing caste on account of poverty, and can offer her friends weak tea and biscuit without any dread of being considered mean and inhospitable. She has the happy conviction that her own personal merit is all sufficing. The young lady who goes to a warehouse or a superior factory is singularly modest in this respect. She seems to imagine that her whole

153 "Religious Influences," I, 87.

154 "Poverty Series," IV, 321. The status differences between these two classes of girls were also observed to operate inside the work situation: Booth spoke of "the manner in which one set of girls keep themselves aloof from another, and in which one factory regards itself as superior or inferior to another." *Ibid.*

future depends on those appearances which must be kept up. When she is left to support herself, the importance she attaches to outside things shows how much more keenly she is actuated by ideal rather than material wants. She starves herself first, living on tea and bread-and-butter; she stints herself in bedclothing and underclothing next, and attributes her colds and bronchitis to original weakness in constitution. And in the reaction that follows, the sickening distaste for drudgery and the struggle, she too often sacrifices maidenhood itself. The substance is thrown away for the shadow. These girls do not sin for bread. They sin for the externals which they have learnt to regard as essentials.[155]

Incidentally, despite an implicit middle-class bias, Booth struck another modern note when, as another aspect of class differences in what we have termed "home ways," he pointed out that the informal, early socialization of children in the home was "an even surer standard by which class can be tested and measured": "As we rise from B to E or F, with each gradation there is less spoiling and less harshness; or in other words, less of want of self-control on the part of the parents."[156]

Yet another dimension of the style of life indicative of class and especially of status was recreation, the use of leisure time. Needless to say, the latter was something of a novelty for the urban masses, and there was considerable controversy over the secularization of "Sunday-pursuits" at the time of the inquiry. The question of holidays was observed to be more discriminating with respect to status differences among the middle and upper strata than in the lower social classes. Whereas they might range from a week or two at the seashore to a winter on the Continent for the former, the working classes were more or less confined to the

155 *Ibid.*, pp. 320–22. The predicament of the lower-middle-class girl was underlined by the empirical finding that "the surplus of women over men is greatest in the districts inhabited by the more well-to-do classes. . . . Whatever the causes may be, the chances of marriage among women in the poorer middle classes are less than among the working girls in the East End. Every girl in the lowest class in the East End can get married and with hardly any exception every girl does. This is not true of the middle classes." *Ibid.*, pp. 321–22.

156 "Industry Series," V, 335.

celebration of Bank Holidays (where their "leisure" was not enforced by the irregularity of their employment). As Booth observed: "Amongst the upper classes holiday-making has been raised to the level of a fine art and invested almost with the character of a religious observance."[157] Nevertheless, even the lower elements of the working classes managed to achieve some sort of holiday activity during the summer months: whole families, for example, migrated to the country to work at hop-picking, and single men often joined the militia to spend a week or two "under canvas."

However, drinking was observed to be the leisure time activity, par excellence, among the poor and working classes. And, while it is often difficult to sift through the middle-class bias that often pervaded this aspect of the inquiry, considerable evidence was amassed to indicate that it played both an intensive and extensive role in the life styles of the poor and working classes.[158]

The public house was not merely the locus of lower-class drinking but the scene of lower-class social life. "Skittle-alley" in the cellar, where an entry fee was paid and a prize of a mutton leg was donated, was a favorite sport. The social character of drinking was further underlined by the tendency for each house to have its own group of patrons:[159]

157 *Ibid.*, p. 336.

158 The concept of "thrift" as the *summum bonum* of middle-class values appeared as almost polar to that of drink. The general impression was given that the absence of thrift (which was considered a primary cause of poverty) was due in large measure to the avocation of drink: in the final analysis the equation read—DRINK = POVERTY! The problem of lower-class drinking loomed large in the middle-class eyes of Booth and his staff. A correlation was also sensed between heavy drinking and prosperity, making for the conclusion that "there is no thrift except putting by for a burst" among the lower classes.

159 In spite of his middle-class bias, Booth was quite fair in his analysis of public houses. For example, there was considerable agitation at the time for legislation to prevent children from going into the pubs to obtain beer for their parents at home. His own view tended to discount their evil influence in this direction: at least the drinking was then done at home and more likely in moderation. He also observed that candy was usually given to the children by the publican, ". . . to induce the child to pass other

. . . every public-house, large or small, has its nucleus of regular customers, its own little *clientele*. With beer-houses this is carried much further, sometimes to the point of exclusion of all others; the business of these houses being almost confined to one particular set of men, so that "even a neighbor would be looked at askance, and would hardly dare to go in.[160]

Most aspects of the life style of the lower classes were not lacking in alcoholic content: whether a wedding or a funeral, drink had its part to play, and even the marketing housewife felt the pressure of this cultural compulsive: "The favorite tipple is gin. There is a butcher's stall close by [to the pub] . . . and those who buy a joint are treated to a drink."[161] On the other hand, while Booth noted (and obviously disapproved of) the fact that women went "freely to the public house," he also emphasized that it was "not to drink in solitary fashion" but rather to "treat a friend or a friend treats them."[162]

Other forms of amusement and recreation were observed to have a class-based quality. The "solid working class," for example, enjoyed a day's outing at Epping Forest and particularly the Sunday afternoon discussion in the public parks:

The London working man is great in all forms of discussion. One cannot frequent the parks and public places without noticing this. Any subject will do, but religious subjects are the most popular, and after the organized debate is over, little groups of men will remain, crowding in, all heads pushed forward, and ears strained to hear the continuation of the debate by those who have not summoned courage enough to mount the stool which has served for a public platform.[163]

On the other hand, the lower elements of this class risked dismissal

---

public houses in order to reach one which was liberal in this respect"; and, he concluded, "It is improbable that any more drink would be sent for because of the child's willingness to go, or that any greater familiarity with the public-house would result . . . from this practice." "Final Volume," p. 66.

160 *Ibid.*, p. 65.

161 "Religious Influences," I, 249.

162 *Ibid., II*, 117.

163 *Ibid.*, I, 87.

from their jobs to take a half-holiday to see the football matches. Bicycle racing and whippet races as well as bird-call competitions were also their favorites. The Sunday morning "bird-fair" at Sclater Street had "all the genial crowdedness of a race-meeting":

It is attended far and wide, but especially reflects the pleasures and habits of the [lower-class people] which largely turns on domestic pets; singing birds, rabbits, and guinea pigs, fowls, pigeons, dogs and even goats are dealt in; any kind of animal that can be kept in or on a house or in a backyard.[164]

Class differences in this area of life also extended, of course, to the children. Those in class E had a backyard for a playground, whereas class D's offspring possessed the "even greater delights of the streets." Among the lower classes, street dancing was a favorite, but organized, formal dancing did not occur below class C, whose "shilling balls" were "eminently respectable." This was, in part, because of the scandalous reputation that "dancing saloons" had at the time.

Betting was an avocation that knew no class lines except in the manner of placing the bets, which, according to the observation that follows, has not changed much in the urban scene:

Tobacconists and newsvendors act as agents on the quiet, and so do barbers (always the confidants of their customers), and a great deal is done in the streets, especially in the dinner hour. . . . Every day the sporting papers have a vast circulation; they are found in every public-house and every coffee-shop. They are read and the news and tips given are discussed before the bets are placed.[165]

Although class differences in reading habits were considered, no data were gathered, but Booth offered the following impression:

Men in every class read nothing but the sporting papers . . . everywhere are also found eager readers of the current trash of the day. The main difference discernable lies in the use by the working classes of a weekly in place of a daily paper, and with the introduction of half-penny papers this distinction becomes each year less marked.[166]

164 *Ibid.*, II, 98.
165 "Industry Series," V, 338.
166 *Ibid.*, p. 335.

More sociologically significant, of course, were Booth's observations about class differences in attitudes and customs governing sex and marriage. Interestingly, Booth and his staff rose above the dominant morality in their analyses of this area of life; their perspective was not only fairly detached but often in the best sociological tradition. For example, in the case of the relative but organized sexual mores of the lower class:

> There are strict rules of propriety, accepted by public opinion, which cannot be violated with impunity by those who wish to live on pleasant terms with their neighbors, though they may not follow the ordinary lines either of legality or religious morality.[167]

Even the causes of the relative immorality of the lower classes were discussed in objective and sociological terms:

> Financial independence and freedom from parental restraint bring about an early escape from the discomforts of home. As boys and girls, and as young men and young women, the sexes meet and keep company together. About this there is little that is vicious, and there is even a good deal of virtuous restraint although the rules are not strict, at any rate in the lower ranks of labour. The mischievous results of Bank Holiday outings are frequently noted in our evidence.[168]

In general among the poor the "natural consequences" of premarital sexual relations led "properly" to marriage, but there was no domestic life until this occurred. And Booth noted that "if these consequences happen, marriage is recognized as the girl's right and the young man's responsibility."[169] In these matters, clear differences were demonstrated between the lowest class and the lower and upper segments of the working class:

167 "Religious Influences," II, 97.

168 "Final Volume," pp. 43–44.

169 *Ibid.*, p. 44. Undoubtedly, this relatively sophisticated attitude of the lower classes stemmed in part from certain aspects of their objective situation—the fact that they lived rather close to life and death: "Amongst this class the mortality is enormous. The mothers discuss the number they have buried with a callousness amounting at times almost to pride in the vastness of their maternal experience. Next to births, the commonest events to the factory girl are funerals; and she enjoys nothing so much as taking part in a funeral procession." "Poverty Series," IV, 325.

With the lowest classes premarital relations are very common, perhaps even usual. Amongst the girls nothing is thought of it if no consequences result; and very little even if they do, should marriage follow, and more pity than reprobation if it does not. As a rule the young people, after a few experiments, pair off and then are faithful, and usually end by marrying.[170]

On the other hand, lower-working-class girls were under "a very definite code of rules" and marriage was expected to follow the premarital relationship; but, the upper-working-class girls,

. . . though not ignorant of evil, are full of pride, and a fall from virtue is a very serious matter for their families and themselves—serious enough to bring very great pressure on the man concerned, who is most likely to be well known. In such cases a prompt marriage may hide all.[171]

Referring to differential class morality and attitudes toward marriage, Booth concluded:

. . . there is no surer test of divergence of standard among the working classes themselves than the way in which this question is answered. There are those to whom a fall from virtue in a daughter or sister is a terrible thing, hardly to be condoned; but the more usual division is between those by whom slips of this kind are spoken of freely, and although not condoned, regarded almost as a matter of course, and those who pass over with as little notice as possible a subject that it is polite to ignore.[172]

At the same time, Booth observed a general and great desire among the lower elements of the working class to have their marriages consecrated by the Church. Perceptively, Booth interpreted this as owing less to a desire for the outward trappings of respectability (as was the case of the upper working class) than to the superstition that pervaded their ranks concerning this and other aspects of life:

It is said that as regards child-bearing, preventive checks are being increasingly used. . . . This does not apply much to the poor, who in these matters are influenced by superstition of the same character as

170 "Religious Influence," I, 55.
171 *Ibid.*, p. 56.
172 "Final Volume," p. 45.

that which brings the poorest kind of women to be churched, "because they don't want a miscarriage next time." . . . So, too, it is not so much amongst the poor as in the artisan class that marriages take place before the registrar. The poor think it unlucky to be without the support of the Church.[173]

While prior to marriage there was some semblance of an organized morality insofar as marriage was expected in the lower working class, more license was granted by public opinion to the evasion of the bonds of marriage by those who had found it a failure; and desertion was quite common. In the working class, premarital sexual relations were observed to lower the age of marriage, whereas in the upper classes such freedom tended to postpone it.

Finally, Booth became especially sensitive to social class differences in the religious life of the people. While much of the material was impressionistic, hardly representative on occasion, and often shot-through with Booth's own religious biases, the whole was not only very pointed but also rang uniquely true. Regardless of the aim of the research, it focussed in fact on class differences in church attendance, attitudes toward religion and the function of religion.[174]

Although the lower classes did not attend church as a rule (with the exception of the Roman Catholics, among whom class lines were less functional in religious matters), they did, especially the women, go to the missions established for them.

Among the quite rough poor, those whose terrible lives affect the imagination and bring about the establishment of Slum Missions, the women eagerly sop up the charitable assistance that is offered and take relief and religion as they come.[175]

The working classes were, on the whole, united in their lack of attendance at either church or mission. Booth formed the general

173 *Ibid.*, p. 46.

174 Discussion of Booth's analysis of the institutional dimension of class differences in religious behavior will be deferred until the next section on "Class and Institutions."

175 "Religious Influences," I, 85. Needless to say, Booth noted that in general it was women who attended church, men being everywhere in the minority.

conclusion that "the great mass of artisans and mechanics hold aloof from the church":

The great section of the population, which passes by the name of the working classes, lying socially between the lower middle class and the "poor," remains, as a whole, outside of all the religious bodies, whether organized as churches or as missions; and as those of them who do join any church become almost indistinguishable from the class with which they mix, the change that has really come about is not so much *of* as *out of* the class to which they have belonged.[176]

Also to be counted among the non-churchgoers, according to Booth's observations, were the great numbers of "non-descript lower middle class clerks" employed in the City and living as lodgers in various parts of London. These were referred to as the "margin of the middle class." It should be noted, however, that despite the workingman's refusal to have anything to do with organized religion for himself, "the children of the respectable working class, even of professed atheists, come regularly to Sunday School."[177]

Before the level of the real middle class was reached, however, another small social stratum was encountered:

. . . what is almost a distinct grade of small-salaried people, minor officials, and the upper ten of the working class world. These people, who are more often on the upward than the downward tack, are sometimes religious, sometimes not. . . . Much depends on their antecedents and on the character of their employment, and much, too, on the habits of those whose way of life they seek to imitate. As a rule this class provides the most hopeful chance for the net of religious fishers of men.[178]

In the genuine middle class, the general rule was that wherever they were found, religious life was sure to be at its highest pitch and most fully developed—"prosperity and religion go hand in hand," as Booth put it. "Those who need "no urging" are mainly

176 *Ibid.*, VII, 399.
177 *Ibid.*, I, 28.
178 *Ibid.*, p. 150

the middle class and it is they who make up the bulk of the good congregations usually obtained."[179]

The upper classes, too, were generally faithful in the matter of church attendance, although not with the vigor of the class below them. Booth went so far as to speak of the "law of class" in the matter of religious observance; and, in the mixed streets, the visiting missionaries soon found that "the character of their reception [was] an index to the class of the inhabitants."[180]

Connected with the differential church attendance was, of course, a set of equally distinctive attitudes in the various classes. In the upper class, religion was observed to play a constant but not large part in their lives: "Their devotional expression is, as a rule, cold and unemotional, but with no class is religion more completely identified with duty."[181] And, on the borders of this class, the *noveau* were noted to involve a status factor in their religious preferences: "If belonging previously to some religious denomination outside the Establishment, they have usually left it behind them and joined the Church of England."[182]

While the place of religion in the middle class was considered to be secure and fully recognized, and while there were many who were motivated by genuine religiosity, status considerations were also often involved. Thus, church attendance and membership assumed something of the nature of a badge of status and respectability: "Many are attracted socially; clerks, for instance, finding in the church a valuable social centre."[183] Or, as put in more general terms: "Among the middle classes there are social advantages that attract, and a social feeling that almost compels a man to put himself in connection with some Christian community. . . ."[184]

Among the working classes generally, the attitude toward

179 *Ibid.*, p. 80.
180 "Poverty Series," I, 149. Cf. also, above, p. 78.
181 "Religious Influences," VII, 395.
182 *Ibid.*
183 *Ibid.*, I, 94.
184 *Ibid.*, p. 90.

religion was more a matter of indifference than aversion to religion. This was demonstrated by their previously noted willingness to send their children to Sunday School and their correlative, complete lack of discrimination in denomination preference:

The parents think it only right that they should, and the children like to come. Carefully washed and brushed and prettily dressed, they troop to the nearest school and are abandoned, without hesitation, to the religious teaching offered there, whatever it may be. . . . The religious bodies try to keep Protestants and Catholics apart, and, with the help of social cleavages, this can generally be done; but as between all forms of Protestantism nothing of the kind is possible, the children go to the most convenient school, or, when rivalry runs high, are fought for by contending visitors.[185]

In the eyes of the working class, religion had a place but a very limited one: they approved of its being taught in the day and board schools and, like the lower classes, felt it had a role to play in connection with the crises of existence—births, deaths, and marriages: "The babies too are usually baptized as 'the fair thing' for the child, with an eye to its future, the parents remembering that they were baptized themselves in their day."[186]

In the final analysis religion and churchgoing tended to be regarded primarily as matters of childhood—"the very choir boys when their voices crack promptly claim the privileges of men and give up churchgoing." There was also an increasing tendency for the working classes to look on the church as a service institution, and the minister was increasingly regarded as another paid professional: as one informant put it, "the clergy are paid from the rates and make a rather good thing out of their jobs."[187] Further, their lack of sophistication made them suspicious of the ethics of any religion. While the middle class sought support in religion, the workingman fought shy of the discipline implied:

Working men have a far more exacting conception of [religion's] ethical obligations. They expect a religious man to make his life

185 *Ibid.*, I, 28–29.
186 *Ibid.*, p. 145.
187 *Ibid.*, p. 89.

square with his opinions. They like their club with its pot of beer, its entertainments . . . and a bet on tomorrow's race, but they look on these things as inconsistent with all religious profession, and every form of religious association thus becomes . . . something from which, in honesty, they must hold themselves aloof.[188]

According to Booth, the characteristic independent attitude of the London laboring man often served further to alienate him from the methods employed by the clergy and their staffs in ministering to the poor. The working-class men wished to "run no risk of being tarred with the charitable brush":

"The poor," it is true, "receive everybody," no matter from what denomination, for every stranger may prove a friend; to them none are Greeks, and all may be welcomed who bring gifts. But the ordinary working-class home is less approachable . . . against anything which could be called charitable assistance, their pride rises swiftly.[189]

While the general attitude of the working class toward organized religion was one of indifference, Booth noted that in some districts of the city hostility was generated by "class feeling" against joining the churches which were assumed to side with the rich. A vicar expressed the opinion that in solid working-class areas many men were deterred from attending church because "the church-goer at once becomes a marked man, the subject of ridicule and chaff."[190]

The members of the lowest class, while they did not go to church, were, of course, the objects of the charitable efforts of the upper and middle classes through the medium of the mission. As Booth soon discovered, their interest was largely in the coal tickets, suppers, entertainments, and so forth, which were handed out. Generally such bounties were expected, and as one clergyman remarked, "Any branch of our [mission] organization that did not have its own particular Christmas party or treat would con-

188 *Ibid.*, p. 89.

189 *Ibid.*, p. 81.

190 *Ibid.*, p. 83. The churches attempted to organize workingmen's clubs but were successful only when all "overt ideas of religion were banished."

sider itself highly aggrieved, not to say defrauded of its rights."[191] Much as the working class did, the lower class went to church only for special occasions, or when they were in trouble. The general opinion was that while a congregation of poor people might be bought, "it melts away as soon as the payments cease."

INSTITUTIONS AND CLASS Beyond the evidence and insights the inquiry provided in relation to the conception of class as culture and to class differences and their impacts on the lives of the people, the force of class in the community was also communicated. Here Booth's naturalistic and fundamentally sociological approach to the organized, collective dimensions of social life as well as his especially perceptive treatment of the relationship between institutions and class differences came into play.

In the first place, Booth provided a picture of institutions not alone in terms of static, formal organization and what has come to be termed, in modern sociological parlance, "manifest function"; rather, process, informal organization, and "latent function" were also implicit (and often explicit) dimensions of analysis.[192] For example, he noted that the Salvation Army had three different functions, the result of specific developments in time:

> It has three aspects: that of a Gospel Mission, that of a religious community, and that of an organization for social work; but these, though distinct and tending to become more so, are closely interconnected. At the outset the last mentioned was unknown, and there was, perhaps no distinction between the other two.[193]

The dynamic quality of institutions was especially emphasized by Booth's observations of ecological shifts—changes in the character of the residential population of an area. The postulate that each religious institution had its particular milieu, the change of which necessitated adaptation for survival, was explicit:

191 *Ibid.*, II, 91.

192 Booth, of course, never employed the concept "institution" in any formal, sociological manner.

193 *Ibid.*, VII, 323.

The natural congregation of Protestant Nonconformist bodies consists mainly of middle class people . . . but . . . they have left, necessitating orientation to the people now living in the district.[194]

. . . their regular supporters have left or are leaving and their church must either adopt missionary methods or close their doors.[195]

The failure of both the Church of England and the Nonconformist bodies in North London was directly traced to changes in the character of the surrounding population:

The middle class has gone, replaced by a non-churchgoing working class. . . . The Nonconformists are not a whit more successful than the Church. . . . Several of the Chapels that prospered here "while the shopkeepers still lived over their shops" [i.e., before the middle class left] . . . have been entirely closed. Their place is taken by special missions, connected, in most cases, with an active church elsewhere. With these missions the regular working class will have nothing to do."[196]

Other examples of Booth's insights into institutional latent functions were the previously noted tendencies of the public house to become the social center for the lower classes; the mission to be less an organization for the preaching of the gospel and more a social service and charity-dispensing institution; and, as will be seen below, the pawnshop to be less a rational economic institution providing occasional credit for an impersonal market than the keystone of the ability of the lower class to adjust income to expenditure through the medium of personal, perpetual credit.

Various observations pointed to the importance of the informal operations within institutions, for example, concerning the university settlements and polytechnics:

The time of greatest leakage among members is found to be after a single term, when no "section" has been joined and friends have not

194 *Ibid.*, I, 30.

195 *Ibid.*, p. 42. Parenthetically, Booth observed that the larger churches, which held a "cathedral position," were often able to continue in the face of such changes because of their ability to draw upon a non-resident population.

196 *Ibid.*, p. 134.

been made. . . . Just one or two men of the right sort to be in and out constantly, learning to know the members, bringing them together. . . . These are the men with the oil cans.[197]

Again, Booth's objective approach to prostitution as an institution allowed a sociological insight into the problem of its control:

[Prostitution's] sole aim is the satisfaction of male sexual passion without the responsibilities of marriage or anything that may be called a social relationship. The woman's passions are hardly involved at all, she is moved neither by excitement nor by pleasure; all questions of "fall" are past. The professional character of the part played by women is very much against rescue work. . . . If, however, the professional character . . . militates against successful rescue work . . . it may perhaps help facilitate regulation.[198]

Finally, even cogent insights of a social psychological nature were not lacking in Booth's consideration of the organized, collective functions of the community. Typical was his discussion of the implications for the approach to charity and the potential conflict with the more rationally motivated groups such as the Charity Organization Society of the specifically "religious" orientation of the sisterhoods:

The spirit of the proselytizer has its genesis in the strong religious convictions of the Sisters, which lead them to be keenly alive to the dangers of false doctrine, and horrified at the neglected and heathen lives of the people among whom they work. The temptation to win souls by whatever means then becomes very great; and the unscrupulous spirit which is evinced obtains the more license from the fact that the Sisters feel themselves to be working not for their own community, but for the church; not for themselves, but for God.[199]

Booth's materials provided four different optics on the relationship between institutions and class differences: in the first place, they suggested that the conditions of life of a class often led to the development of unique, class-specific institutional arrangements; in the second place, they exemplified the tendency for an

197 *Ibid.*, VII, 387.
198 "Final Volume," pp. 126–27.
199 "Religious Influences," VII, 353.

institution to assume a characteristic form for each class insofar as it served a range of classes; a third perspective noted the manner in which a specific or concrete institutional form adapted to the simultaneous involvement of two or more classes, either by a differentiation of function apropos each class or by other means to allow such multi-class involvement; and a fourth optic, one less perfectly developed, adumbrated the notion that each class had its own institutional complement or set. Together, these postulates supported not only the more general conception of class as life style or culture but especially the lesson of class as a force in the social organization and process of the lives of the people.

Regardless of the ultimate causes of their poverty—industrial, physical, social, or moral—Booth discovered that the expenditures of the lower classes for the necessaries of life generally exhausted their incomes. And, the consequence of this objective dimension of their class situation was the development of special, class-specific institutional arrangements as well as, correlatively, considerable insight into the economic organization of lower class life: the pawnshop and the moneylender, the provident and loan clubs, and the friendly and "sharing-out" societies were cases in point.

Indeed, both the formal and informal loan organizations were direct outgrowths of the limits of the lower-class economic situation. These institutions allowed lower-class people to obtain needed credit without recourse to the more formally and rationally organized banks. The "sharing-out" societies, for example, made it possible for the members to receive larger single sums with which to make special purchases. Interesting in this connection was the discovery that many of the informal "thrift clubs" were organized among the patrons of a particular beer or public house, the proprietor typically serving as the treasurer. The following is an example of what Booth termed "publican's thrift":

> A number of men meeting weekly at some public house form a society with treasurer (usually the publican), trustee, check steward, and secretary; 3*d* entrance fee is paid and 3*d* more for the book of rules, including a card on which loans and repayments are noted. Each share taken up involves a weekly subscription of 6*d*; the number of shares

that may be taken by one member is generally limited. There is also a small quarterly subscription fee for working expenses. The funds so subscribed, week by week, are available for loans to the members who stand security for each other. The interest on the loan (5 per cent) is deducted when the amount is borrowed. . . . Fines are levied if repayments and subscriptions are not punctually met . . . and great care is exercised not to lend more than is safely secured. The result at the end of the year is a profit of 3*s* or 4*s* per share, and if not in debt to the society at the time, each member receives also the 1£ 6*s* accumulated. . . . The money is divided at Christmas. . . . Every member is obliged to borrow to some extent, otherwise he would obtain would be thought an unfair advantage in the division of profit.[200]

The "sharing-out" society, on the other hand, was a simpler version and popular among the factory girls of the lower working class:

. . . a number . . . club together weekly 6*d* or 1*s* each, the whole sum being taken by one of the members in rotation by lot. The object is to get a large enough sum at once to make spending profitable; to buy a hat, or boots, or have a fling of sorts.[201]

The more formally organized and larger friendly societies and their less formal brethren, the "dividing societies," were also noted to play a large role in the lower classes' attempt to achieve some sort of surplus, or a degree of financial security:

. . . death clubs with a weekly subscription of ½*d* to 2*d* per head are very commonly subscribed to, and there are instances of a system by which tradesmen are paid small sums all through the summer against the winter expenditure at their shop, receiving the money on a deposit card, and acting in fact as a sort of savings bank. But, such cases are exceptional; the reverse would be the rule, credit being given in winter against repayment in summer. Most benefit societies, death clubs, goose clubs, etc., are held at public-houses.[202]

200 "Poverty Series," I, 111.

201 *Ibid.*, p. 112.

202 *Ibid.*, p. 46. Booth noted that the "Total Abstinence Benefit Societies" literally "lived by their lapses, being able to trust with scientific certainty to a proportion of their members breaking the pledge." *Ibid.*, p. 108. Perhaps in these communal roots lie the viability of English socialism as well as "the welfare state."

On the subjective level, it was noted that the large, impersonal friendly societies were not as popular as the informal dividing societies among the lower classes. To the latter, the long-range benefits of such institutionalized arrangements seemed "mythical"; and the Government-sponsored prudential system, while admittedly more liberal as to terms, involved "methods [which] do not suit the poor so well."

Because of the discrepancy between income and outgo, credit and numerous small purchases were the means invented to fill in the gap. An analysis of family budgets showed that on the average the number of trips to buy tea at the local shop varied directly with the class of the purchaser: ". . . there were in five weeks, 23 journeys to the shop in class B, 10 in D, and 6 in E."[203] Even the rent collector was observed to make his collection *every* morning in the poor districts. And, another of the products of this situation in the lower class was the traditional practice of pawning the "Sunday Clothes." According to Booth, "the Monday morning business of the pawnshops was a sight to see":

> The weeks earnings come in on Saturday; Sunday clothes are then taken out of pawn, pressing claims met, and Sunday dinner bought. This accomplished, the men drink till all is spent. On Monday, the clothes go back into pawn and the rent paid, and the club money too will be called for and paid.[204]

> . . . they, every week, put in and take out of pawn the same set of garments, on which the broker every time advances 16*s*, charging the no doubt reasonable sum of 4*d* for the accommodations . . . for the comfort of having a week's income in advance.[205]

Not only did the objective economic situation of the lower classes produce such unique institutional arrangements, but the entire area of their economic life became permeated by essentially traditional, non-rational norms. Again, in the matter of the pawnshop,

> . . . a poor man would not hesitate to enter an establishment in a principal street if he had anything of recognized value to dispose of,

203 *Ibid.*, p. 140.
204 "Religious Influences," I, 54.
205 "Poverty Series," I, 140.

but if he has only clothes to "put away," he goes to a shop where he is known, because he will get more there than elsewhere.[206]

In contrast to the middle and upper classes, the organization of the economic dimension of the lower-class life style was observed to be personalized to a unique degree.

Religious, economic and recreational organizations provided excellent examples of institutional adaptation to class differences by change of form. Thus, there was a tendency for the mission to serve the lower classes, the church to serve the middle classes, and the cathedral to serve the upper classes. Speaking of a typical local church in North London, Booth remarked:

[It] maintains its congregation in the usual way with old Parish churches in London, drawing from a wide area. . . . Practically all who come are middle class, and women preponderate. The poor do not come at all. For them there is the mission-church.[207]

Further, the organizational and activity programs of each church were specifically adapted to the tastes of the class involved. The social interest, typical of the middle class, was catered to by an elaboration of organized activities on this level, recreational activities being particularly characteristic:

. . . it seems to be regarded as part of the duty of the church to supply decent amusements and the entertainments in wintertime are described as "incessant"; consisting of dances, balls, concerts, plays, and . . . these entertainments pay for themselves and sometimes leave a surplus. In summer there are excursions without end, and the cricket clubs are extremely numerous.[208]

The class-denoting qualities of such extra-religious developments were explicitly noted. As Booth put it, such activities "are notable . . . as indicating the passing . . . from working class with a substratum of poverty, and great lack of social initiative, to middle class activity and domination."[209] Not only were the services (as might be expected) adapted to class tastes but other aspects as

206 "Final Volume," p. 82.
207 "Religious Influences," I, 91.
208 *Ibid.*, p. 102.
209 *Ibid.*, p. 103.

well. Thus, pastor "personality" was suggested to be an important consideration in the middle-class Nonconformist churches:

Pulpit appearance is of great importance. For example, we read, "Fine head and great shock of hair;" "Plain, bright, humorous face;" "Frank, almost jovial tone;" "Good presence, muscular, attractive;" "Massive, gray-haired man;" and with more than one a non-clerical appearance is mentioned. . . . Though frequently said of Nonconformist ministers, it is not often that such things are considered and come to be reported of the clergy of the Church of England.[210]

Again, in the middle-class churches, the young were a great concern and served as the focus of much of the extra-religious activity: football, cycling, and lawn tennis clubs were characteristic. Indeed, this sort of adaptation was termed the "congregationalist method," to refer to the use of social life in connection with religious work and congregational unity; it was a mark of middle-class religious life wherever found.

On the other hand, though equally characterized by extra-religious activities, the missions for the poor or lower classes tended to emphasize activities of a charitable and philanthropic nature: begging and giving were the operations, par excellence, and the proliferation of such industries was the hallmark of the missions. Grocery, bread, and coal tickets—in some instances, soup kitchens, clinics, legal advisors, employment bureaus, and blanket societies for the lending of blankets in winter—were the stock in trade of almost every mission. Not only did such corporeal operations prevail but there was also an increasing tendency for the missions to take over the management of loan clubs formerly held by the publicans. Thus, the operation of thrift clubs and sick-benefit and burial societies became a popular mission activity, directly aimed at the class of clients involved; it was regarded as a proper field for mission work. There were also, of course, temperance societies and above all the "mothers' meeting," which was ubiquitous:

The women . . . are reached in a special way, the "mothers" meeting being everywhere a successful institution. It is sometimes said that

210 *Ibid.*, p. 129.

those who come are "bribed" to attend, but the word is unnecessarily hard. If applicable here, there is hardly any social function to which it does not apply. Some of the clergy would like to add a greater touch of discipline; would like to insist on regularity of attendance; on coming to church; even on church membership; but most are wisely content to accept for what it may be worth the willingness of the women to meet and work together under religious influences.[211]

Mothers' meetings are almost exclusively for the poor. . . . It is unusual for the wives of regularly employed, well-to-do working men to attend them. . . . The singing of hymns is a pleasure to the women and a reverent attitude is maintained . . . but religious truths have hardly any more grip on the mother than on the children. Religion is rarely taken home . . . saving is fostered and economy made more possible for the women by coal and clothing clubs, while tea parties and excursions pleasantly bind the whole together.[212]

Each activity was aimed at the class involved or to specific segments of it. Just as there was the "mothers' meeting," there was a variety of clubs for childern (e.g., "The Band of Hope," a temperance society; boy and girl "Brigades," etc.). As previously noted, denominational differences counted for little when it came to mission organization and functioning:

. . . whatever religious body . . . Church, Non-conformist, or Independent Evangelical, the methods adopted are very similar. . . . The same ideas prevail and the same methods succeed.[213]

. . . the Mothers' Meeting and its adjuncts; the Sunday School and all that goes with it; these form the staple work of every mission, whatever the denomination, and there is a good deal of overlapping; for wherever the poor are, there are the missions crowded together.[214]

Since religious institutions achieved minimum success among the working classes, except with the children in Sunday school, where interest was occasionally aroused, certain adaptations were

211 *Ibid.*, pp. 29–30.
212 *Ibid.*, VII, 277.
213 *Ibid.*, I, 46.
214 *Ibid.*, p. 136. Booth discovered at least one instance of a lower-class child who was baptized by the Catholics, Wesleyans, and the Church of England.

imperative. Above all, this meant concentrating on the secular rather than the sacred. As Booth observed, "the Total Abstinence Society can fill its rooms unless it is a religious sort of a meeting."[215] And, the "P.S.A." (Pleasant Sunday Afternoon) was noted to be the only development in which the working class took any interest, but here emphasis was definitely on a secular type of program: teas, concerts, entertainments of various sorts.

The great numbers of clubs for boys and girls were consciously aimed at the working class in the hope of prolonging the churches' hold on the children, and the same was true of the treats and excursions. In some churches, as another example of institutional adaptation to the working-class life style, the hour of morning service was fixed at an earlier time in recognition of the fact that the wives were also the cooks and that Sunday dinner was the most important meal of the week in working-class homes.

Needless to say, similar sorts of adaptations were noted in the case of the lower classes: even the drapery sales at the missions were, of necessity, organized in a manner suited to their economic limitations—the goods were paid for gradually and only taken away when the payment was complete. Even the architecture of some of the missions was directed to assumed lower-class tastes, one being built like a lighthouse, displaying a revolving light! In general, all the various churches, in their mission activity, regarded social work as necessary and acceptable as an intermediary to higher things. And, whether it was a matter of attracting and holding the middle, working, or lower classes, the type of extra-religious activity was a function of class-specific tastes and needs.

The retail shop was another social institution noted to be adapted to specific classes; this was true not only of shops in general but also of specific types of shops:

> . . . broad differences may be noticed between class and class, on a sliding scale from A or B to F. For instance, very poor people hardly ever venture into any but the smallest description of shops, and for each shop there is a corresponding grade. This is a rule, rarely broken, which applies to all ranks of society.[216]

215 *Ibid.*, II, 94.

216 "Industry Series," V, 333.

Drapers' shops vary in style—low medium, and high class—according to the customers for whose wants they cater, or, more roughly, according to the neighborhood in which they are situated. Walworth is as much above Bermondsey New Road as Lewisham or Holloway would consider themselves above Walworth; and a widening gulf separates these from the shops in Kensington, in Oxford Street and in Regent Street. It would be easy to fill up the intervals with other shops which would compete more or less with those above and below. . . .[217]

While such shops generally served needs that were more or less universal, cutting across class lines, there were distinctive types of shops which catered to class-specific needs which, incidentally, were a reliable index to the class of the neighborhood:

A poor neighborhood is also stamped by its shops. Bird-fanciers are mostly to be found in the mixed streets which lie near black districts. Fried fish, and still more stewed eel shops commonly mark the vincinity of great poverty, and a catmeat shop is seldom far removed from it. The cats themselves may be taken as a last test.[218]

Prostitution also illustrated the tendency of a general activity to adapt itself to the class it served, each social grade having its own particular form:

At the top of the scale, there are the fashionable brothels. . . . There are not many of them, and they are located where they are least likely to be noticed as a nuisance. Their *clientele* is private and personal; those who seek them know where to find them. They are solely West-End institutions. In this mode of life they represent fashion. . . . Below these are large numbers of less fashionable but still mostly West-End houses, well known to the police. . . . These girls are not so closely looked after as those in the class above. . . . From this level there is a descending scale, in which the organized brothel plays a decreasing part, and the houses of accommodation an increasing one. Falling lower still, the bully protector . . . becomes a common factor. . . . The descending scale is represented by locality, and again by the class of women employed, as also by their age, and each locality, each class and each age presents specific difficulties to the reformer.[219]

217 *Ibid.*, III, 68–69.
218 "Poverty Series," II, 83.
219 "Final Volume," pp. 123–26.

In regard to the third optic, religious institutions again served as the best example. The simultaneous participation of a number of classes usually occurred in parishes of mixed population, especially in the case of the Church of England. The inevitable result was the recognition of class differences sometimes explicitly, sometimes implicitly, and a consequent adaptation on the part of the institution. In the first place, class lines were often objectified in terms of different levels of function or of participation. This was best illustrated by the non-denominational missions: "In this matter there are three parties concerned; those who give their money, those who carry on the work which the money enables them to do, and "the poor" who are the recipients."[220] In general, these categories corresponded to the wealthy and middle-class patrons, the lower-middle-class volunteers and professional workers, and the lower-class clients. "The duty of the rich to the poor" still played a major part in the organization of London's religious life:

> . . . as a rule, wherever poverty is found scattered in patches, each patch furnishes the opportunity for one or more missions. Most of these centers of religious and philanthropic efforts are connected with, and supported by some wealthy church or chapel in the vicinity.[221]

The functional relationships among the classes were well summarized in the following generalization:

> . . . what [money] has been raised has almost invariably come from the parson and his private friends, from the middle class members of the congregation. . . . The working class accept the services of the Sunday school and the treats that are offered their children . . . but themselves take no part or interest in the mission work of the church; while the poor are ready to receive whatever is to be had. . . .[222]

Despite their fundamentally more universal orientation, even the Catholic churches exhibited adaptations to multi-class participation; as Booth observed, "[people] sort themselves more or less

220 "Religious Influences," II, 22.
221 *Ibid.*, I, 177.
222 *Ibid.*, VII, 281.

according to class in the hour at which they came together."[223]

Where two or more classes participated in the same capacity, for example in the Sunday schools, class lines were quite evident as among the middle-, working-, and lower-class children. Whereas in the middle-class district of North East London the adults who attended church were generally of one social level,

> . . . with the Sunday school and mission class distinctions come in. The little children of the members get religious education "at mother's knee" and do not go to Sunday school, though those who live near may attend. The Sunday school, however, is mainly filled with working class children from roundabout, while poorer people's children go to the missions.[224]

The tendency of the Sunday schools to recognize class lines and to explicitly adapt to class differences was pointed out again and again:

> In the Sunday schools there are two classes: the children of their own coming in the afternoon, and those of a rougher description in the evening.[225]

> The intermixture of class in many localities . . . is shown by the need of divisions according to grade in Sunday schools, gymnasiums, etc. We are told that contingents from different streets would never mix. In one case as regards the Summer treat, three divisions are made: "no treat," "pay towards it," and "pay nothing," and in another case the gymnasium is open on three nights for different grades of children.[226]

The force of class was further demonstrated by the invasion of clubs designed for lower-class young people by those of another class, with the result that a mission club for girls sometimes became "too successful, as the rough girls for whose sake it was started find themselves almost out of place in it."[227]

223 *Ibid.*, I, 87.
224 *Ibid.*, p. 122–23.
225 *Ibid.*, II, 124. In some instances even finer divisions were made among the poor. Thus, one school was ". . . attended mainly on Sunday evening when some six hundred of the poorest children are gathered in. Classes for those not quite so poor are held on week nights." *Ibid.*, p. 72.
226 *Ibid.*, I, 150.
227 *Ibid.*, II, 90.

The final optic, which was noted to be only implicit in the inquiry, did much, however, to make explicit and to elaborate the concept of class as style of life. Indeed, something of a functional perspective was introduced by the postulate that certain sets of institutions hung together, so-to-speak, because of their class basis. Thus, in the lower classes there was the mission with its perennial adjuncts—the "Mothers' Meeting," thrift clubs, coal clubs, etc.; in the economic sphere there was the pawnshop, the informal provident and loan club; on the recreational side, there was the beer house, the low-grade public house; for education, the ragged school and the district visitor; and last, the public hospital, workhouse, and street market.

With the working class, the church, except for Sunday school for the children and the religious day school, in contrast to the board or "ragged" school, was conspicuous by its absence. Consumers' cooperatives, trade unions and friendly societies, as well as social and political clubs were part of the specific institutional set of this social stratum. In contrast to the publican's thrift of the lower classes, there was more apt to be the savings bank; and, where religious interest was present, it took the form of the gospel center. Finally, the polytechnic and endowed secondary school catered to the educational needs of the working class on a higher level.

Correlatively, the middle class was noted particularly by the reappearance of the church and the disappearance of the public house; there was the butcher's shop in contrast to the street market and the large, centrally located retail establishment instead of the small general shop.

An Assessment

No man or his work better illustrates the truth of Myrdal's observation that "the social sciences have all received their impetus much more from the urge to improve society than from simple curiosity about its working" than Charles Booth and his classic study of the life and labour of the people in London.[228] Not

228 Gunnar Myrdal, "The Relation Between Social Theory and Social Policy," *British Journal of Sociology*, 4 (September, 1953): 210.

the least of Booth's relevance for the development of sociology stems from his emphatic empirical concern. However unplanned and often implicit, the questions, both theoretical and methodological, which such an approach inevitably raised, became central to the sociology which emerged, primarily in America, a generation later.

Because he focussed on the problems of an urban community in an industrial society; because of his use of statistical data and methods to describe, to compare, and to chart the course of change of the social structure and functioning of the (then) world's largest city; because he rationally organized and pursued a collective research effort; and, finally, because despite his abiding concern to bring about reforms he developed a very sophisticated sociological eye and scientific attitude toward "social facts," the materials in the seventeen volumes strike a very modern note.

To be sure, Booth was human enough not to escape completely the ideological bonds of his own tradition and experience in his view of man and society. Yet his instinctive explicit choice of the problem of poverty and implicit choice of the problem of the city as the locus of social life have been vindicated not only by the run of events but also by the foci of contemporary sociologists and sociological research.

His specific concern with the city as a physical fact as well as with the centrality of social class in its social organization and functioning suggests his work as a proper antecedent of much that has taken place in sociological thought and research in the decades that have followed. If Booth stands between the encyclopaedic and philosophical concerns of an earlier social science and the more limited empirical interests of a later sociology, he also adumbrated, by his focus on poverty in the midst of urban plenty, the return of an established academic discipline to the most salient and pressing problematic aspects of the society in which it lives and has its being. This surely would have pleased Charles James Booth—husband, father, businessman, public servant, and *sociologist!*

CHARLES BOOTH

THE LIFE AND LABOUR OF THE PEOPLE IN LONDON: SELECTED WRITINGS.

I. Poverty Series

1

INTRODUCTION

The inquiry of which I am now able to publish the results, was set on foot in 1886, the subject being the condition and occupations of the inhabitants of London, and my grateful thanks are due to those friends who helped me at the outset in laying down the principles on which the inquiry has been conducted. It was decided to employ a double method, dividing the people by districts and again by trades, so as to show at once the manner of their life and of their work. Most of 1886 was occupied with preliminary work, 1887 sufficed to complete the district inquiry in East London, and 1888 was spent on the trades and special subjects.

The special subjects connected with East London have started into great prominence during the time I have been at work. On the question of the "Unemployed" we have seen a house-to-house inquiry instituted by Government, which took as one of its selected districts St. George's-in-the-East. On the influx of poor Jews, under the name of "Foreign Immigration," we have had a Committee of the House of Commons; and there has been the Committee of the House of Lords on the "Sweating system," which is still prolonging its labours. In addition, the whole question of Poor Relief has been laid open by another Committee of the House of Commons, and we have seen a succession of Mansion House inquiries on the same subject. To meet this evident demand for information I offer the pages which follow. The facts as given have been gathered and stated with no bias nor distorting aim, and with no foregone conclusions.

Reprinted from "Poverty Series," I, 3–7, 24–27.

For the district inquiry, resulting in the division of the people into 8 classes, I have relied upon information obtained from the School Board visitors, of whom there are 66 in the East London district, and my tables are based on three assumptions:

1. That the numbers of married men with school children in each section by employment imply a similar proportion in the same sections of married men without school children, and of other male adults. For the choice of employment is made before the epoch of school children, and the period of employment continued long after; the fathers of the school children of the day are but a section of a block which contains, all the while, old men and young, married and single, those with children and those without, in every trade. Hence, having scheduled the heads of families with school children, I feel justified in dividing the other male adults in similar proportions.

2. That likewise the number of children of school age in each section implies the existence of brothers and sisters, older and younger, to be found living under the same home conditions. Hence I have added children and young persons of 13–20 to each section in proportion to the number of school children scheduled.

3. That the condition as to poverty of those with children at school in each section will safely represent the condition of the whole section; the younger men in some employments, and the older men in others, earn less money than those of middle age who are the fathers of the children at school, but both are at less expense. On the whole, therefore, the condition of the bulk will be better than that of the part we are able to test.

I have, however, assumed that as is the condition of the tested part—which amounts to fully one half of the population—so is the condition of the whole population; and I may here say that I have throughout my inquiry leaned to the safe side, preferring to paint things too dark rather than too bright, not because I myself take a gloomy view, but to avoid the chance of understating the evils with which society has to deal.[1]

[1] I undoubtedly expected that this investigation would expose exaggerations, and it did so; but the actual poverty disclosed was so great, both in mass and in degree, and so absolutely certain, that I have gradually become equally anxious not to overstate.—C. B., 1902.

The School Board visitors perform amongst them a house-to-house visitation; every house in every street is in their books, and details are given of every family with children of school age. They begin their scheduling two or three years before the children attain school age, and a record remains in their books of children who have left school. The occupation of the head of the family is noted down. Most of the visitors have been working in the same district for several years, and thus have an extensive knowledge of the people. It is their business to re-schedule for the Board once a year, but intermediate revisions are made in addition, and it is their duty to make themselves acquainted, so far as possible, with new comers into their districts. They are in daily contact with the people, and have a very considerable knowledge of the parents of the school children, especially of the poorest amongst them, and of the conditions under which they live. No one can go, as I have done, over the description of the inhabitants of street after street in this huge district (East London), taken house by house and family by family—full as it is of picturesque details noted down from the lips of the visitor to whose mind they have been recalled by the open pages of his own schedules—and doubt the genuine character of the information and its truth. Of the wealth of my material I have no doubt. I am indeed embarrassed by its mass, and by my resolution to make use of no fact to which I cannot give a quantitative value. The materials for sensational stories lie plentifully in every book of our notes; but, even if I had the skill to use my material in this way—that gift of the imagination which is called "realistic"—I should not wish to use it here. There is struggling poverty, there is destitution, there is hunger, drunkenness, brutality, and crime; no one doubts that it is so. My object has been to attempt to show the numerical relation which poverty, misery, and depravity bear to regular earnings and comparative comfort, and to describe the general conditions under which each class lives.

For the trade inquires and special subjects, I have been fortunate in obtaining the aid of others, and their work will speak eloquently for itself.

If the facts thus stated are of use in helping social reformers to find remedies for the evils which exist, or do anything to prevent the adoption of false remedies, my purpose is answered. It was not my intention to bring forward any suggestions of my own, and if I have ventured here and there, and especially in the concluding chapters, to go beyond my programme, it has been with much hesitation.

With regard to the disadvantages under which the poor labour, and the evils of poverty, there is a great sense of helplessness: the wage earners are helpless to regulate their work and cannot obtain a fair equivalent for the labour they are willing to give; the manufacturer or dealer can only work within the limits of competition; the rich are helpless to relieve want without stimulating its sources. To relieve this helplessness a better stating of the problems involved is the first step. "We are a long way towards understanding anything under our consideration, when we have properly laid it open, even without comment."[2] In this direction must be sought the utility of my attempt to analyze the population of London.

In order that the true, and not more than the true, significance and value may be given to the facts and figures produced, it may be useful to explain exactly the method that has been adopted in collecting them.

The 46 books of our notes contain no less than 3400 streets or places in East London, and every house and every family with school children is noted, with such information as the visitors could give about them.

From notes such as these the information given in our schedules was tabulated, and from them also was coloured the map which now forms a part of that published in connection with these volumes. The people—that is those of them who had school children—were classified by their employment and by their apparent status as to means; the streets were classified according to their inhabitants. Such is the nature of our information, and such the use made of it. It was possible to subject the map to the test of criticism, and it was mainly for this purpose that it was prepared. It was exhibited at Toynbee Hall and Oxford House, and was seen and very carefully studied by many who are intimately acquainted,

2 "Autobiography of Mark Rutherford."

† St. Hubert Street. (Class A—*coloured black on map.*) ‡

			Class.	Section.
1. Casual Labourer......	1 room	2 school children	B.	2
	(Now gone hopping.)			
Charwoman	1 room, widow	1 child at school and 1 baby......	B.	33
	(The widow's sister also lives with her.)			
....	1 room	1 family, no children at school		
2. Bootmaker	1 ,, wife helps,	2 school children......................	C.	11
Casual Labourer	1 ,, ...	1 child at school and 2 babies ...	A.	1
	(Very low family. Also have one child at Industrial School.)			
?	1 room, widow...	1 child at school	B.	35

		Class.	Sect.
42. Railway Ticket Collector	3 school children (1 an idiot)	F.	13
43. Carman	2 ,, ,, 2 babies........................	E.	5
44. Engineer	2 ,, ,, 1 baby	E.	9
Carman	1 child at school....................................	E.	5

General Character.—All the houses consist of 7 rooms and scullery and let at 13s per week. The people are all in good circumstances, and the houses well-built and commodious as a rule, but a few new houses are jerry built.

† The real names of the streets are, for obvious reasons, suppressed.

‡ Note.—The system of colour used on the map to indicate the class of each street is as follows:—*Black*—the lowest grade; *Dark Blue*—very poor; *Light Blue*—ordinary poverty; *Purple*—mixed with poverty; *Pink*—working-class comfort; *Red*—well-to-do; and *Yellow*—wealthy.

not with the whole, but each with some part, of the district portrayed. Especially, we obtained most valuable aid in this way from the Relieving Officers and from the agents of the Charity Organization Society. The map stood the test very well. There were errors, but on reference they were, in almost every case, found to be due to mistake in the transfer of verbal into graphic description, or consequent on our having made a whole street the unit of colour, whereas different parts of the same street were of very different character. The map was revised, and now equally represents the facts as disclosed by this inquiry, and as agreed to by the best local authorities.

Our books of notes are mines of information. They have been referred to again and again at each stage of our work. So valuable have they proved in unforeseen ways, that I only regret they were not more slowly and deliberately prepared; more stuffed with facts than even they are. As it was, we continually improved as we went on, and may be said to have learnt our trade by the time the work was done. At first, nothing seemed so essential as speed. The task was so tremendous; the prospect of its completion so remote; and every detail cost time. In the Tower Hamlets division, which was completed first, we gave on the average 19¾ hours work to each School Board visitor; in the Hackney division this was increased to 23½ hours. St. George's-in-the-East when first done in 1886 cost 60 hours' work with the visitors; when revised it occupied 83 hours. At the outset we shut our eyes, fearing lest any prejudice of our own should colour the information we received. It was not till the books were finished that I or my secretaries ourselves visited the streets amongst which we had been living in imagination. But later we gained confidence, and made it a rule to see each street ourselves at the time we received the visitors account of it. With the insides of the houses and their inmates there was no attempt to meddle. To have done so would have been an unwarrantable impertinence; and, besides, a contravention of our understanding with the School Board, who object, very rightly, to any abuse of the delicate machinery with which they work. Nor, for the same reason, did we ask the visitors to obtain information specially for us. We dealt solely with that which comes to them in a natural way in the discharge of their duties.

The amount of information obtained varied with the different visitors; some had not been long at the work, and amongst those who had been, there was much difference in the extent of their knowledge; some might be less trustworthy than others: but taking them as a body I cannot speak too highly of their ability and good sense. I also wish to express my warm thanks for the ready manner in which all—the Divisional Committees themselves, the District Superintendents, and the Visitors; lent themselves to my purpose. For without this nothing could have been done. The merit of the information so obtained, looked at statistically, lies mainly in the breadth of view obtained. It is in effect the whole population that comes under review. Other agencies usually seek out some particular class or deal with some particular condition of people. The knowledge so obtained may be more exact, but it is circumscribed and very apt to produce a distortion of judgment. For this reason, the information to be had from the School Board visitors, with all its inequalities and imperfections, is excellent as a framework for a picture of the Life and Labour of the People.

The population brought directly under the schedule—viz., heads of families and school children coming under the ken of the School Board visitors, with the proportion of wives and of older or younger children all partly or wholly dependent on these heads of families and sharing their life—amounts to from one-half to two-thirds of the whole population. The rest have been scheduled by other means or in proportion, according to the three assumptions already noted.

The special difficulty of making an accurate picture of so shifting a scene as the low-class streets in East London present is very evident, and may easily be exaggerated. As in photographing a crowd, the details of the picture change continually, but the general effect is much the same, whatever moment is chosen. I have attempted to produce an instantaneous picture, fixing the facts on my negative as they appear at a given moment, and the imagination of my readers must add the movement, the constant changes, the whirl and turmoil of life. In many districts the people are always on the move; they shift from one part of it to another like "fish in a river." The School Board visitors follow them as best they may, and the transfers from one visitor's book to another's are very numerous.[3] On the whole, however, the people usually do not go far, and often cling from generation to generation to one vicinity, almost as if the set of streets which lie there were an isolated country village.

The inquiry as to Central London was undertaken by a committee of six, and that for Battersea by Mr. Graham Balfour; the method adopted in each case being the same as had been employed in East London.

3 A return prepared by one of the School Board visitors, who has a fairly representative district in Bethnal Green, shows that of 1204 families (with 2720 children) on his books, 530 (with 1450 children) removed in a single year.

2

STATISTICS OF POVERTY

BEFORE giving the figures by which I have sought to measure the poverty existing in London, it may be well to refer once more to their validity. The methods employed in the collection and tabulation of the information have been already indicated. These methods were adopted as suited to the peculiarities of the subject and the materials with which we had to deal; but are doubtless open to criticism from many points of view. Not only is exactness in this case out of the question, but even the most general results obtained are open to dispute. At every turn the subject bristles with doubtful points. For each one of these, as it has arisen (if it has been observed) the best available solution has been sought, or what has seemed the most reasonable course has been taken.

But it is manifest that in an inquiry such as this, a very slight bias may lead to serious error, and the bias might be quite unconscious. I can only say we have done our best to keep clear of this danger.

It is to be remarked further that apart from bias two distinct mental attitudes continually recur in considering poverty; and either of these, if not safeguarded in some way, might prove very misleading. On the one hand we may argue that the poor are often really better off than they appear to be, on the ground that when extravagances which keep them in poverty are constant and immediate in their action, the state of things resulting cannot reasonably be called poverty at all. For instance, a man who spends ten or fifteen shillings in drink one week, cannot be called poor because he lacks the money for some necessity a few days later. In support

Reprinted from "Poverty Series," II, 18–24.

of this it is certainly true that in many cases the homes appear no whit less poor whatever the earnings at the time may be. It often occurs too that the ordinary earnings are increased by accidental receipts capable, if judiciously applied, of meeting the occasional extra demands which keep men's pockets empty. On the other hand we may as logically, or perhaps more logically, disregard the follies past or present which bring poverty in their train. For how distinguish between degrees of folly more or less recent or remote? In this temper we prefer to view and consider these unfortunates only as they actually exist; constantly put to shifts to keep a home together; always struggling and always poor. And turning in this direction the mind dwells upon the terrible stress of times of sickness or lack of work for which no provision, or no adequate provision, has been made. According as the one or other of these two points of view is taken, thousands of families may be placed on one or the other side of the doubtful line of demarcation between class and class among the poor.

Of these two ways of looking at the same facts, the second is that which we have in theory adopted, and although in practice this theory will have been more or less modified, it is still probable that a good many families have been reported as poor, who, though they are poor, are so without any economic necessity. On the other hand it is likely enough that many a painful struggling life hidden under a decent exterior has passed in our books as "comfortably poor," to borrow a phrase used by one of the most sympathetic of the School Board visitors. Thus in the end, when I consider the figures, and the tale they tell, though I sway this way or that according to the mood of the moment, I am fully satisfied that the general conclusions are not very far from the truth, and I believe that my readers may fairly accept them in this light. In so far as there is any general error it will I think be found on the safe side; —that is, in overstating rather than understating the volume of poverty which exists, or existed when the inquiry was made; and it is satisfactory to know that since the inquiry was made, times have been good, and poverty less pressing, than was the case previously.

The inhabitants of every street, and court, and block of buildings in the whole of London, have been estimated in proportion to the numbers of the children, and arranged in classes according to the known position and condition of the parents of these children. The streets have been grouped together according to the School Board subdivisions or "blocks," and for each of these blocks full particulars are given in the tables of the Appendix. The numbers included in each block vary from less than 2000 to more than 30,000, and to make a more satisfactory unit of comparison I have arranged them in contiguous groups, 2, 3, or 4 together, so as to make areas having each about 30,000 inhabitants, these areas adding up into the large divisions of the School Board administration. The population is then classified by Registration districts, which are likewise grouped into School Board divisions, each method finally leading up to the total for all London.

The classes into which the population of each of these blocks and districts is divided are the same as were used in describing East London, only somewhat simplified. They may be stated thus:—

A. The lowest class—occasional labourers, loafers and semi-criminals.

B. The very poor—casual labour, hand-to-mouth existence, chronic want.

C. and D. The poor—including alike those whose earnings are small, because of irregularity of employment, and those whose work, though regular, is ill-paid.

E and F. The regularly employed and fairly paid working class of all grades.

G and H. Lower and upper middle class and all above this level.

The Classes C and D, whose poverty is similar in degree but different in kind, can only be properly separated by information as to employment which was obtained for East London, but which, as already explained, the present inquiry does not yield. It is the same with E and F, which cover the various grades of working-class comfort. G and H are given together for convenience.

Outside of, and to be counted in addition to, these classes, are the inmates of institutions whose numbers are specially reported in every census, and finally there are a few who, having no shelter, or no recognized shelter, for the night, elude official enumeration and are not counted at all.

The description of these classes given already as to East London, may be taken as applying with equal force to the whole population. Much might be aded to make the description more complete, but nothing need be taken away. The numbers of the lowest class (A), it is admitted, are given at a very rough estimate; they are hardly to be counted by famlies and so partly escape the meshes of our School Board net. They are to be found in the common lodging-houses and in the lowest streets, and a very full description of their lives and habits is given in the special chapters which treat of these subjects. Class B is fairly counted, and of what it consists, many examples are given in the description of specimen streets, but neither it nor any of the working classes, C, D, E, or F, can be dealt with properly apart from their trades or employments, as the conditions under which these people live, depend mainly upon the conditions under which they work or fail to find work. An account of the life of each of the several classes that are grouped under the letters G and H would be very interesting, but is beyond the scope of this book. I am, however, able to make a division in the figures which answers pretty closely, though not quite exactly, to that between upper and lower middle class. This division is provided by the line of rental value, beyond which the School Board do not go in making their schedules. Out of the 750,000 people included in Class G and H, as nearly as possible 250,000 live in scheduled and 500,000 in unscheduled houses. These figures may be counted as representing roughly the lower and upper middle classes respectively. The wealthy classes are included with the upper middle class.[1]

Assuming these these figures are accepted as approximately correct, the view that is taken of them will depend partly upon what may have been pre-supposed. I imagine that bad as is the

[1] The unscheduled population has been estimated in proportion to the number of houses in some cases, and assumed by way of remainder in other cases, and in every instance the assumed number of servants has been added to Classes E, F, to which by position they may be taken to belong.

state of things they disclose it is better than was commonly imagined previous to the publication of the figures obtained for East London. On the other hand they are probably worse, especially in regard to the numbers of Classes C and D, than may have been anticipated by those who have studied and accepted the East End figures.

That is to say, the poverty of the rest of London as compared to East London is perhaps greater than most people have supposed. For myself it was so. In 1888 I made an estimate based on the facts as to East London, and the comparative density of population in other parts, on the theory that density would probably coincide with the degree of poverty. The result was to show a probable 25 per cent. of poor for all London, or nearly 6 per cent. less than we now get. South London and the district about Holborn are mainly responsible for the difference.

The 100,000 people counted in institutions belong rather to the whole of London than to the particular district in which they are found. They may be divided under four heads:—

(1) Indoor paupers	45,963
(2) Inmates of hospitals, asylums, homes, &c., supported mainly by charitable donations, past or present	38,714
(3) Inmates of prisons	5,833
(4) Troops in barracks, &c.	9,320
Total	99,830

These people do not belong to the active population, and have therefore been omitted from the percentages given, but if for some purposes it is desirable to introduce them, it will not be unreasonable to include the inmates of the prisons with Class A, the in-door paupers with Class B, those in hospitals, &c., with Classes C and D, and the troops, &c., with Classes E and F. The revised percentages would then stand as follows:—A, 1.0 per cent.; B, 8.4 per cent.; C and D, 22.7 per cent.; E and F, 50.5 per cent.; G and H, 17.4 per cent.

3

POINT OF VIEW

East London lay hidden from view behind a curtain on which were painted terrible pictures:—Starving children, suffering women, overworked men; horrors of drunkenness and vice; monsters and demons of inhumanity; giants of disease and despair. Did these pictures truly represent what lay behind, or did they bear to the facts a relation similar to that which the pictures outside a booth at some country fair bear to the performance or show within? This curtain we have tried to lift.

It will be observed that the attempt has in the main been confined to showing how things are. Little is said as to how they come to be as they are, or whither they are tending. The line of inquiry which we have neglected is perhaps more interesting than that which we have taken up, and is certainly more commonly adopted. An inquiry as to tendency appeals controversially, and therefore attractively, to two opposite schools of thought. One of these holds that the condition of the people is becoming year by year more deplorable and its problems more pressing, and casts a backward glance upon some Golden Age of the past; while the other finds on all sides proof of marked improvement, preaches patience as to the evils which still remain, and will say, when pushed, that "if Golden Age there be, it is to-day."

It is manifest that this alternative has an important bearing whether considered simply as a difference of opinion, and so concerning only he on-looker, or positively as a difference of fact. Seen from without, the same habits of life, amount of income, method of expenditure, difficulties, occupations, amusements, will

---

Reprinted from "Poverty Series," I, 172–78.

strike the mind of the on-looker with an entirely different meaning according as they are viewed as part of a progress towards a better and higher life, or of a descent towards a more miserable and debased existence. Felt from within, a position will be acceptable and even happy on the upward road, which on the downward path may be hardly endurable. The contrast with that to which men have been accustomed is doubtless the principal factor in sensations of well or ill being, content or discontent; but we have also to take account of the relation of the present life, whatever it may be, to the ideal or expectation. It may happen that on the upward path, where, on our hypothesis, contentment ought to reign, the ideal so far outstrips the advance as to produce discontent and even discomfort. Or the opposite may happen, and a slipping downwards be accompanied by a feeling of greater ease, a sense of relief. In all this what is true of the individual is no less true of the class. To interpret aright the life of either we need to lay open its memories and understand its hopes.

Nor have we yet exhausted the complicated relativities which are crowded into the phrase "point of view"; for we have to take into account the condition of the on-looker's mind and of public sentiment generally, and the changes of feeling that occur, in this or that direction, by which it becomes more sensitive or more callous. On these three points—(1) the relation to past experience; (2) the relation to expectation; (3) the degree of sensitiveness of the public mind—we have room for great gulfs of difference in considering the same facts.

These points apply with varying force to the condition of each class or industry, and to the terms of each problem involved. In a general way, I find that with few exceptions, those who have had a lengthened experience of East London, agree that its state was much worse when they first knew the district than it is now. Beyond this, such glimpses as we can obtain of a remoter past seem to tell a similar story of improvement, and however we test the question the same answer is given; so that I am inclined to think that if an inquiry, such as the present, had been made at any previous time in the history of London, it would have shown a greater proportion of depravity and misery than now exists, and a lower general standard of life. But let us take the subject piecemeal.

Whatever the miseries of Class A, they are not the result of a too exalted ideal, nor due to any consciousness of degradation. This savage semi-criminal class of people had its golden age in the days when whole districts of London were in their undisputed possession. They mainly desire to be let alone, to be allowed to make an Alsatia of their own. Improvement in our eyes is destruction in theirs. Their discontent is the measure of our success. On the other hand, the impression of horror that the condition of this class makes upon the public mind to-day is out of all proportion to that made when its actual condition was far worse, and consequently the need to deal with the evils involved becomes more pressing. This, moreover, is no mere question of sentiment, but (if we admit a general all-round improvement) an imperative need of the rising standard of life. What might be an admissible state of things in days past is admissible no longer. It drags us back, and how to put an end to it has become a question of the first importance. The outcasts themselves are sufficiently conscious of this, and opposing, dumbly, the efforts of philanthropy or order, their instinct of self-preservation seeks some undisturbed sanctuary where they can still herd together, and, secured by the mutual protection of each other's character for evil, keep respectability at bay. This it is that must be prevented. No sooner do they make a street their own than it is ripe for destruction and should be destroyed. Destruction of such property involevs no general loss. The houses in which they live have, in truth, a negative value, and merely to destroy them is an improvement. The owners may perhaps lose, but there can be no reasonable vested interest in a public nuisance, and the penalty of destruction paid once, might have a widespread effect in a clearer recognition of the responsibilities of ownership. A glance at the map will show the extent of the "black" streets. It does not follow that all of these need to be destroyed, but even if they were, the total destruction would not be a very serious matter. The numbers of this class are not large. I think the 11,000 (or 1¼ per cent.) given in my schedules an ample estimate. To add more to it would be to take away the lowest section from Class B. Persistent dispersion is the policy to be pursued by the State in its contest with them, for to scatter them is necessarily to place them under better influences. The chances for their children, especially, would be better; the hereditary taint less inevitable.

Class A must not be confounded with the criminal classes. Every social grade has its criminals, if not by conviction, at least by character. Of these the lowest grade mix freely with Class A, and are not to be distinguished from it. But there are many of Class A who are not criminals, as well as plenty of criminals who have nothing to do with Class A.

Class B is more than any other affected by the relation of present to past experience. It is not a class in which people are born to live and die, so much as the drift from other classes. It follows that what they feel is the contrast between their lives and those of others. If the condition of other classes improves, the contrast is intensified, and with it the misery, except in those cases where a higher standard of life is felt burthensome, and to "wallow in the mire" more comfortable. Such cases are not uncommon, but on the whole I regard the individuals of Class B as suffering severely from loss of position and of the comforts to which they have been accustomed, although as a class it is possible that they are better off than ever before.

To the sufferings of these unfortunate casually employed people increasing attention is paid. The discredit into which the system of charitable doles has fallen deprives the public conscience of its customary anæsthetic and leaves it to bear its full burthen of sympathetic sensitiveness as best it may, since no satisfactory alternative has been found. The result is that in proportion as our feelings lack the relief of action they become more impulsive and variable, by turns hyper-sensitive and callous. Out of this gusty atmosphere the problem of how to mend the lives of these poor people needs to be lifted, and to this end a mere statement of proportionate numbers and the condition of their lives has its value apart from an estimate of suffering, which, as I have tried to show, is complicated beyond the possibility of analysis.

Here, in Class B, we have the crux of the social problem.

Every other class can take care of itself, or could do so, if Class B were out of the way. These unfortunate people form a sort of quagmire underlying the social structure, and to dry up this quagmire must be our principal aim.

If Class A are not to be confounded with criminals, so Class B must not be confounded with paupers. They are rather the material from which paupers are made. Other classes contribute to pauperism, but those who drop down from the classes above may be supposed to pause for a time in Class B before they finally succumb. A study of the sources of pauperism, by means of an analysis of paupers, would be interesting, and might lead to valuable and suggestive results.

Class C, with its irregular employment and improvident habits, is that which is most hardly judged, and perhaps, also, most hardly used. "If we got our deserts, which of us would 'scape whipping?" and perhaps in nine cases out of ten these unfortunate people get no more than they deserve. Towards their misfortunes modern sentiment turns its hard side of moral condemnation. The more it knows of them the harder becomes the line drawn between "deserving" and "undeserving," and the fewer they be who rank with the deserving. Those who are industrious and thrifty usually need no help. It is for the most part with those who fall below the ideal standard of energy, prudence, or sobriety that we are attempting to deal. To select the few picked cases or even the larger number who are comparatively deserving, and simply to admonish the rest, is not enough. To raise this class we need some larger plan.

Class D does not deserve the less consideration because it is troubled neither by its own past experience of better things, nor by what is expected of it, nor by an unattainable ideal. But it even more than Class C can only be helped by a movement which shall succeed in raising the whole standard of life. It is chiefly for the sake of these two classes that my proposals for dealing with Class B are made. They are my clients, and to their service especially I dedicate my work.

Class E contains those whose lot to-day is most aggravated by a raised ideal. It is in some ways a hopeful sign, but it is also a danger. Here, rather than in the ruffianism of Class A, or the starvation of Class B, or the wasted energy of Class C, or the bitter anxieties of Class D, do we find the springs of Socialism and Revolution. The stream that flows from these springs must not be dammed up, and therefore it is to this class and its leaders in Class F that I particularly appeal in favour of what I have called "limited Socialism"—a socialism which shall leave untouched the forces of individualism of the sources of wealth.

Finally there are two ways of looking even at mere figures, by which very different impressions may be produced by the same facts. It may with some show of reason be regarded as not so very bad that a tenth of the population should be reckoned as very poor, in a district so confessedly poverty-stricken as East London; but when we count up the 100,000 individuals, the 20,000 families, who lead so pinched a life among the population described, and remember that there are in addition double that number who, if not actually pressed by want, yet have nothing to spare, we shrink aghast from the picture. The divergence between these two points of view, between relative and absolute, is in itself enough to cause the whole differnce between pessimism and optimism. To judge rightly we need to bear both in mind, never to forget the numbers when thinking of the percentages, nor the percentages when thinking of the numbers. This last is difficult to those whose daily experience or whose imagination brings vividly before them the trials and sorrows of individual lives. They refuse to set off and balance the happy hours of the same class, or even of the same people, against these miseries; much less can they consent to bring the lot of other classes into the account, add up the opposing figures, and contentedly carry forward a credit balance. In the arithmetic of woe they can only add or multiply, they cannot subtract or divide. In intensity of feeling such as this, and not in statistics, lies the power to move the world. But by statistics must this power be guided if it would move the world aright.

4

CLASSIFICATION AND DESCRIPTION OF STREETS

SEVEN SHADES of colour are used on the map to indicate the general condition of the inhabitants of each street. These colours correspond with the classification of the people as given in Chapter 2.

Black.—The lowest grade (corresponding to Class A), inhabited principally by occasional labourers, loafers, and semi-criminals—the elements of disorder.

Dark Blue.—Very poor (corresponding to Class B), inhabited principally by casual labourers and others living from hand to mouth.

Light Blue.—Standard poverty (corresponding to Classes C and D) inhabited principally by those whose earnings are small (say 18*s* to 21*s* a week for a moderate family), whether they are so because of irregularity of work (C) or because of a low rate of pay (D).

Purple.—Mixed with poverty (usually C and D with E and F, but including Class B in many cases).

Pink.—Working class comfort. (Corresponding to Classes E and F, but containing also a large proportion of the lower middle class of small tradesmen and Class G.) These people usually keep no servant.

Red.—Well-to-do; inhabited by middle-class families who keep one or two servants.

Yellow.—Wealthy; hardly found in East London and little

Reprinted from "Poverty Series," II, 40–41, 43–51, 83, 86–87, 94–98, 139–41, 172–75, 214–15, 225, 228, 229–30.

found in South London; inhabited by families who keep three or more servants, and whose houses are rated at £100 or more.

Here and there an attempt has been made to give a little more elasticity to the system by combining the colours. Dark blue in especial will frequently be found with a black line upon it, to indicate that great poverty is mixed with something worse; or a red line has been introduced in connection with pink or yellow to show the presence of a middle-class element amongst working class or wealthy surroundings. At best the graphic expression of an almost infinite complication and endless variety of circumstance, cannot but be very imperfect, and a rainbow of colour could not accomplish it completely. But in order to group and mass our information we need to sink minor differences, and to this end the shades and combinations used may be taken as representing so many types of streets inhabited for the most part by the corresponding classes of people.

Summary of London.

—	Streets.	Population.	May be compared with.	
Black . . .	128	26,903	Class A. .	37,610
Dark Blue + Black	118	47,657	,, B. .	316,834
Dark Blue . .	1,014	165,867		
Light Blue . .	2,707	508,238	,, C and D.	938.293
Purple . . .	3,148	1,077,346		
Pink . . .	5,606	1,361,035	,, E and F.	2,166,503
Pink + Red . .	1,001	257,195		
	13,722	3,444,241		3,459,240
Red . . .	not counted.	—	,, G and H.	749,930
Yellow . . .	,,	—		
—	—	—		4,209,170

[Note.—It is noteworthy that the multiple needed to turn number of children of school age into total of population, which is 4·6 for the whole of London and also for the S.W. district, requires to be 5 for N.W. and sinks to 4·2 for N.E. and S.E. The poorer the districts the larger are the families on the whole.]

The preceding table enumerates the streets of each colour (from Black up to Pink with a Red line), for the whole of London, with an estimate of the numbers of their inhabitants. Side by side with these figures, for the sake of comparison, are repeated those which give the classification of the people in the same divisions. It will be seen that in all we count 13,722 streets (or parts of streets, for where a street runs through from block to block it is counted twice). The estimated population of these streets falls slightly short of that of classes A to F, showing that on the balance there is a small proportion of the upper artisan class to be found in the unenumerated streets.

In comparing the one set of figures with the other it must be borne in mind that *every* street is more or less mixed in character, that the Black streets taken together contain some of *every* class from A to F, or (including the publicans) even G; the same thing is true of the Pink streets also, and even those with a red line are not without a sprinkling of poor people mixed with the better-to-do.

For those of my readers who are intimately acquainted with any district of London in which streets are to be found which take the various colours on our map, description is hardly needed. There are no doubt differences; there is dark blue and dark blue, light blue streets vary in character, and there are many shades of black; but the likeness far transcends the differences, and those who know well how the poor or vicious live in one district know pretty well how they live in all other districts. I would even venture to say that the conditions of life do not vary very much in any of our great cities, and the picture I shall try to give for the benefit of those who have no such detailed personal experience may, I believe, be taken as applicable in Liverpool or Manchester or Birmingham, and even in the poorer parts of much smaller places. Everywhere the same conditions repeat themselves, and although crossing the sea makes a difference, the description of a city slum in New York might almost serve as an illustration to this book.[1]

1 "The roadway and sidewalks and doorsteps swarmed with children; women's heads seemed to show at every window. In the basements over which flights of high stone steps led to the tenements were shops in proportion to the small needs of a poor neighbourhood. Ash barrels lined the sidewalks and garbage heaps filled the gutters; teams of all trades stood idly about; a pedlar of cheap fruit urged his cart through the street and mixed his cry with the joyous screams and shouts of the children and the scolding gossiping voices of the women; the bulky blue figure of a

Parish by parish a very large part of London is visited systematically, and by the kind assistance of the clergy and their lay-helpers, I have obtained a detailed description of a number of streets of various colours sufficient to serve as samples. There are over seventy of these streets, viz.:

5	selected	from those	coloured	Black.
5	"	"	"	Dark Blue with Black.
21	"	"	"	Dark Blue.
20	"	"	"	Light Blue.
20	"	"	"	Purple.
4	"	"	"	Pink.

The particulars for the most part include every house in each street with a short account of every family in each house, or where only part of a street has been done care was taken to choose a section complete, as far as it goes, and fairly representative. In addition to the sample streets we have similar particulars concerning eight blocks of buildings of various types from dark blue to pink.

In the statistical tables at the end of this chapter the complete figures for the sample streets are given, but the details are too lengthy for publication in full, and are greatly cut down in the following pages. Even so they are rather bulky, but in no other way has it seemed possible to tell the story of the streets as completely as is needed for my purpose. It will be understood that where names are given to the streets or the people described, they are, for obvious reasons, not the real ones, those of the streets which immediately follow being the only exception. In the invention of new names the flavour of the originals has been retained as far as

---

policeman defined itself at the corner; a drunkard zig-zagged down the sidewalk towards him. It was not the abode of the extremest poverty, but of a poverty as hopeless as any in the world, transmitting itself from generation to generation, and establishing conditions of permanency to which human life adjusts itself as it does to those of some incurable disease like leprosy. . . . I must say they don't seem to mind it. I have not seen a jollier crowd anywhere in New York. They seemed to have forgotten death a little more completely than any of their fellow-citizens."—From "A Hazard of New Fortunes," by W. D. Howells.

possible. Scotch or Irish names have been replaced by others of the same character, Welsh by Welsh, and any of foreign nationality by the like. With English names similar care has been taken. Nothing is more remarkable or more characteristic of our race than the prevalence of old family names among the poorest classes. In every workhouse, it is said, as well as in manor house and parsonage, you find these names.

Streets Coloured Black

SHELTON STREET On the map of Central London there is a group of streets coloured black of which I need not hesitate to give the true names. They are Macklin Street, Shelton Street, and Parker Street, all running out of Drury Lane to the east. Shelton Street has been entirely destroyed, and its place will know it no more. I myself have never seen it as it is here described, but only as a yellow strip of broken bricks and crumbling mortar intermixed with here and there a tattered piece of wall paper. The open space was railed across near Drury Lane, but the gates were open and I could walk through to the other end where there is still the exit, through upright iron bars and down stone steps, into Newton Street. On either side of the site of Shelton Street lie Parker Street and Macklin Street. Many of the houses in each have been pulled down and others are doomed. Before long little will be left standing of what did exist when my inquiry was made; moreover, in seeking particulars of these streets and their inhabitants I have gone back a little and I trust that nothing I shall say will hurt the susceptibilities of any of my readers. I propose to take the reader from end to end of each of these streets and some adjoining courts, and to tell the story, house by house, as I have received it from the City missionaries, who, the one for 11 and the other for 29 years, have made it their business to visit here, carrying the Gospel with impartiality to willing and unwilling ears. Shelton Street was just wide enough for a vehicle to pass either way, with room between curb-stone and houses for one foot-passenger to walk; but vehicles would pass seldom, and foot-passengers would prefer the roadway to the risk of tearing their clothes against projecting nails. The houses, about forty in number, contained cellars, parlours, and first, second, and third floors, mostly two rooms on a floor, and few of the 200 families who lived here occupied more than one room. In little rooms no more than 8 ft. square, would be found living father, mother and several children. Some of the rooms, from the peculiar build of the houses, shallow houses with double frontage) would be fairly large and have a recess 6 ft. wide for the bed, which in rare instances would be curtained off. If there was no curtain, anyone lying on the bed would perhaps be covered up and hidden, head and all, when a visitor was admitted, or perhaps no shyness would be felt. Most of the people described are Irish Roman Catholics getting a living as market porters, or by selling flowers, fruit, fowls or vegetables in the streets, but as to not a few it is a mystery how they live. Drunkenness and dirt and bad language prevailed, and violence was common, reaching at times even to murder. Fifteen rooms out of twenty were filthy to the last degree, and the furniture in none of these would be worth 20*s*, in some cases not 5*s*. Not a room would be free from vermin, and in many life at night was unbearable. Several occupants have said that in hot weather they don't go to bed, but sit in their clothes in the least infested part of the room. What good is it, they said, to go to bed when you can't get a wink of sleep for bugs and fleas? A visitor in these rooms was fortunate indeed if he carried nothing of the kind away with him. The passage from the street to the back-door would be scarcely ever swept, to say nothing of being scrubbed. Most of the doors stood open all night as well as all day, the passage and stairs gave shelter to many who were altogether homeless. Here the mother could stand with her baby, or sit with it on the stairs, or companions would huddle together in cold weather. The little yard at the back was only sufficient for dust-bin and closet and water-tap, serving for six or seven families. The water would be drawn from cisterns which were receptacles for refuse, and perhaps occasionally a dead cat. At one time the street was fever-stricken; the mortality was high, and the authorities interfered with good effect so that the sanitary condition of the street just before it was destroyed was better than it had been formerly. The houses looked ready to fall, many of them being out of the perpendicular. Gambling was the amusement of the street. Sentries would be posted, and if the police made a rush the offenders would slip into the open houses and hide until danger was past. Sunday afternoon and evening was the hey-day time for this street. Every doorstep would be crowded by those who sat or stood with pipe and jug of beer, while lads lounged about, and the gutters would find amusement for not a few children with bare feet, their faces and hands besmeared, while the mud oozed through between their toes. Add to this a group of fifteen or twenty young men gambling in the middle of the street and you complete the general picture. House by house the story is as follows:—

No. 2, *Shelton Street.* The ground floor was last occupied by Mr. Mulvaney and his wife, without children at home. He was a shrewd Irishman and stepped in when it was known the houses were coming down — fitting up a small shop with a view to compensation. He is one to make money and stick to it. He collected the rents from other occupiers. The shop was on one side of the door and there was a small room opposite in which the Mulvaneys lived At back there was a very small yard with water-tap, &c., below was a basement, which seems not to have been occupied. On the first floor, living in one large room (there being no division) were a man and wife with one daughter almost grown up. These people, like the Mulvaneys, were Irish Roman Catholics and not very friendly to English or Prostestants. Were inclined to drink but were tidier than some, and before Mulvaney's time the man acted as deputy in collecting the rents. In the second floor room lived some time since a widow and her three children, who made a fair living as a costermonger. Very clean and careful, and though a superstitious Irish Catholic, very friendly and kindly disposed towards the Protestant English missionary. After their mother's death the children opened a small greengrocer's shop in Drury Lane, and since that various people have occupied the room, coming and going and leaving no record behind. The third floor was divided into two rooms, very small in size, with roofs sloping to the floor, and here to the one side lived a Covent Garden porter with his wife and three young children, and on the other side two women. All these were Irish Roman Catholics. The market porter, though of the roughest, was disposed to be friendly, and the wife a good-humoured woman, though feckless. He had been a great drunkard, signing the pledge from time to time and after a while breaking out again. He would earn a little in the morning but would spend nearly all of it in drink before he came home, would then swear and knock his wife about. The room this family occupied, besides being very small, was destitute of comfort and as dirty as could be, and full of vermin, yet the walls were covered with little pictures. One of the children, a boy of five years, fell ill, and being taken to the hospital died on the way there in his mother's arms, arriving at the hospital past help. The parents had neither money nor goods, but borrowed sufficient for the wax candles to burn near the body and light the poor little soul to paradise. The two women in the adjoining room lived together for economy, sharing the rent which would be 2*s* 6*d* or 2*s* 3*d*. They bore the appearance of widows, and got their living by begging or picking up odds and ends in the street. Their room was almost destitute—all it contained would not fetch 2*s*—and dirty to the last degree. Both these women were fond of drink. One of them claimed to be an officer's widow, or rather that he had deserted her and she did not know whether he was living or dead. She was of French origin and was always called "Madam." She spoke beautiful English and her appearance justified her tale to some extent. Such is the story of No. 2. Most of these people had been known to the missionary for many years and most of them received his visits kindly.

No. 4, *Shelton Street.* In one of the ground floor rooms lived Mr. and Mrs. Shane and their four children, the eldest of whom was fourteen at the end of the seven years during which my informant was acquainted with the family. Like so many more in this neighbourhood they were Irish and Catholics and costermongers. The man took cold from exposure and was groaning in bed for nearly nine months with pain in head as well as limbs, and finally died. During his illness and since his death Mrs. Shane obtained a living for them all by selling watercresses. This family was rather tidier than some, though the woman was given to drink at times and said she "believed in it when she could get it." An older boy "got into trouble" and coming out of prison was not long before he was re-committed. For the opposite room on the ground floor there are no particulars. The first floor consisted again of one large room and in it another family of Irish Roman Catholic costermongers. These were less friendly and would only open their door wide enough to afford a glimpse of wall covered with pictures and shut it again. The costermongers of this neighbourhood, it may be here observed, usually hire their barrows and borrow the money to purchase stock. They buy in the early morning at Covent Garden, bring home what they buy, sort it over, and then turn out to sell; work very hard early and late and for the most part drink hard. A risky trade, sometimes making, sometimes losing. Used to make more at it than now, it is said, because there are too many at it. They often go far a-field into the outskirts of London to sell.

On the second floor of No. 4, Shelton Street, there was, six months before the house was pulled down, a very sad case—a woman with four small children whose husband had gone to America. The children were without boots or food, and their mother had to lock them in the room while she went to sell oranges in the streets. On the third floor, in two small rooms, lived a family whose record goes back eleven years—father, mother, and two children now grown up. A powerfully built man, but, in consequence of drink, smitten four years ago with paralysis, helpless and almost speechless. He said he had been "a bad 'un," but he went to mass now and hoped to reach heaven. His wife was very friendly. After his father's paralysis the son, who was in a bakery in Camden Town, kept the family. The daughter had a child. Her husband, or the man with whom she lived, died soon after and the child died also. The rooms of this family were filthy, and the occupants lived like pigs. Both sights and smells were sickening.

Of the ground floor at *No.* 6, *Shelton Street*, and also of the first and second floors, there is nothing particular to note; families came and went, usually costers, almost always Irish Roman Catholics, living in dirt, fond of drink, alike shiftless, shifty and shifting. At the top, on the third floor, there lived for five years Mr. and Mrs. Casson and their four children, all in one small attic. The father earned little, but most of this he spent in drink; the mother was very clean and industrious, and careful, but the children were at times without food. In the adjoining room there lived also for some five years a man by the name of Smith, a carman at about 20*s* a week, and the woman with whom he lived. They were not married; the banns were once published, but on the morning when the marriage should have been solemnized the two fell out and he blackened her eye, so the ceremony had to be postponed, and, the man dying suddenly, it never came off. He was an Army Reserve man, and would drink, but in spite of all was not a bad fellow, and the woman, who had been married before, was also a nice person.

So far as we have gone it will be thought that "black is not so very black," but we have but just begun. I fear that I may tax the patience of my readers, but my aim is to show the street and its inhabitants as it existed—not selected cases, nor the mere resultant of an average, however carefully drawn out.

Dark Blue Streets with Black Line

The look of great poverty which stamps all the dark blue and most of the black streets may be resolved first into two elements—the people and the houses. With the people it is the children who mark the greatest contrast, and then the women; the appearance of the men is less affected by poverty. With the houses it is naturally the windows and the doors that tell the tale. The windows are cracked and patched, and are imperfectly screened by dirty and ragged blinds stretched across, or by falling curtains of the very commonest description. The doors usually stand open —in tenement houses it is always so—and afford glimpses of the poverty within. But more than all else, the brickwork round about each door carries the stamp of poverty. The surface of each brick by the rubbing of arms and shoulders takes a black polish, but the mortar frays away and remains clean until, as the houses age, it is picked out or wears away into a cavity which becomes as dark as the rest. When such houses are "done up," the pointing and refacing of the brick is a principal item in the change effected.

A poor neighbourhood is also stamped by its shops. Birdfanciers are mostly to be found in the mixed streets which lie near black districts. Fried fish, and still more stewed-eel shops commonly mark the vicinity of great poverty, and a catsmeat shop is seldom far removed from it. The cats themselves may be taken as a last test. People are poor indeed whose cat looks starved. I have seen the catsmeat-man on his round in a very poor street, and not less than a dozen cats were strolling about with raised tails confidently awaiting their turns.

Burdock Road. A few years ago Burdock House and its garden became, in the hands of a local speculator, the "Burdock Estate," and was sold with a stiff ground rent to a builder who covered it with houses for the working classes, of that cheap description which gives the most immediate return in rent. The result is now Burdock Road, which, bending at right angles, occupies most of the old grounds of Burdock House. Each house in this street consists of three floors, and each floor is a separate tenement, consisting of two rooms to the front and a small one to the back.

At first there was a fairly good class of tenants, the houses were respectable and such as working people might live in with decency and comfort. But after a year, two or three bad lots got in on the odd number side, and then the street changed as by magic. The better folk left and the people came who had hardly any furniture—the rejections of other districts. One family, by whom the deaconness was called in to dress a wound, had no furniture, only an empty cask; no bed-clothes and not even a basin or any utensil for the water she needed, except a tin pot. In some of the houses the banisters have gone to feed the fire, and in some the iron stoves have gone, leaving nothing but an open hearth of brick below the chimney. The inhabitants are continually on the move. If the rent presses they leave. In summer they go hopping. They are very rough and very dirty. On Saturday and Sunday the place is dreadful indoors and out. The houses swarm with vermin, and are not pleasant places to visit.

Burdock Road.

No.		Rms.	Pers.			
1 & 3 one hse.	ground shop & 2	3		(E)	Man, wife, and step-mother.	Small grocer's shop. Man collects rents. Comfortable.
	first floor	3	10	(B)	Man, wife, and 8 children.	Sawyer, usually out of work. Seems good for nothing. Wife wretched and slovenly. Very poor; always moving.
	second floor	2	4	(E)	Man, wife, and 2 children.	Baker. Very respectable.
		1	1	(E)	Single man lodger.	Works with the baker above.
5	ground floor	3	6	(D)	Man, wife, and 4 children.	Labourer. Wife works 4 days a week. Recently come.

No.		Rms.	Pers.			
	first floor	3	7	(B)	Man, wife, and 5 children.	Labourer in and out of work. Very poor and very dirty.
	second floor		8	(C)	Man, wife, and 6 children.	Butcher, often out of work for months. Drinking and gambling more or less. Very often starving. Woman dirty, but does what she can and does not drink much. Man had a good business at one time.
7	ground floor	3	2	(C)	Elderly couple.	Coal porter. Had prostitute lodging with them.
	first floor	3	9	(B)	Man, wife, and 7 or 8 children.	Labourer. In irregular work. Has a bad leg. Children at ragged school. Very rough and dirty family.
	second floor	2	4	(D)	Widow and 3 children.	Scrubber at infirmary. Three older children have been found places away. One earns 6*s* or 7*s*.
	second floor	1	4	(B)	Man, wife, and 2 children.	Labourer. Always out of work. Children are sickly and miserable. One boy got to sea.
9	ground floor	2			No information.	
	first floor	2	8	(B)	Man, wife, and 6 children.	Compositor. Exceedingly dirty, but decent people, probably Irish. Big girl of 17 and 5 small children.
	second floor	2	8	(B)	Man, wife, and 6 children.	Builder's labourer. Has been a soldier, and had sunstroke. Tries to keep sober, but when drunk smashes everything. Wife struggling woman. Very dirty. Lost baby recently. Two boys work at coal yard, and also sing in music-halls.

The other side of the street has a different landlord. It used to be very bad, but was cleared out and left empty until better tenants could be found. 11 inhabited houses in all.

Dark Blue Streets

SUMMER GARDENS This place lies at the back of Fount Street. The particulars given apply to the inhabitants of Summer Gardens, but for the purpose of description it will be convenient to describe Fount Street as well, and even to touch upon Baxter Street, the leading business street to which the other two in some sense pertain. Fount Street and Summer Gardens are both coloured dark blue. Baxter Street is black, the houses which are interspersed with the business premises having a bad character. The three together are part of one of the poorest districts in all London, a district where poverty is almost solid.

Summer Gardens is a narrow street, all dwelling-houses. Fount Street is mostly dwellings, but has some places of business, and a mission-house. Baxter Street seems full of business—cheap cabinet-work, furniture, and chairs. Cart and barrow-loads of roughly shaped wood or sawn boards are in the roadway, and men pass about with great bundles of chair-back or legs. In the centre of this street are the large church mission-buildings. There was soup going at the mission-house in Fount Street, a very large old house with wooden front, the boards overlapping like the sides of a boat. At each of its two doors a group was gathered; one, of women with jugs, the other of children who brought no jugs and would doubtless carry the soup in a more simple manner when it could be given them. Both groups had to wait. I passed several times and still the same women, and I think the same children, stood waiting in the freezing air. The children looked well enough, more common than wretched. The women looked exceedingly cold, and no wonder, for they seemed to have run over from their houses without throwing on either bonnet or shawl, in their working aprons, bare-armed as well as bare-headed, dangling their jugs and gossiping till their turn might come. At the corner as I passed along two boys met. "'ad dinner?" said one. "Yes." "What did you 'ave?" "Soup." "Was it good?" I put in, and the answer came promptly, "No." I had seen another crowd of children pushing into a third mission at the end of Baxter Street, and seeming very eager. It may have been one of these who afterwards turned critical. It was "black Monday," and before I left the bell of the Board school had rung and the children with much lagging were trooping into school. The sweet-shop opposite the entrance was doing a brisk trade.

Many of the houses in these streets have been formerly occupied by weavers, and have the usual large upper windows and spacious rooms (as originally built) needed for the looms. Now these large rooms are partitioned up into small ones. With these old houses are mixed others of different type. The new buildings are principally missions or schools. In Summer Gardens there live some costermongers, and in Fount Street also, empty barrows stood about and one or two baked potato vans, ready to turn out at night. Before one door stood two barrows well loaded with oranges ready for a start (12.30); the man may have returned to dinner, but more likely his hours begin and end late. Summer Place, the next street to Summer Gardens, is more completely in the occupation of costers. Here, and still more in the yet smaller courts round about, the roads are much littered with paper unwrapped from the fruit. Amongst the scraps of paper and garbage and frozen dirt there is as usual a great quantity of bread strewn about (surest sign of extreme poverty all over London). The streets are all covered and the gutters filled with frozen dirt; harmless in its present condition and impossible for any vestry to deal with, but more or less it would be there at all times.

In one street is the body of a dead dog and near by two dead cats, which lie as though they had slain each other. All three have been crushed flat by the traffic which has gone over them, and they, like everything else, are frozen and harmless. The houses in Baxter Street and Fount Street are interspersed with little shops. Except the old clothes shops, every shop, whatever else it deals in, sells sweets, and with most of them the sweets seem the "leading article." They differ only in what else they offer. With some it is toys; with others oranges and onions; with others dripping, cheese and ham; with others again loaves of bread or temperance drinks. In almost every case cakes of some kind are sold, or little open tarts.

The particulars given below are for part of one side of Summer

Gardens, compiled from the notes of one who knows the street and its people very well.

On the ground floor of No. 2 lives Mutton, a builder's labourer; he had had no work for a month, and his wife was just confined. There were four children. Came from Weymouth. The wife gave up attending the mothers' meeting connected with the Church because of the bad language of other members. Above is the office of the landlord. The man in charge, a pleasant little fellow, lives elsewhere. Complained of difficulty in collecting his rents; some tenants owe thirteen weeks and have no goods worth distraining. There is also a room occupied by man and wife. The man a dirty, disreputable looking old fellow with a sharp wit. Not at all religious. Said his brother had served the Lord till seventy-four years old and "then He thought fit to choke him." The old man's trade is doll making, but having no dolls to make is in the meantime a shoeblack. He "should be busy when the Germans were all dead." Imported dolls came cheaper than they could be made in England. He was born not far away and had always lived in the neighbourhood. His father (a toy maker) employed eighteen men and rented four houses. Our old man inherited the business, but failed, and is now very poor. He is over sixty. His wife does a little charing.

No. 4. On the ground floor lives a hawker with eight children; the eldest, a girl of seventeen, and a quiet gentle creature, was at home with the two youngest. She makes boot boxes. Wife was out doing half a day's work. A grown-up son lives in Fount Street. The first floor is occupied by Green, a dock labourer, with wife and four children. They subscribe to a clothing club connected with the church. At the top lives Marston, a chair maker, with wife and four children. They also are in the clothing club. The wife makes match-boxes. She has just been confined, but the baby is dead.

No. 6. On the ground floor live Mr. and Mrs. Meek. Meek is a hatter and was engaged in dyeing children's hats in a portable boiler. A cheery little man. With the help of his wife he dyes, re-blocks, and trims old hats, which they sell in the streets at 3*d* each. Wife had been selling them in New Cut. Had taken 6*d*—last night 3*d*—so she said. There are six children. Rent 6*s* for two rooms; had to shift from another house where they owed rent. One of the rooms now occupied should be a shop, but the shutters are up on account of broken glass. Get free breakfast tickets and other help from church. On the first floor lives a widow who does washing. She had two sons at home out of work. The second floor is occupied by the Martins; the man was in the infirmary and his wife was away at work, leaving only the daughter at home. On the top, in one room, lives Barge, a bricklayer's labourer. Had only had one week's work since Christmas. He has a wife and five children, of whom one earns 4*s* a week. Rent 3*s*. Helped by Church. In the other room lives Grantly, a costermonger, with three young children. The wife gets four days a week at a laundry. Seem very respectable.

No. 8. This is an eighteen-room house. On the ground floor two rooms are occupied by the Robsons, a young couple with two children. The man is a coster, but was out snow-sweeping. The wife makes boxes. Decent, industrious people. At the back lives Mrs. Helmot, whose husband, formerly an optician, is now at Haswell suffering from suicidal melancholia. The woman has had several children and supports herself by washing and charing. She has charge of two children belonging to one of her daughters. Of these she takes home the youngest every evening, but the eldest (being by a former husband) stays altogether with the grandmother. This child had not been to school lately, having no boots, and only came out from behind the table when told that "it was not the School Board man." In the kitchen to the right, sub-let by the Robsons at 1*s* 6*d*, lives Mr. Thomas and Mrs. Flanaghan, two miserable looking widows, who share the rent. Mrs. T. sells fruit or flowers in Paternoster Row, but had this day (in February) taken nothing and got very wet-footed. Mrs. F. does washing and charing occasionally. On the walls of the room hung a portrait and two other prints. Mrs. T. had just pawned two aprons and a pocket handkerchief to pay the rent. She wore a pair of odd boots—bought one at a time; don't keep the wet out. Was at church last three Sundays and doubtless hoped a reward in this world as well as the next. Could only afford, she said, "Just a cup of tea sometimes." Mrs. F. does not go to church. "Has got no Sunday clothes." Good clothes all pledged. Rent 7*s* 6*d* in arrear. Born in Hatton Garden. Had been here two years. Her father was in good circumstances, a tailor employing over sixty hands, working for a large retail house. She had married against her father's wish and been discarded. The father has been dead now sixteen years. Mrs. Thomas was also born in London—at Snow Hill.

On the front floor at back was Mrs. Brandon, formerly and better known as Smith. Her husband (Brandon), a French polisher, and great drunkard, deserted her on Christmas Day, and is now living with a girl at a low lodging-house. His wife still had the remains of a black eye and two cuts on the forehead by which to remember him, but does not herself bear a very good character. Living at home with her was a boy of fourteen who went out with a bookstall man. Doing nothing now because of bad weather. There was also a married daughter with an infant who pays her mother 10*s* a week. This young woman's husband enlisted on the day she was confined, being then only sixteen and a half and she barely eighteen. He had signed for seven years and was at Malta. Mrs. Brandon had worked in the kitchen of a City restaurant.

Streets Coloured Light Blue

GINGER STREET This is a very rough and untidy place. The main employment is fish curing. Dirty barrows stand about and the side walks are lumbered up with Billingsgate boxes, empty and full, but all reeking of fish. Men may be seen in the street and in the houses disembowelling haddock. Fishes' heads, and sometimes their entrails, bestrew the gutters. The houses are ill-cared for and shabby. Broken windows abound, and the people need to be better off than their surroundings would at first sight suggest, to justify the light blue colour under which this street appears on the map. The street, however, has a poorer end, where there is a block of buildings which is described in the next chapter. Those that follow are the upper ten of Ginger Street. The houses are all of two rooms—one up and the other downstairs.

Nos. 1 to 15 have been pulled down and replaced by "Ginger Street Dwellings." *No.* 16 is used by Rorke (No. 18) for fish curing.

No. 17. On the ground floor, Hartley, an old man, occupies one room. His wife, who died recently, used to keep a mangle, and since her death his grand-daughter has worked it for him. On the upper floor lives Grant, a labourer, himself an elderly man, who married Hartley's daughter. Grant has a big boy and girl at work besides the girl (of thirteen) who turns the mangle, and three younger children. There is not much mangling to be done, and the earnings of the boy and girl are what the families live on mainly. Grant cannot or does not find work.

No. 18. Rorke, smoker and hawker of haddocks, lives here. He smokes his fish at the back here as well as at No. 16. He has a wife and one infant. The home, which might be comfortable, is miserable through drink.

No. 19 is occupied by an old man who only lately lost his wife. Since her death the visitor has not been admitted. He does not ask for any relief.

No. 20 is occupied by a brother of Rorke, of No. 18. These men belong to a clan, very strong in this neighbourhood, who help each other, working together. They are a drinking set. This man has a wife and three children, one at school. His father lives here, infirm and almost bed-ridden. These people appear very poor, especially as to clothes, probably through drink.

No. 21. No information.

No. 22 is occupied by Wright, a labourer, in fairly constant work, and, so, better off than the average here; but his wife is very delicate and does no work. They have five children, all at school except the baby, who is sickly. They pay for the doctor.

No. 23. Smart lives here, a costermonger and a leader among these people. He is known as the King of the Costers. He has a wife, but no children living, having lost some. They drink heavily, or might be well off. They are quite comfortable.

No. 24. Percy, hawker, lives here with wife and two young children. Seem comfortable, but the earnings are not so regular as with their neighbours at No. 26.

No. 25. This house is occupied by old Mr. Binney and his wife, the parents of the man at No. 26, and they are probably employed in a similar way.

No. 26. Binney, the son, lives here. He is a hawker and does fairly well. Has a wife and four young children, three at school, one an infant.

No. 27. Rand, a labourer, lives here. He has a wife and six children, all going to school. The eldest boy goes out with papers out of school hours. One girl helps at home. Two girls are out at service. The man is a casual worker and has done very little lately. Very poor.

No. 28. A Roman Catholic family, with whom the visitor is not acquainted.

No. 29. Boyle, a labourer, with wife and two little children. The wife goes out hawking a little. They probably earn 20*s* between them, and are pretty comfortable. They have lost one child.

No. 30 is occupied by David, a coal porter at docks. During the summer he was at night work. For some weeks past has been out of work. He has a wife and six children. The oldest girl has been in service, but is out of place. All the others are of school age, or under. The wife would be glad to do "cleaning," if she could get it to do. They are very poor.

No. 31 is occupied by an old couple, without children, Roman Catholics.

No. 32 is occupied by a blind man, a basket maker. He had a blind wife, who used to sing in the streets, taking one of the children with her. She was, not long since, run over by a cab and killed. The man succeeded in placing all his children in schools, and married again—another, blind woman. His earnings are pretty good and he seems comfortable.

No. 33. Towle, a licensed messenger, lives here. He does not earn much, one day 3*d*, another, only 2*d*, as he is not yet well known. He had good employment, but the firm failed. He had very good testimonials, and has been helped to start as messenger. There is a wife and two children. The wife has tried for work without success. One of the children, a girl, works in the City, earning 4*s* a week. These are very respectable people, but are behind-hand. Owe seven weeks' rent.

No. 34 is occupied by Thompson, a labourer of some kind. His wife does not work. They have one baby. They are newcomers. Do not need charity.

No. 35. Green, another costermonger or hawker, doing fairly. His wife goes out cleaning two or three days a week. They have one big girl at work, and another who should be in service, but is often at home. Two boys are at school. They are comfortable for costers. Drink a great deal.

No. 36. Mrs. Wood, a widow, who sells in the streets, making her profit mostly on Saturday night. She has a daughter living with her of about twenty, who goes to business daily. They are fairly comfortable when both are in work.

There are 7 more houses.

Streets Coloured Purple

We find in these streets a very wide range of character. All may be represented in the samples to be given, but we cannot say exactly in what proportions the various kinds exist. In some the mixture of poverty is to be found almost in every house, lying very commonly, though not always, floor by floor, in strata. In other streets it goes by houses and then is more easily distinguished. In others, one whole side of the street is better off than the other. In some again, there is one special bit poorer than the rest, perhaps because of bad building, more often from the contaminating influence of other poor property lying near by at the affected point. Finally, we have streets which are poor only at one end, with some of which we have been able to deal on the map. Thus Lady Street, described among the dark blue streets, changes its colour, becoming first purple, and finally pink before the eastern end of it is reached.

The greatest difference in type lies in the size of the houses, especially as regards the number of floors, and this distinction is much enforced when, as is often the case, the larger kind of house has been built for people of larger means than those who now inhabit them, and a dwelling intended for one family is arranged as best may be for two or three families, or even more. Distinctions arising from the number of floors, and from the character of the original design, apply to the light and dark blue streets, and even in some instances to the pink streets, but it is to the purple streets that they apply most.

CUTTER'S ROW This street is partly filled by business premises. It has some saw mills and places where wood is sold to the cabinet trades, and one side consists almost entirely of the backs of the large shops in the High Street. It has also a cats meat shop, a dried fish shops, and a fried fish shop in close proximity; also two or three sweets shops. It is a street with plenty of life of its own.

No. 18. Fishmonger's shop, kept by Bloxham, who employs a youth as assistant. Mr. and Mrs. Bloxham live on the first floor above the shop; have one boy at school. On the top floor, front room, lives Mrs. Grantly, a widow, who makes toy whips at 1*d* each, or 5*s* 6*d* a gross. Busy about Christmas, when publicans take a lot to give away to the children as presents, just as they give sweets on Sundays at some of the public-houses. The husband has been dead six years. Mrs. Grantly has four children married, one of whom allows her 1*s* weekly. Another son lives with her, and sells papers near the railway station.

Rent 2*s* 6*d*. In the back room lives Halhead and his wife. He is an "out-of-work." Used to be cigar-box maker, but trade declined, owing to use of paper packets — women's work. Has lately been working at the docks. They have a girl at service. In the second floor front room lives Pantin, a marble mason, out of work. His wife gets four days a week as laundress; looks thin and wan. Grandmother looks after the two children when their mother is at work. Seem respectable, but have only been here six months.

No. 20. Entrance to large wood yard occupies the ground floor. On top floor lives Peel, a bill-poster, who has been out of work for twelve months, but is now doing a little. There is a wife, but no children. They owe four months' rent, and have had to sell a bedstead. Were burning old boots for fuel when visitor called. Peel drinks.

No. 22 is occupied by the offices of the wood yard.

No. 24. A toy shop. The man Brown hawks toy whips. Trade is bad. His wife and he are elderly people, very decent and struggling.

No. 26. Public-house, changed hands lately, which has been an improvement.

No. 28. Baker's shop, kept by Stein and his wife; they have a grown-up daughter and some young children, and have been here for years. Stein worked for his predecessor. Very respectable people.

No. 30. Second-hand boot shop, kept by Shaw, an elderly man. There is his wife and one daughter at home, and he has three sons married. Lived here many years. No lodgers.

No. 32. Haberdasher's shop, kept by Bird. The wife and daughter do dressmaking, as well as mind shop. The man goes out to work. Very respectable.

No. 34. Ground floor, occupied by Grind, a looking-glass frame maker, as shop. He lives at the back, and has a sick wife and five children, one, a girl at service, and four at home. Very friendly. He sometimes works to order, but more frequently on own account, and then takes his wares round. Works sixteen hours a day, and earns 25*s* to 30*s* a week. The first floor of this house is occupied by the Steads. Stead himself is a waterside labourer, but acts also as scene-shifter at the Royal Theatre. His wife used to be a pew-opener. They have two children, a girl, who is a mantle-maker, but now out of work and a boy, who is at home. The wife's mother lives with them. She is widow of a Freeman (Clothworkers' Company), and receives 6*s* a week pension. She sells lights at the corner of a street in the City, where she had a stall for thirty-four years. The daughter was educated at Cripplegate School. On the top floor there was a dock labourer, with wife and twins, both very poorly. These people are badly off. The man, when last visited, had been out on strike four weeks.

No. 36. The ground floor is occupied by Hilton, a fishmonger and greengrocer, who has his shop next door, and does a fair trade. Has wife and children, of whom two are at work. Very nice man; abstainer. He complained of the number of loafers about in the street. The first floor front was to let, and the occupant of the back room out. On the top floor lives Appleby, a shoemaker, busy now, but had no work for five weeks previously. His wife makes match-boxes. They have one girl at home. Rent, 4*s*; owe two weeks. Mrs. Appleby attends church.

No. 15 is a lodging-house, kept by Baker and his wife, helped by their son. It is said to be respectably managed. Service held here every Sunday by a missionary.

No. 13. Public-house.

No. 11. Large dwelling-house. On the ground floor lives Kerr, a general labourer, who is out of work. He worked twenty-one years for a wholesale chemist, and cannot now find employment because of his age (56), although well and hearty. Seems a respectable man. Has a wife and one child. There are three other families in the house (Jews).

No. 9A. Lower part stables. On the first floor, Park a printer's labourer, with wife and baby. Attend church, pay 3*s* for room and small kitchen. At the top lives Gardner, a dealer in sawdust. His wife is an Irish Roman Catholic. She goes out cleaning. They have one girl at service and three children at home. The husband drinks.

No. 9. Barton and his wife live here. Mrs. Park, who lives next door, is their daughter, and they have another daughter, who lives at home, and works with her mother, mending up second-hand clothes for a tailor in Virginia Row. No information as to Barton himself. The Bartons have lived twenty-five years in the neighbourhood. On the top floor lives Slattery, a shunter on the railway. Both Barton and Slattery are Roman Catholics.

No. 7. Mr. and Mrs. Penrose live here. Mrs. Penrose was another daughter of Mrs. Barton. Respectable people.

No. 5. The Mayfields occupy both floors of this house. They have seven children. Have been here about twelve months, having come from Spitalfields. Said they had been very poor, but were doing better now. Accept the occasional teas offered to those who join mothers' meetings or attend mission services, as "of course." Seem very respectable. No information as to husband's business.

Nos. 3 *and* 1 do not exist any longer.

Altogether there are 25 houses in this street.

Streets Coloured Pink

The examples which follow are not satisfactory or sufficient. The sources of information from systematic visiting apply more fully to poor streets, and it was with regard to the poorer streets that we chiefly sought information.

Chesterfield Street, which is described at length, is in truth so much mixed that it might be coloured purple. Mutimer Street amongst the purple examples is better off. Mutimer Street we originally had as pink, and the details were gone into because the vicar of the parish thought our view of it incorrect. We altered the colour, but the street lies on the line, and might very well be placed in either category.

Some admixture of poverty is found very frequently in the pink streets; our figures show it; but on the average it will be less than the following examples show, and in whole districts, where the general conditions approach those of middle class life, little or none will be found.

CHESTERFIELD STREET This street has a pleasant look. Most of the houses on the sunniest side have creepers hanging from them, and the wide areas make light basements. The windows are well kept. They contain a few business cards, one of a shirt and collar dresser promising "highly polished work." There are few signs of poverty. Only one side of the street is detailed below, but this side gives a fair picture of the whole. The people are poorer at the end most remote from the main street. The houses have a frontage of 15 feet.

Nos. 1 *and* 2. Just built, and only one family come in.

No. 3. Occupied by two Scotchmen and their wives, each having also one child. They came up to London together, employed upon the same piece of work. There are four rooms in the house.

No. 4 is occupied by Burgess, a printer, who is old and suffers from paralysis. His wife keeps him by taking in washing. This is his second wife; the first family has grown up. Four rooms.

No. 5 is occupied by Barton, a policeman, with wife and four or five children, the eldest being about seven. The wife's mother lives with them and sells milk, carrying it out. Mrs. Barton did this also before her marriage.

No. 6. In one room of this house an old couple live, Roman Catholics, who in their younger days kept a greengrocer's shop in this street. The man now works as a carman. An old woman, too old to work, and a son, who keeps her, live in two rooms; while a poor widow, a needlewoman, has the fourth.

No. 7 is a larger house, having six rooms and two attics. A woman named Baker kept the house during her husband's life, and still retains it. She has six children, three of whom go to work and are her main support. Knowles, a saddler with wife and three little children, has two rooms. He has slack work in certain seasons, and is probably poor. A back room is occupied by an old man, a Roman Catholic, who receives a little parish relief. He has a son who used to live here, but has left.

No. 8 is occupied by a printer, who earns good money, but both he and his wife are too fond of drink. They have five children — one son a pupil teacher, a daughter in service, and three others at school. Would be very comfortable but for the drink; are able to accommodate two lodgers, but they have been unsatisfactory, continually changing.

No. 9. Partly occupied by Barnes, a man who is employed in the City. His wife used to take shirt and collar dressing, as the man did not do much, but she has given it up now. There are three children, two at school and a baby. Two rooms in this house are occupied by a man working at the saw mills. The wife in this case used to work for some time after her marriage; she is now employed with two little children. In another room lives Mrs. Park, a widow, who does washing, but mainly lives on charity.

A Summary of Sample Streets

The tabels which follow summarize the sample streets colour by colour (omitting the black streets which are beyond such arithmetical treatment). In these tables the streets are arranged according to the proportion found in them of classes A and B, plus half of C and D. This plan seems to yield the most truthworthy order of poverty.

Summary of Sample Streets (*Purple and Pink.*)

Name.	A.	B.	Per cent.	C.	D.	Per cent.	E.	F.	Per cent.	Population.
Peel Street	—	41	33	7	46	43	30	—	24	124
Back Park Row	—	37	27	4	58	46	31	6	27	136
Bank Street	3	13	35	—	14	30	6	10	35	46
Gordon Road	—	47	21	48	53	45	42	33	34	223
Norman Passage	—	41	24	3	60	37	66	—	29	170
Roussillon Road	—	41	15	74	82	55	53	32	30	282
Marshall Passage	—	105	30	44	44	25	105	51	45	349
Tramp Road	—	8	19	13	5	43	11	5	38	42
Patriot Street	—	11	7	38	53	59	47	6	34	155
Ross Street	—	16	10	28	56	54	57	—	36	157
Upwell Road	—	66	16	58	107	39	120	65	45	416
Avon Road	—	5	4	22	48	59	40	3	37	118
Carver Street	—	61	14	93	62	37	196	8	49	420
Mutimer Street	—	15	7	26	86	49	80	21	44	228
Major Road, &c.	—	8	7	12	35	44	36	16	49	107
Turner Road	—	11	7	25	47	42	82	7	51	172
Cutters' Row	—	6	7	10	16	31	36	15	62	83
Meldrum Street	—	3	4	18	6	34	31	13	62	71
Shakespear Place	—	—	—	16	18	39	46	8	61	88
Flatter Street	—	8	4	23	23	23	75	71	73	200
Total Purple	3	543	15	562	919	42	1190	370	43	3587
Chesterfield Street	—	19	7	61	55	41	143	7	52	285
Martin Street	—	18	9	6	49	28	117	5	63	195
Weaver Street	—	10	8	6	10	12	55	51	80	132
Cherry Street	—	—	—	—	2	2	12	81	98	95
Total Pink	—	47	6	73	116	27	327	144	67	707

Classification of Inhabitants of Selected Streets.—Summary.

	A.		B.		C.		D.		E.		F.		Total.	
	Nos.	Per cent.	Nos.	Per cent.	Nos.	Per cent.	Nos.	Per cent.	Nos.	Per cent.	Nos.	Per cent.	Popula-tion.	Per cent. of Poverty.
Dark blue and black	125	12	436	43	192	19	179	18	82	7	13	1	1,027	92
Dark blue	47	1	1,371	42	780	24	638	20	413	12	22	1	3,271	87
Light blue	44	1	660	20	626	19	1,015	31	773	23	194	6	3,312	71
Purple	3	—	543	15	562	16	919	26	1,170	33	390	10	3,587	57
Pink	—	—	47	6	73	10	116	17	327	46	144	21	707	33
	219	—	3,057	—	2,233	—	2,867	—	2,765	—	763	—	11,904	—

An application of these percentages to the total figures for the different coloured streets seems to show (though the calculation is a rough one), that the selected sample is rather poorer than the bulk.

Those who may study closely the particulars of the sample streets will find that the colours overlap each other a little, and this is shown very clearly in the summary tabels just given. There are one or two blue streets which might have been purple, and *vice versâ,* whilst in at least one instance an exchange should have been made between purple and pink to make description and colour tally exactly. These cases, however, are exceptional, and do not affect the general results.[2] Absolute agreement between the accounts given by the School Board visitors and by the clergy was not to be expected, considering that entirely different methods were employed, and that an interval, extending in some cases to three or four years, had elapsed between the first inquiry and its revision.

It should also be said that those who gave the information did not know what use would be made of it, nor were they asked to decide in what class each family should be placed. The accounts of each street and its inhabitants were noted with "running pen"; and the result is a very vivid picture, without doubt honestly drawn, and I believe true, but perhaps hardly fit for statistical analysis. The method of analysis, as well as the value of the picture itself, lies open to the judgment of the reader.

2 If the figures for the whole 66 sample streets, from dark blue mixed with black to purple, be taken together, the two methods yield practically the same results. The School Board visitors' figures give 29 per cent. A and B, 44 per cent. C and D, and 27 per cent. E and F, while the district visitors' reports come out, 26 per cent. A and B, 45 per cent. C and D, and 29 per cent. E and F. So close an agreement is more than could be expected. It will be observed that the degree of poverty noted is on the whole rather less from the second point of view.

II. Industry Series

5

GENERAL CLASSIFICATION OF THE PEOPLE

IN THE INTRODUCTION to my first series it was pointed out that a double method of inquiry was needed, in order that the condition of the people might be tested in two ways, and the facts be ascertained, first, as to how they live, and next, as to how they work.

The first of these two methods, although carried out for the whole of London with sufficient fulness in the first and second volumes of that series, was felt to require the check afforded by statistics obtained in some different manner; the second test was, save in a few exceptional cases, left on one side until I could make use of the more recent and comprehensive statistical basis to be afforded by the occupation returns of the Census of 1891.

Thanks to the kindness of the Registrar-General my hopes in this respects have been fulfilled; and I have been permitted to make a very complete use of the census figures in classifying the people of London.[1]

In the Census of 1891, each head of family or occupier living in less than five rooms was asked to state the number of rooms occupied; and, in London at least, this information was in most instances obtained by the enumerators. The result is embodied in the Report lately issued by the Registrar-General, showing that

---

Reprinted from "Industry Series," I, 1–4, 11–16.

1 In thanking the Registrar-General for the great courtesy he has shown me in this matter, I perhaps ought to say that while supplying me with all the information I needed for my purpose, he has never placed in my hands any original documents, or supplied any of the facts, except in such form as to preclude all possibility of individual identification.

there were 630,569 occupied tenements of less than five rooms, and giving the particulars as to the numbers of persons compared to the number of rooms in each tenement.

Rooms in Tenement.	Number of Tenements with less than Five Rooms.	Number of Occupants of each Tenement.					
		One.	Two.	Three.	Four.	Five.	Six.
1	172,502	60,114	55,766	29,005	16,111	7,409	2,871
2	189,707	16,106	46,075	40,168	32,486	24,013	15,526
3	153,189	5,522	27,246	29,151	26,796	22,657	17,293
4	115,171	1,864	12,049	16,645	18,896	18,175	16,294
Total ...	630,569	83,606	141,136	114,969	94,289	72,254	51,984

Rooms.	Number of Occupants of each Tenement (*continued*).					
	Seven.	Eight.	Nine.	Ten.	Eleven.	Twelve or more.
1	879	231	72	27	10	7
2	8,863	4,195	1,590	488	138	59
3	11,953	7,078	3,446	1,377	470	200
4	12,801	8,952	5,203	2,573	1,150	569
Total ...	34,496	20,456	10,311	4,465	1,768	835

It must be noted that by "head of family" is meant anyone claiming to fill up an independent return or "householder's schedule." The "house" indirectly referred to may be but one room, and the household its single occupant; but boarders do not usually expect or obtain separate schedules, and thus as a rule it may be taken that those by whom or for whom the kitchen fire is used form one census family.

The method which I have adopted in re-stating the facts for the purposes of this classification is as follows: So far as the population are living in less than five rooms per family, the classification is based on the number of persons to each room; so far as they are employers of domestic indoor servants, it rests on the number of persons served to each servant; while those who live in five or more rooms, but keep no servants, form a central class.

On this plan those living in each district, or engaged in each trade, fall into three broad divisions, which again may be subdivided.

I. Lower Class—			Families occupying less than 5 rooms.
(1.)	4 or more persons to each room		
(2.)	3 and under 4 persons to each room		
(3.)	2 ,, 3 ,,		
(4.)	1 ,, 2 ,,		
II. Central Class—			
(5.)	Less than 1 person to each room		
	Families occupying 5 rooms or more without servants		Families employing domestic indoor servants.
(a.)	4 or more persons to 1 servant		
III. Upper Class—			
(b.)	3 or less with 1 servant 4 ,, more with 2 servants		
(c.)	3 ,, less ,, 2 ,, 5 ,, more ,, 3 ,,		
(d.)	3 ,, 4 ,, 3 ,, 5 ,, 6 ,, 4 ,, 7 ,, more ,, 5 ,,		
(e.)	1 ,, 2 with 3 servants 3 ,, 4 ,, 4 ,, 5 ,, 6 ,, 5 ,, 7 ,, more with 6 servants		
(f.)	1 ,, 2 with 4 servants 3 ,, 4 ,, 5 ,, 5 ,, 6 ,, 6 ,, 6 ,, 7 ,, 7 ,,	and other families where number of servants about equals that of members of the family	
(g.)	1 ,, 2 ,, 5 ,, 3 ,, 4 ,, 6 ,, 4 ,, 5 ,, 7 ,,	and other families with 8 or more servants, where members of family equal the number of servants	
(h.)	1 ,, 2 ,, 6 ,, 1, 2, or 3 persons with 7 servants And all families with more than 8 servants, where the members of family are less in number than the servants		

In the central class I have included on the one hand, those who, though occupying less than five rooms, are fewer in family than the number of rooms occupied, and on the other hand have counted also those who, though keeping one servant, are not less than four in family. For the former are fully as well housed, and the latter are in very much the same social position, as those who without servants occupy a house of five or more rooms.

This classification embraces the whole population in families as they live, leaving outside of it only the inmates of institutions, hotels, &c. It can be applied equally well to the whole population or to any district or trade, or if desired could be applied to any trade in any of the 127 registration sub-districts in London. In it every individual inhabitant of London has his place.

The original classification has the advantage of being directly aimed at poverty, with which domestic crowding is not entirely coincident, but was based on *opinion* only— that is, on the impression made on the minds of the school board visitors and others by what they had seen or heard as to the position in the scale of comfort of the people amongst whom they lived and worked, whereas the new classification is based on a direct enumeration of the facts.

Some doubt, it is true, is thrown by the Registrar-General on the trustworthiness of the information given in the census as to the numbers of rooms occupied, the numbers of employers and employed, and as to the description by occupation. It is pointed out in the Report (1893) that in spite of the very exact instructions issued, defining the words "house" and "tenement"—the former as the space between the external and party walls of a building, the latter as any house or part of a house separately occupied—confusion seems to have arisen. This is true, but the danger of inaccuracy is not greater in the case of this return than may be urged with equal, or perhaps even greater, force against the returns as to civil condition, age, or place of birth. No one of these is immaculate. As to age, no doubt *some* figure is filled in, but in how many cases is this done by the enumerator? Or, if filled in by the householder, what guarantee that the ages are known, or, if known, are truthfully recorded? So far from the data being accurate, they bear on their face the stamp of inaccuracy, as witness the concentration upon even figures, such as thirty-five, forty, &c., and the evident and natural error in the ages returned by young women, who wish only to be "as old as they look," or not quite that. As to civil condition, marriage and widowhood are terms very loosely used, and as to birthplaces, what reliance can be placed on detailed accuracy? Yet these returns are used without cavil for calculations and deductions of the most elaborate character, connected with vital problems and the movements of population.

Primâ facie, the statistics we are using have an advantage over those concerning age and civil condition, in that the information is common property. Age is known at best only to the individual, or, in the case of children, to the parents; the neighbours do not know, the enumerator can only guess. But the number of rooms occupied is well known, and not to be hidden. In nine cases out of ten the enumerator would not need to ask the question if it were his business to fill in the schedule. It is therefore to be supposed that when the enumerator's work was carefully done, the errors on this point would not be either serious or widespread, and if omissions or blunders have been made, they would be due to the fact that the question was novel.

To meet the difficulty of novelty, and to make sure that the enumerator's work was carefully and intelligently performed, at any rate in London, I obtained the Registrar-General's permission to place myself in communication with the Registrars in each sub-district of the metropolis, and through them with the enumerators themselves. I personally saw all the Registrars more than once, and discussed the subjects with them, pointing out the object to be attained, and the important uses that could be made of the material to be collected; and my appeal was very heartily responded to both by them and by the enumerators. Amongst so many men (there were over three thousand enumerators in all) there could not be uniform excellence, and no doubt some may have performed the work in a perfunctory manner, but, on the whole, I was assured, and feel quite satisfied, that the work was well and conscientiously done. To some extent its quality could be seen when we came to edit the results; and the process of editing served not only as a test, but enabled us also to make current corrections of evident errors or omissions.

On the whole, therefore, I am confident that any errors which may have crept in could not materially affect the general merits of the classification, and that the numbers counted in the census as occupying each tenement, and the number of rooms in each tenement of less than five rooms, may, for all practical purposes, be taken as correct; whilst the value of the return for comparative purposes is strengthened by the fact that the rooms occupied by the poor are usually similar in size.

As to wealth, the new classification has every advantage; indeed, the previous one made no attempt in this direction, but lumped together all the servant-keeping classes, and even some out of the lower middle classes, who, though keeping no servants, live in middle-class streets, and send their children to middle-class schools. The numbers of servants and the numbers in family as given by the census, are undoubtedly correct, and although the number of servants kept is no certain test of wealth, it is at any rate a very fair test of expenditure, and an almost absolute indication of the style of life.

Old Classification.		*New Classification.*			
		Class (1.) More than 8 to a room	1,000		
		8 to a room...............	2,000		
		7 ,, ...	6,000		
Classes A and B	354,000	6 to a room, &c.	20,000	340,000	
		5 ,, ,, ...	57,000		
		4 ,, ,, ...	102,000		
		½ ,, (2.) 3 ,, ,, ...	152,000		Lower, 2,257,000
		½ ,, (2.) ,, ,, ,, ...	152,000	934,000	
,, C and D	938,000	,, (3.) 2 ,, ,, ...	782,000		
		Common Lodging-houses		20,000	
		Class (4.) 1 ,, ,, ...	963,000		
		,, (5.) Less than 1 to a room	153,000		
		,, (6.) More than 4 rooms ...	982,000		
,, E and F	2,167,000	Persons living in large shops, &c.	15,000	2,547,000	Central, 1,584,000
,, G	500,000				
		Servants	206,000		
		,, (a.) Over 4 persons, 1 servant	228,000		
,, H	250,000	(b.) to (h.) 3 or less persons to 1 servant...............	248,000	274,000	Upper, 274,000
	4,209,000	Hotels and boarding-houses, &c................	26,000		
Inmates of Institutions	100,000	Inmates of Institutions		97,000	
	4,309,000			4,212,000	

The numbers of the "*crowded*" are, as we have seen, very similar to those of the "*poor*" in London, but if all families with three or more persons per room are to be counted as *very crowded*, the number of these considerably exceeds that of the "*very poor*" as they were previously estimated. In this there is nothing unreasonable. A man and his wife and one child, or a widow with two children, may occupy only one room; or a family of six or seven may have only two rooms; and yet not be "very poor" in the sense of suffering "chronic want." But when four or more persons live in one room or eight or more in two rooms, there must be great discomfort, and want of sufficient food, clothing, and firing is probably a frequent incident. I have, therefore drawn a line at this point. Further, of the 300,000 who live three or from three to four in a room, it may be that half would be correctly placed in the same category. If so, we have about 340,000 in all of "very poor," amongst the crowded, a number which compares closely with the 350,000 of the old classification.

Amongst those who live four to a room, there may be some instances in which the room is unusually large, or the family, as in the case of a widow, may consist of only one adult and three small children, but such exceptions will be comparatively rare, and apart from them the whole 100,000 persons can only be described as overcrowded.

Still more certainly must this be true of the 50,000 or 60,000 persons who are living five in one room or nine to ten in two rooms. And beyond these we have no less than 20,000 persons living six in one room, or over ten together in two rooms. Into the cases of still greater crowding—the 6000 living seven in one room, or the 2000 living eight in one room—I will not go at present. That such cases exist is known to every relieving officer, and it will be found that many of them are rather aggravated than explained by the character of the "room" occupied. Finally, we have 1000 persons returned as living nine, ten and over ten in a room. These cases, as already stated, are very probably erroneous or misleading in some way. There may be isolated cases of the kind, but the total cannot be regarded as correct.

Of the third section of the lower class, those who live two in one room or four or five in two rooms—or any other combination which yields two and a fraction per room—some may be "very poor," just as, on the other hand, some of the very crowded would not be found to be so very poor, but, on the whole, they will be simply "poor," *i.e.* obtaining with difficulty the bare necessaries of life, but succeeding in obtaining them. Of these, we have in London 780,000, or if we add to them one-half of those who live three, &c., to a room, omitted above as not belonging to the very poor, we have 930,000 or 940,000, comparing exactly with the 938,000 "poor" of the old classification.

As to section four of the new classification it is not possible to make any direct comparison with the old arrangement. There are nearly a million of them (962,780) living one person in each room, or at most three people in two, five in three, or seven in four rooms. They are part of the 2,200,000 "comfortable working classes" recognized in the old figures, and to their numbers may be added three-fourths of the "central class," of which the remainder then compares with the lower middle class (G) in the former classification.

There is little real difference in condition between the three sections of which this central class is composed. Families in which one servant (generally a young girl) waits upon, or helps to serve, four or more persons, are not on any different level socially from families who occupy a whole house and do all the domestic work themselves, with occasional aid from a charwoman or a girl who comes only in the day, going home to sleep. The difference is rather an accident in the constitution of the family, such as the presence of a baby or the absence of grown daughters, than any question of income or class. And amongst the classes who do not keep a servant, there is not much to choose between those who, living in four rooms or less, have fewer individuals in family than the number of rooms occupied, and those who with five rooms or more (*i.e.* a whole house) have an indefinite number of persons.

Finally, we have the 275,000 of the upper classes, of whom 26,000 are visitors—inmates of hotels, &c.—comparing closely with the roughly estimated 250,000 of class H.

Taking the whole number of these classes we cannot but be

struck by its insignificance, being only 6 per cent. of the population, and if we analyse it further this becomes still more marked. Of the 250,000, more than 50,000 live in households with only one servant, fully another 50,000 in families where two servants wait upon six or ten or more persons, and, again, 50,000 in smaller families with only two servants; thus leaving in all less than 100,000 who enjoy such an amount of luxury as is connected with the employment of three or more servants. Of these, again, 20,000 live in largish families with three servants, and 20,000 more in small families with three servants, leaving out of over 4,000,000 only 60,000 persons, all told—men, women and children—who enjoy the luxury of an establishment with at least four servants, and with less than half of these is the number of indoor servants greater than that of those they serve.

6

AN EXAMPLE: DEALERS AND CLERKS

Preliminary Statement

THIS PART is occupied principally with small shop-keepers and street sellers on the one hand; and with merchants, brokers, and bankers, and those they employ, on the other. Their numbers, age, and sex are given in the tables that follow.

Persons represented: (A) Census Enumeration.

ENUMERATED BY AGE AND SEX.

DEALERS.	10—	15—	20—	25—	55—	65—	Total.
Males	889	4423	4367	19,200	2805	1491	33,175
Females	247	1571	1330	4948	1023	535	9654
Total	1136	5994	5697	24,148	3828	2026	42,829
COMMERCIAL.							
Males	2376	22,606	22,265	62,805	6408	2625	119,085
Females	107	2227	3039	3767	145	45	9330
Total	2483	24,833	25,304	66,572	6553	2670	128,415
Grand Totals	3619	30,827	31,001	90,720	10,381	4696	171,244

Reprinted from "Industry Series," III, 241–58.

More than half of those returned as general shop-keepers are females, as are also nearly one-third of the street sellers. The other sections consist mostly of males. Amongst the 43,000 employed in "dealing," there are 22,000 heads of families, and amongst the 119,000 "commercial," there are 54,000 heads.

Persons Represented: (B) Enumeration by Families.

No.	Sections.	Heads.	Total numbers (excluding Servants).	Per family (excluding Servants).	Servants.
55	Ironmongers, china dealers and pawnbrokers	4724	21,221	4·50	1726
56	Coal, wood and corn dealers	4360	20,384	4·67	1604
57	General shop-keepers and dealers.....................	7137	31,244	4·37	503
58	Costers and street sellers ...	5825	23,695	4·07	65
	Total dealers.........	22,046	96,544	4·38	3898
59	Merchants, bankers, brokers	13,278	58,212	4·39	13,722
60	Commercial clerks	40,737	169,779	4·16	11,810
	Total commercial...	54,015	227,991	4·22	25,532
	Grand total	76,061	324,535	4·27	29,430
	Servants		29,430		
	Total population		353,965		

In the census of 1861 general dealers are combined with costers and street sellers, and in the returns for the other decades there is evidently some overlapping between the different sections of dealers. Taking the class as a whole, however, the increase is steady and consistent from 26,800 in 1861 to 42,900 in 1891, an addition of 60 per cent. in the thirty years.

The number of commercial clerks shows great increases each decade, but especially from 1861 to 1871, when it more than doubled. In the same decade merchants, &c., increased consid-

SOCIAL CONDITION OF FAMILIES OF MERCHANTS AND CLERKS.

Class	Condition	Number	Per cent	Group per cent	
Lower Classes.	4 or more persons to 1 room	2241 or ·9 °/ₒ		2·7 °/ₒ	Crowded: 9·4 °/ₒ
	3 and under 4 ,, ,,	4538 ,, 1·8 °/ₒ			
	2 and under 3 ,, ,,	16,909 ,,	6·7 °/ₒ		
	1 and under 2 ,, ,,	40,558 ,,	16·0 °/ₒ		Not Crowded: 90·6 °/ₒ
Central Classes.	Less than 1 person to a room	11,142 ,, 4·4 °/ₒ		50·2 °/ₒ	
	More than 4 rooms	80,507 ,, 31·7 °/ₒ			
	4 or more persons to 1 servant	35,858 ,, 14·1 °/ₒ			
Upper Classes.	Less than 4 persons to 1 servant and 4 or more to 2 servants	21,645 ,,	8·6 °/ₒ		
	All others with 2 or more servants	14,593 ,,	5·8 °/ₒ		
	Servants	25,532 ,,	10·0 °/ₒ		
		253,523 ,,	100 °/ₒ		

SOCIAL CONDITION OF FAMILIES OF DEALERS AND STREET SELLERS.

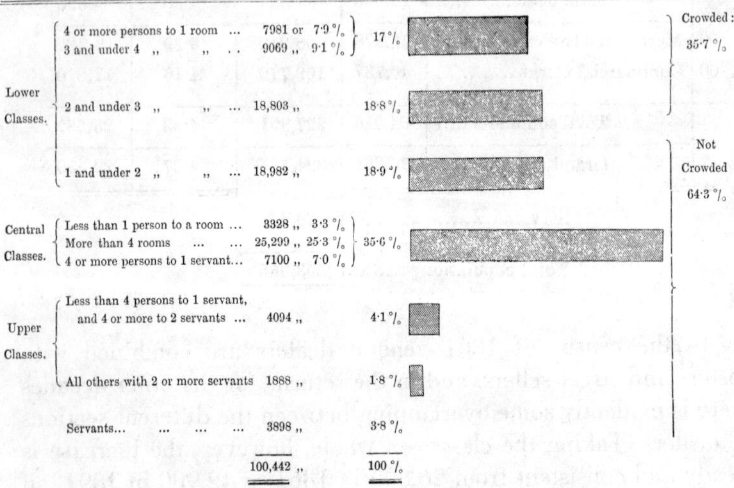

Class	Condition	Number	Per cent	Group per cent	
Lower Classes.	4 or more persons to 1 room ...	7981 or 7·9 °/ₒ		17 °/ₒ	Crowded: 35·7 °/ₒ
	3 and under 4 ,, ,, . .	9069 ,, 9·1 °/ₒ			
	2 and under 3 ,, ,, ...	18,803 ,,	18·8 °/ₒ		
	1 and under 2 ,, ,, ...	18,982 ,,	18·9 °/ₒ		Not Crowded 64·3 °/ₒ
Central Classes.	Less than 1 person to a room ...	3328 ,, 3·3 °/ₒ		35·6 °/ₒ	
	More than 4 rooms	25,299 ,, 25·3 °/ₒ			
	4 or more persons to 1 servant...	7100 ,, 7·0 °/ₒ			
Upper Classes.	Less than 4 persons to 1 servant, and 4 or more to 2 servants ...	4094 ,,	4·1 °/ₒ		
	All others with 2 or more servants	1888 ,,	1·8 °/ₒ		
	Servants...	3898 ,,	3·8 °/ₒ		
		100,442 ,,	100 °/ₒ		

erably, but during the last twenty years the numbers have altered very little, there being a slight decrease since 1881.

Among dealers there are about 5300 employers to 20,000

Social condition (by Sections).

Section.	3, 4, or more persons to a room.	2 and under 3 persons to a room.	1 and under 2 persons to a room.	Less than 1 to a room. More than 4 rooms, or 4 or more persons to 1 servant.	Less than 4 persons to a servant.	Servants.	Total.
Ironmonger, China, &c.......	1228	2275	3520	11,505	2693	1726	22,947
Per cent......	5½	10	15½	50	11½	7½	100
Coal, &c., Dealers	1372	2705	3618	10,100	2589	1604	21,988
Per cent......	6	12½	16½	46	11½	7½	100
General Shop-keepers	5930	6851	7200	10,663	600	503	31,747
Per cent......	19	21½	22½	33½	2	1½	100
Costers & Street Sellers	8520	6972	4644	3459	100	65	23,760
Per cent......	36	29	19½	14½	½	½	100
Merchants, &c....	1221	3140	6110	27,705	20,036	13,722	71,934
Per cent......	2	4½	8½	38½	27½	19	100
Clerks	5558	13,769	34,448	99,802	16,202	11,810	181,589
Per cent......	3	7½	19	55	9	6½	100

Order of apparent poverty.

Trade.	Employers and Employed.	Employed only.
	Crowded.	Crowded.
Costermongers and Street Sellers ...	65·2 per cent.	69·5 per cent.
General Shopkeepers	40·3 „ „	46·7 „ „
Coal, Wood, and Hay Dealers	18·5 „ „	28·7 „ „
Ironmongers, China Dealers, &c.......	15·3 „ „	22·2 „ „
Clerks	10·6 „ „	10·8 „ „
Merchants, Brokers, &c.	6·1 „ „	8·7 „ „

employed, and no less than 17,500 who are neither employers nor employed. Among the commercial class we lack particulars of those who are neither employer nor employed. The proportion of clerks to those who may be employers is five to one.

CENSUS ENUMERATION, 1861-1891, FOR EACH SECTION.

	1861.	1871.	1881.	1891.
Ironmongers, China Dealers	4800	5800	7800	9200
Coal, Wood, Hay Dealers ...	7300	9100	8400	6600
General Shopkeepers	14,700	10,200	14,600	14,200
Costers and Street Sellers ...		10,800	9,300	12,900
Merchants, Bankers & Brokers	12,600	18,500	20,300	20,000
Clerks	35,500	72,900	84,400	108,400
Total	74,900	127,300	144,800	171,300

IRONMONGERS, GLASS AND CHINA DEALERS, COAL, WOOD, AND CORN DEALERS, AND GENERAL SHOPKEEPERS The amount of poverty indicated by the room test in these sections is naturally proportioned to the size of the shops. Ironmongers' and pawnbrokers' shops are seldom very small, and amongst glass and china dealers there are a proportion that are of some pretension. It is the same with hay, straw, and corn dealers; but as to coals, the far greater proportion are of the smallest kind; and with what are called general shops—selling cakes and sweets, dripping and bacon, toys and small wares, ginger pop or lemonade, and perhaps milk—very few indeed are other than of the smallest kind.

As to the wages received by the employees of the largest of these shops I have not obtained any particulars. They will, doubtless, be found to be in proportion to those paid for regular employment in any other trade—varying that is from 20*s* to 50*s* a week, according to the responsibility of the position, and proportionately less if board and lodging are included, supplemented in the higher branches by a commission on sales.

Nor have I any information as to those smaller shops in which the proprietor and his family do most of the work. They enjoy, or suffer, a very varying fortune. Many a small inheritance, and many a sum of savings slowly accumulated in some other occupation, is dispersed and lost by the rash entering into a "little business" of those who are entirely ignorant of the social services demanded from a retail trader, or devoid of the qualities needed to fulfil

IRONMONGER, GLASS AND CHINA DEALER. (*Section* 55.)

Persons Represented.

Census Enumeration.

Census Divisions, 1891.	Females. All Ages.	Males. −19	Males. 20—54	Males. 55—	Total.
(1) Ironmonger..	118	511	2484	297	3410
(2) Glass & China	431	130	1038	211	1810
(3) Pawnbroker..	66	1075	1365	109	2615
(4) Works of Art, &c.	221	96	811	201	1329
TOTAL.. ..	836	1812	5698	818	9164

The noticeable feature, as shown on the age chart, is the large proportion of young men employed, who are mainly pawnbrokers' assistants.

DISTRIBUTION.

E.	N.	W. & C.	S.	Total.
1248	2534	2233	3149	9164

DETAILS OF OCCUPATIONS (FROM THE CENSUS DICTIONARY).

(1) Hardware dealer, grindery dealer, scrap-iron, old iron dealer.
(2) Earthenware, porcelain, terra cotta dealer, bottle merchant, pottery salesman, dealer, medical glass dealer.
(3) Unredeemed pledge salesman.
(4) Dealer in antiquities, curiosities, coins, stamps, and bric-a-brac; Japanese wares worker, importer, dealer, and manufacturer; picture dealer, cleaner, liner, mounter, restorer; figure caster, plaster moulder, wax modeller; bird and beast stuffer, dried flower preparer, marine florist; shell merchant, polisher, worker, shell box maker, skeleton articulator.

Enumerated by Families.

Sex	Males		4522	Heads of Families, 4724.
	Females		202	
Birthplace	In London ..	55 %	2621	
	Out of London	45 %	2103	
Industrial Status ..	Employer	32 %	1495	
	Employed	53 %	2509	
	Neither	15 %	720	

TOTAL POPULATION CONCERNED.

	Heads of Families.	Others Occupied.	Unoccupied.	Servants.	**Total.**
Total	4724	5190	11,307	1726	22,947
Average in family..	1	1·10	2·40	·36	4·86

CLASSIFICATION.

For full details see Appendix (Pt. III.).

Numbers living in Families.		%
3 or more to a room	1228	5·4
2 & under 3 ,,	2275	9·9
1 & under 2 ,,	3520	15·3
Less than 1 ,, / More than 4 rooms / 4 or more persons to a servant ..	11,505	50·2
Less than 4 to 1 servant, and 4 or more to 2 servants	2000	8·7
All others with 2 or more servants ..	693	3·0
Servants	1726	7·5
	22,947	100

	Inner.	Outer.	Together.
Crowded ..	24 %	10 %	15 %
Not ,, ..	76 %	90 %	85 %

DISTRIBUTION.

East ..	Inner	2495	3021
	Outer	526	
North	Inner	1400	6430
	Outer	5030	
West..	Inner	520	3870
	Outer	3350	
Central	Inner	1486	1486
South-East	Inner	460	3621
	Outer	3161	
South-West	Inner	1416	4519
	Outer	3103	
			22,947

Inner 7777, or 34 %
Outer 15,170, or 66 %

Status as to Employment (according to Census Enumeration).

Census Divisions (1891).	Employers. Males.	Employers. Females	Employed. Males. Under 20.	Employed. Males. Over 20.	Employed. Females of all Ages.	Neither Employer nor Employed. Males.	Neither Employer nor Employed. Females	Total.
(1) Ironmonger	670	21	511	1935	78	176	19	3410
(2) Glass and China Dealer..............	337	56	130	640	293	272	82	1810
(3) Pawnbroker	310	21	1075	1130	38	34	7	2615
(4) Dealer in Works of Art	248	12	96	413	182	351	27	1329
	1565	110	1812	4118	591	833	135	9164
TOTAL..........	1675		6521			968		

them. Thus the sale of bankrupt stock has become almost a business in itself. On the other hand, a well-situated and carefully managed shop often affords a comfortable livelihood to one family for generations, or to successive owners, each of whom will pay on entering a substantial sum for the "goodwill" connected with the premises. Whether the capital employed is fruitful or dwindling

COAL, WOOD, AND CORN DEALERS. (*Section* 56.)

Persons Represented.

Census Enumeration.

Census Divisions, 1891.	Females. All Ages.	Males. —19	Males. 20—54	Males. 55—	Total.
(1) Coal and Coke	110	98	983	308	1499
(2) Timber, &c...	67	135	1243	256	1701
(3) Corn & Flour	300	360	2305	399	3364
TOTAL....	477	593	4531	963	6564

Owing to the fact that the numbers here given consist largely of employers and small dealers, there is an excessive proportion of men over 40 years of age. (*See* diagram.)

DISTRIBUTION.

E.	N.	W. & C.	S.	Total.
1124	1464	1267	2709	6564

DETAILS OF OCCUPATIONS (FROM THE CENSUS DICTIONARY).

(1) Coal agent, contractor, shipper, wharfinger.
(2) Chip dealer; hazel rod dealer; sawdust collector; shavings dealer; barrel and cask dealer; hoop and stave merchant; tan dealer; timber measurer.
(3) Fodder dealer; rush, cane, willow dealer; hay compresser; straw mat maker; straw joiner; chaff cutter; farina maker; pea splitter; rice cleaner; bran dealer; maccaroni maker, importer; groat manufacturer; hop sampler, dealer.

Enumerated by Families.

Sex	Males		4220	Heads of Families, 4360
	Females		140	
Birthplace	In London	52 %	2285	
	Out of London	48 %	2075	
Industrial Status	Employer	37 %	1618	
	Employed	41 %	1783	
	Neither	22 %	959	

TOTAL POPULATION CONCERNED.

	Heads of Families.	Others Occupied.	Unoccupied	Servants.	Total.
Total	4360	4421	11,603	1604	21,988
Average in family ..	1	1·01	2·66	·37	5·04

CLASSIFICATION.

Numbers living in Families.		%
3 or more to a room	1372	6·2
2 & under 3 „	2705	12·3
1 & under 2 „	3618	16·4
Less than 1 „ / More than 4 rooms / 4 or more persons to a servant ..	10,100	46·0
Less than 4 to 1 servant, and 4 or more to 2 servts.	1605	7·3
All others with 2 or more servants ..	984	4·5
Servants	1604	7·3
	21,988	100

	Inner.	Outer.	Together.
Crowded..	31 %	12 %	18½ %
Not „ ..	69 %	88 %	81½ %

DISTRIBUTION.

East..	Inner	2877	3575
	Outer	698	
North	Inner	714	5085
	Outer	4371	
West	Inner	394	2999
	Outer	2605	
Central	Inner	836	836
South-East	Inner	1008	5094
	Outer	4086	
South-West	Inner	1454	4399
	Outer	2945	
			21,988

Inner 7283, or 33 %
Outer 14,705, or 67 %

Status as to Employment (*according to Census Enumeration*).

Census Divisions (1891).	Employers. Males.	Employers. Females	Employed. Males. Under 20.	Employed. Males. Over 20.	Employed. Females of all ages.	Neither Employer nor Employed. Males.	Neither Employer nor Employed. Females	Total.
(1) Coal and Coke*....................	481	28	98	362	43	448	39	1499
(2) Timber, &c.	502	12	135	574	42	423	13	1701
(3) Corn, Flour, &c.	903	43	360	1501	227	300	30	3364
	1886	83	593	2437	312	1171	82	6564
TOTAL........	1969		3342			1253		

* The small number of employed persons here given is owing to the fact that the coal porters and carmen are returned and described elsewhere. (*See* Part V., Chapter II.)

away makes little difference as to the physical comfort in which the shopkeeper lives. It may often be that those who are losing live better than others who are making money. Thus, in a view of London such as is here attempted, all these persons are to be counted as comfortably off.

GENERAL SHOPKEEPERS. (*Section* 57.)

Persons Represented.

Census Enumeration.

Census Divisions, 1891.	Females All Ages.	Males. —19	Males. 20—54	Males. 55—	Total.
(1) General Shopkeeper and dealer........	4974	1376	5920	1100	13,370
(2) Rag gatherer, dealer........	354	63	393	61	871
TOTAL....	5328	1439	6313	1161	14,241

The age line here is peculiar—a normal proportion of lads, a marked deficiency of young men, and an excess of males over 40. Amongst small shopkeepers, boys and youths are commonly employed, and they, as they grow up, largely find their way into other branches of dealing. (*See* diagram.)

DISTRIBUTION.

E.	N.	W. & C.	S.	Total.
3758	2318	3049	5116	14,241

DETAILS OF OCCUPATIONS (FROM THE CENSUS DICTIONARY).

(1) Shopkeeper's assistant, shopwalker, shopman. Co-operative stores service. Wholesale dealer, miscellaneous dealer, money taker (undefined). Small ware dealer. Outfitter. Chandler. Marine store dealer, sorter.
(2) Ragman, rag cutter, sifter, sorter.

Enumerated by Families.

		%		
Sex	Males		5784	Heads of Families, 7137.
	Females...............		1353	
Birthplace	In London	68 %	4859	
	Out of London..	32 %	2278	
Industrial Status ..	Employer	13 %	913	
	Employed	26 %	1872	
	Neither........	61 %	4352	

TOTAL POPULATION CONCERNED.

	Heads of Families.	Others occupied.	Unoccupied.	Servants.	Total.
Total.	7137	7586	16,521	503	31,747
Average in family ..	1	1·06	2·31	·07	4·44

CLASSIFICATION.

Numbers living in Families.		%
3 or more to a room	5930	18·7
2 & under 3 ,,	6851	21·6
1 & under 2 ,,	7200	22·7
Less than 1 ,, / More than 4 rooms / 4 or more persons to a servant ..	10,663	33·6
Less than 4 to 1 servant, and 4 or more to 2 servants	410	1·3
All others with 2 or more servants ..	190	0·5
Servants............	503	1·6
	31,747	100

	Inner.	Outer.	Together.
Crowded..	48 %	29 %	40 %
Not ,, ..	52 %	71 %	60 %

DISTRIBUTION.

East ..	Inner	8727	9960
	Outer	1233	
North	Inner	1076	4509
	Outer	3433	
West..	Inner	735	3099
	Outer	2364	
Central	Inner	3086	3086
South-East	Inner	941	4277
	Outer	3336	
South-West	Inner	4050	6816
	Outer	2766	
			31,747

Inner 18,615, or 58 %
Outer 13,132, or 42 %

Status as to Employment (according to Census Enumeration).

Census Divisions (1891).	Employers. Males.	Employers. Females	Employed. Males. Under 20.	Employed. Males. Over 20.	Employed. Females of all ages.	Neither Employer nor Employed. Males.	Neither Employer nor Employed. Females	Total.
(1) General Shopkeeper and Dealer	689	254	1376	1794	2909	4537	1811	13,370
(2) Rag Gatherer and Dealer	96	9	63	240	330	118	15	871
	785	263	1439	2034	3239	4655	1826	14,241
TOTAL..........	1048		6712			6481		

With regard to the quite little "general" shops, of which many are kept by women, who in this way try to either support themselves or to increase the family income, one may be sure that there is present a great deal of real and even acute poverty. Of the business carried on in one such shop I have seen something, and it may prhaps be accepted as representative of many.

This shop, which exists no longer, was situated in a rather poor street, out of which open some still poorer courts, while nearly opposite is a common lodging house for single men.[1] The frontage of the street itself is partly occupied by a tobacco factory and some printing works. The houses on both sides are respectably occupied, and being old-fashioned—built when the neighbourhood experienced better days—afford apartments or lodgings for working men. Two or three of the cellars of these houses are used as shops, and the one of which I speak had been so used for many years by a couple who, living in a small house up the adjacent court, obtained a living out of the sale of provisions. The man, who had formerly figured on the stage as a clown, drank heavily; and after his wife's death the business went to pieces. He is now in the work-house. The fixtures and such goodwill as clung to the premises were sold by the occupant of the house (who sublet the shop) to friends of mine for 40*s*. A wooden screen betwixt door and fire, two tables, a counter, small and large scales and weights, a good corner cupboard, and some odds and ends, were thus acquired. The shop, which was fully half its height below the level of the street, measured about 14 ft. by 11 ft. by 7 ft., and the rent, which had been 3*s*, was raised to 3*s* 6*d*.

The previous occupants had been continually hard up, frequently borrowing the money needed to buy the stock; but so far as was known they had no other source of income. At first my friends did fairly well, though never well enough to have made a living out of the profits; but after twelve months an opposition shop was started in a neighbouring cellar, and cut so much into the money earned, that finally it was not worth while to continue the business. Moreover, in comparing the profits made during the year which came under observation with those which presumably had been made previously, it seems probable that there had been a

1 It is noticeable how indigenous is the general shop to the more central poor districts of London. Although the "inner ring" has only a little over a third of the total population of the metropolis, it contains 58 per cent. of the general shopkeepers. (*See* Table of persons represented.)

gradual diminution in the amount of trade done, due partly, perhaps, to more enterprise and lower prices at the large shops in the main streets, but mainly to the establishment of workmen's cocoa-rooms close by, at which, or from which, better and cheaper supplies could be obtained by the factory girls at mid-day, or by men in the common lodging-house at supper-time. It is said also that the late occupier took the risk of selling on credit.

My friends, a married pair without children, whose house was higher up the street, were accustomed to get a rather meagre living by letting their spare rooms to single men, who paid for board as well as lodgings, and they took the shop in order to add to their resources. One or other of them had to be at the shop from 6 in the morning to 11 at night, and so long as they carried on the business a girl was needed to help in the work of the house. It was necessary to keep open early and late, and on Sundays as well as week days, because it was before and after ordinary working hours, when the larger shops are closed, that custom was most active. Except sometimes on Saturdays, trade was seldom very brisk, and in the middle of the day the person in charge might sit and sell nothing, nor even exchange a word with anyone, for hours together. This dull time fell mostly to the lot of the husband —a man advanced in years and past regular work—for his wife, a much younger woman, was employed the later morning and mid-day hours over her household or in buying the stock, and, when she was more needed at the shop, sent him to keep house at home. Saturday evening was of course the busiest time, and in preparation for Saturday and Sunday the stock was brought up to its maximum every Friday.

Of Friday stock I twice took an account, and full particulars of it are appended as taken on June 1st. On the second occasion, four weeks later, the total value was a few shillings less. The articles dealt in show the nature of the business.

The very small sum needed to stock a shop of this kind is no less remarkable than the high average rate of profits. The two are closely interconnected, for if the rate were not high the sum earned on each transaction would be infinitesimal. There are about forty different descriptions of stock enumerated, and of the sales a large proportion were in penn'orths and ha'porths. Nevertheless, the sum taken amounted to fully £3 in a good week, and for months averaged about £2. 15*s*. It will be seen that the weekly turn-over was thus half as much again as the total stock at any one time, and we have a veritable instance of the supposed rare combination of large profits with quick returns. It must be said, however, that the average profit is not quite so high as a cursory glance at the figures might suggest, for it depends on the proportion in which the articles were sold. Bread and sugar only carry 14 per cent., and those things which pay 25 and 33 per cent. possibly out-weigh in amount sold those which yield the higher rates of 50, 100, and 200 per cent.

Stock was purchased from day to day as requisite, with a general replenishing on Friday. The quantities bought were thus never very large—nor could large quantities have been accommodated at all on the shelves of the shop, which contained altogether far less than the store-room of an ordinary middle-class family. But as they were regular continuous weekly purchases, and as cash was paid, the prices were not much above those of the wholesale market.

The ginger beer and milk were delivered at the door by carts, which made a regular round among their customers. The bread and flour came from the baker close by. Onions were bought at a public market, and dripping from the cook at a large drapery shop where the employees took their meals on the premises. All the other articles were purchased at shops which combine wholesale with retail business. From one came the chandlery stores—from another tea, and from a third other groceries; butter and eggs from a fourth, and so on. Althogether there were about twelve sources of supply, most of them to be found in the adjacent main streets, and not distant more than half a mile.

The buyers were the immediate neighbours. Two or three of them kept an account, paying on Saturday. Otherwise no credit was given, and no bad debts were made. A great deal of the money was spent by children, both on their own account on sweets and tarts, for which ha'pence are plentiful even among the very poor, and also as emissaries of their parents. "Well, Jennie, what is it?"

Stock in Shop on Friday Evening.

Articles.	Quantities.	Total value.	Cost price.	Sale price.	Percentage of Profit on cost.
Ginger beer	6 doz.	4 0	8*d* per doz.	1*d* each	50
Vinegar	1 gallon	0 9	9*d* per gallon	by ha'porths (say)	100
Salt	—	0 2	2*d* per loaf	by ha'porths & farthings	100
Mustard	1 doz.	0 8	8*d* per doz.	1*d* each	50
Tea	Loose	0 8	1/4 per lb.	6*d* per ¼ lb.	25
Tea	in oz. & ½ oz. pkts.	1 6	1/- ,,	1*d* per oz.	33
Rice & pearl barley	—	0 4	1½*d* ,,	5 oz. for 1*d*	100
Sugar	12 lbs. in pkts	1 9	1/9 per doz. lbs.	2*d* per lb.	14
Currants	—	0 2	1½*d* per lb.	5 oz. for 1*d*	100
Coffee	—	0 6	1/- ,,	4*d* per ¼ lb.	33
Soap	—	1 1½	4½*d* per bar	cut into 12 pieces at ½*d*	33
Blue	2 doz. packets	0 4	2*d* per doz.	¼*d* each	50
Blacking	1 doz. packets	0 2½	2½*d* ,,	½*d* ,,	140
Matches	3 doz. boxes	0 6	2*d* ,,	¼*d* ,,	50
Candles	1½ packets	1 6	11*d* per pkt. of 60	4 a penny	36
Washing powder	1 doz. packets	0 4½	4½*d* per doz.	½*d* each	33
Black lead	,, ,,	0 2	2*d* ,,	¼*d* ,,	50
Epsom salts	,, ,,	0 2	2*d* ,,	¼*d* ,,	50
Senna	,,	0 2	2*d* ,,	¼*d* ,,	50
Fire-wood	3 doz. bundles	0 6	2*d* ,,	4 a penny	50
Baking powder	1 doz. packets	0 2	2*d* ,,	¼*d* each	50
Flour	6 packets	0 7½	1/3 per doz. pkts. (fell later to 1/-)	1½*d* & 2*d* per packet(1½*d*)	50
Bread	6 loaves	0 7½	1/9 per doz.	2*d* each	14
Margarine	3 lbs. (best)	1 10	7½*d* per lb.	10*d* per lb.	33
,,	2½ ,,	1 3	5½*d* ,,	8*d* ,,	42
Cheese	3 ,,	1 3	5*d* ,,	8*d* ,,	60
Eggs	—	1 0	6/6 per 120 in summer	1*d* each and 2 for 1½*d*	25 (about)
Dripping	—	1 8	4*d* per lb.	6*d* per lb.	50
Bacon	6¼ lbs.	2 8	4½*d* ,,	8*d* ,,	77
Onions	—	1 0	10*d* or 1/- per 20 lbs.	1*d* ,,	80
Pickled onions	1½ jars	1 8	Home made	by ha'porths (say)	100
Jam	—	0 9	4*d* for 2 lbs.	6*d* per lb.	200
Milk	1 gallon	0 9	9*d* or 10*d* per gal.	2*d* per pint	60
Cotton, tapes, &c.	—	1 0	Various	—	—
Hair oil	—	0 7	7*d* per bottle	by ha'porths	—
Cigarettes	—	—	6 doz. for 1/-	¼*d* each	50
Sweets	—	3 0	3*d* and 4*d* per lb.	½*d* for 1½ oz.	50
Cakes	—	1 0	Various kinds	—	30-50
Tarts	—	0 3	4½*d* per doz.	½*d* each	33
		1 16 7½			

"Please, mother wants"—some soap, or whatever it may be. Almost everyone who comes is known, and greeted by name.[2] The dullness of the life when there are no customers is heightened by contrast with the pleasantly social nature of the business at those times of day when every few minutes a friend drops in for some small purchase and a little talk. For a man who neither reads nor knits there is, during the dull hours, nothing to be done but to stand at the door for the chance of a word with some passer-by.

The business lasted about fifteen months, but during the last three became much less profitable owing to the opening of the rival shop already mentioned. The family who thus started an opposition had been themselves regular customers, and besides their own requirements they, having somewhat the better position, intercepted a large portion of the trade. They had, moreover, the advantage of living above their shop. It is probable that neither of the two shops did much good while they divided the trade. The takings of my friend fell to 25*s* or 30*s* a week, and the profits were then barely enough to pay the rent and meet the expenses of hiring a girl to help in the house-work. So they lost heart and gave it up. Never to have a day's holiday; never an evening to yourself; to give up the Good Templar meetings; and never, or hardly ever, to get to church, made too severe a life, and it was only the consciousness of some much-desired accumulations in the savings bank that made it bearable at all. At the end of the twelve months there was £25 in the bank, whereas when the shop was taken there had been nothing.

What portion of this sum saved can be counted as coming from the shop and what from the house it is not possible to say exactly. An attempt was made, at my request to separate the two accounts by keeping two purses, and letting the house pay for all its supplies, but it failed; and what the house used was never considered part of the takings of the shop. Moreover, food eaten on

2 Children get many a sweet given them. It is a kind of commission paid to retain their patronage. Amongst publicans a little stock of sweets is sometimes kept for this purpose beneath the bar counter, and it is certainly well that the child's lips should be saved in this way from the temptation of taking a surreptitious sip from the jug.

the premises came naturally out of the stock. It seems probable that the shop paid fully 10*s* a week beyond its rent, and that the money from the lodgers paid for the maintenance and rent of the dwelling-house, and for all living expenses; or perhaps it might equally be said that the house earned 10*s* a week profit, if we burthen the shop with all the food consumed by the master and mistress. At any rate, the saving was strictly due to the combination of the two, and was earned by hard work and very abstemious lives.[3]

A shop doing such a business as this appears to afford a fair living for one person, but not for two. There must, however, be two persons more or less employed—one of whom is able to attend the shop when the other is out replenishing the stock. It thus lends itself to family effort. A young girl or an old grandmother can see to the shop, and, if shop and home are not divorced, it may be possible to go on with other work above or in a back room, and come to serve customers when summoned. It is manifest that a much larger business than that described might be done in such a shop, and possibly if less profit were sought on each transaction, the custom would increase, but I rather doubt it. Those who prefer to deal at the large shops would probably continue to do so; and those who find the little shop's situation and hours and friendly ways convenient—those whom it does not suit to keep stores of anything; to whom an expedition, fuly dressed, into the busy world of a main street is a serious undertaking, and the entrance into a large shop an affair of shyness and alarm—such as these do not strain at a slight difference in quality or in price. Nor would the difference in price be so very great to them, as in no case would they buy in anything but the smallest quantities. The shops

3 An exact account for four weeks' working—stock being taken at the beginning and end of the period—showed a profit of £3. 18*s* 3½*d* as having been made between house and shop beyond expense of living. This average, if maintained, would yield no less than £50 surplus in a year. The average was not maintained. Money has to be spent from time to time on furniture and on clothes, and at times several rooms in the house were not occupied for weeks together. The margin of possible saving is, however, remarkable and very suggestive.

which lay themselves out for supplying smaller shops must, and do, as a rule, protect their wholesale customers by maintaining full retail prices, and only reduce them when the quantities bought justify special terms.[4]

4 That they are ready to reduce on occasion is shown by the fact that my friends, although now buying for the house only, have been able to maintain the prices paid for the shop on articles which they are able to buy in fair quantities. For bread they pay 10½*d* for six loaves, and get "two-shilling tea" for 1*s* 4*d* a pound.

A PICTURE OF PAUPERISM

The Rooney family and its connections MARTIN ROONEY, aged eighty-six, now in Bromley Workhouse, married Ellen King, and this family has been prolific in paupers.[1]

First there is Mary Rooney, the wife of Martin's brother James, who was deserted by him in 1867 and has had relief in various forms since, including residence in the sick asylum for several years. She also applied on behalf of her married daughter, Mrs. Wilson, and her son Michael appears on the books; but with this branch we do not go at present beyond the second generation.

The old man Martin, who is now blind, applied for admission in 1878. His wife was then in hospital, having broken her leg when intoxicated. He had been a dock labourer, and had received £21 from the Company in 1857 on breaking a leg. He was admitted to Poplar Workhouse. A month later his wife, who is twenty-four years his junior, came out of hospital and was also admitted. The relieving officer made a note that he did not know a more drunken disreputable family than this one. He had seen the woman "beastly drunk" at all times of the day. From this time the old man remained in the house, but the woman went out several times, and when out was more than once seen in the streets in a drunken condition. She worked sometimes at the Lead Works, sleeping occasionally with her sons, at other times in various places—in water-closets, on stairs, &c. When her son Patrick was sent to prison for two months she went into the house. In 1888 she

---

Reprinted from "Industry Series," IV, 317–22, 394–97.

1 Fictitious names are used.

absconded, but in March, 1889, applied for readmission; she had fallen down and cut her face on the Saturday night before.

This couple had three children—Patrick, James, and Bridget. Patrick, born in 1853, by trade a stevedore is now in Poplar Workhouse. He was living with his mother in 1886, and she made application for medical attendance for him. He was suffering from rheumatism. He became worse and was sent to the sick asylum; was discharged, but again admitted a month or two later. Next year he was sent to Bromley Workhouse. He bears a bad character, and was in prison two months in 1888, and had one month in 1889 for attempting to steal some ropes. On coming out of prison he again applied for admission to the workhouse, and was sent to Poplar. He had a bad leg. He got work on the day he was discharged from the sick asylum, injured his leg, and was readmitted to workhouse. He served fourteen or fifteen years in the Royal Marines, and was discharged in 1885 for striking a petty officer. He was for this sentenced to six months' imprisonment by court-martial.

James, the second son, is a labourer, not married. He used to live with a woman name O'Reill, but left her, or she him, and is at present living with another woman.

Bridget, the eldest, born 1847, married John Murdock, a bricklayer's labourer, eight years older than herself, and there are four children, all boys. Murdock deserted his wife several times, and has been sent to prison for it. She in turn left him in 1877, and has been living with another man since. After this he was in Bromley House with the children. The two eldest were emigrated to Canada in 1880. The man's sister married Richard Bardsley, whose mother, a widow, is living at Bromley, and whose brother and brother's wife both had relief there.

Murdock had also a brother George, a general labourer, who lived with Anna Peel, a prostitute, whose parents are now in West Ham Workhouse. This woman applied in 1878 for sick asylum or medical relief for the man, and six months later wanted an order for the sick asylum herself. The relieving officer visited her two days later, but she had gone to her father at Stratford. In 1885 she came again and was admitted, suffering from syphilis. She had been living at a brothel in James Street for three years. George Murdock is now dead.

Murdock's mother married again, and both she and the man she married, Thomas Powles, are now in Bromley House. Powles, a dock labourer, had an accident, being burnt on a barge at Gravesend in 1875. He came to London then, and was admitted to the sick asylum. In 1877 he applied for relief, saying he had been knocking about, sleeping in barges, &c. He was admitted to the house. The next record was in 1883, when he asked for medicines for his wife. She had had a fall and was very ill. The relieving officer visited and found the home (one room) clean and comfortable; medical relief was given. In 1884 the man was admitted to the asylum, having met with another accident. He had been out of work some time then. In 1886 the man was ill again. He had not worked for five weeks, and they had lived by selling their things. He became worse, and was sent to the sick asylum in April. He did not stay long, but in two months' time applied again for relief outside. He had only earned 8*s* in the two months. Three days later the doctor recommended his removal to the sick asylum. Later in the same year his wife was taken ill: and finally they were both admitted to Bromley Workhouse.

We may now come to the relatives of Eliza King, Martin Rooney's wife. She had three sisters—Susan, Jane, and Sarah Anne. Of Susan we only know that she was in service at Guildford. Jane married Thomas Milward. In 1879 Milward applied for medical aid. He could not pay. Whatever money he gave his wife she spent in drink, and if he did not give her money she sold the furniture. Relieving officer made a note that he knew the woman as a notorious drunkard. On visiting he found her in the room drunk, while another woman (Mrs. Harvey of Spring Street) was "reclining on a heap of something which served as a bed," speechlessly drunk. The sick man was sitting by the fire. He always found the room thus, with no furniture, although the man earned from 30*s* to 40*s* a week. A month later the woman came and said her husband was dead, and that she wanted him buried by the parish. During 1880 and 1881 Mrs. Milward had medical relief frequently. She went to the Lead Works, and this work and drink seemed to be telling on her. Some time in 1882 she picked up with a man named Robert Belton, a carpenter, and she lived with him at intervals until 1885. This man was in Bromley Workhouse with a bad leg in 1879, and again later, and died in the sick asylum in 1885. Mrs. Milward says he was a great drunkard, which was pot calling kettle black. After Belton's death she injured her shoulder, and having sold up Belton's home and spent the money, applied for admission. She was sent to Poplar Workhouse, and since then has been in and out several times. She hurt her shoulder three times when out from the workhouse, probably through falling while drunk. On two occasions she walked to Guildford to see her sister.

Sarah Anne, the remaining sister, married Thomas Searle, who broke his neck falling downstairs when drunk. It is even said that some of his relatives threw him down in a quarrel. The family was reported as utterly disreputable and very drunken. Left a widow, she kept herself by washing, and does not seem to have any assistance from the parish herself. She had three children—Edward, Martha, and Francis. Of Edward there is happily no record. Martha married Peter Connor, and her aunt, Mrs. Milward, applied on her behalf for medical aid in 1882, she having hurt herself from falling from a ladder at the Lead Works. She had separated from her husband about three years before. He was a 'bus driver and lived at Notting Hill. After leaving him she lived a while at his sister's, and then went to her mother's in South London, and when her mother moved to this neighbourhood came with her. She was, however, living at the time with a dock labourer in a common lodging-house—a connection which did not last long.

Francis Searle cohabited with a woman named Augusta Hendy from 1877, he being then twenty-two, and he married her in 1885. They had three children. The woman asked for medical aid for her child Wilfrid in March, 1880. The relieving officer found the room filthy, with a bed on the floor. In May of the same year the man applied on behalf of the woman. She was found to be suffering from his ill-usage, had black eyes, and had been beaten much. From this time there were frequent applications for medical aid. In July, 1881, the woman was admitted to Poplar Workhouse, and was there confined of her third child Edith. In July, 1882, their landlady made application, saying that Francis Searle and Augusta Hendy were ill at her house. The relieving officer visited with the doctor. The woman came downstairs without shoes or stockings, a miserable-looking creature. The man, woman, and child were sent to Poplar. After this there were no more applications till 1886, when the man came for medical aid for his child Constance. In 1887 the man applied for medicine for the children; he said he "was married now." During the greater part of 1888

STEPNEY PAUPERISM

The method adopted for tabulating the causes of poverty was as follows. To each cause I affixed an alphabetical symbol, using a capital letter where the cause given is the principal one, and a small letter where it is contributory, thus:

Cause.	Principal.	Contributory.	Father or Husband.	Mother or Wife.	Both.
Crime	C	c	c^1	c^2	c^3
Vice	V	v	v^1	v^2	v^3
Drink	D	d	d^1	d^2	d^3
Laziness	L	l	l^1	l^2	l^3
Pauper association	P	p	p^1	p^2	p^3
Heredity	H	h	h^1	h^2	h^3
Mental disease	M	m	m^1	m^2	m^3
Temper (queer)	Q	q	q^1	q^2	q^3
Incapacity	I	i	i^1	i^2	i^3
Early marriage (girl)	G	g	g^1	g^2	g^3
Large family	F	f	...	...	...
Extravagance	E	e	e^1	e^2	e^3
Lack of work (unemployed)	U	u	u^1	u^2	u^3
Trade misfortune	T	t	t^1	t^2	t^3
Restlessness, roving, tramp	R	r	r^1	r^2	r^3
No relations	N	n	...	...	...
Death of husband	W	w	...	...	...
Desertion (abandoned)	A	a	...	...	...
Death of father or mother (orphan) . .	O	o	o^1	o^2	o^3
Sickness	S	s	s^1	s^2	s^3
Accident	X	x	x^1	x^2	x^3
Ill luck	Y	y	...	...	...
Old age	Z	z	z^1	x^2	z^3

As a further indication of character when the opposite of a fault is intended, the letter can be enclosed in brackets thus: (l) for industry, (d) for known sobriety or teetotaller.

There are few stories that cannot be very forcibly expressed by married condition, age, and three letters. As for example:

Martin Rooney . . .	M	86	I z d	Incapable old man, who drinks.
Patrick Rooney . . .	S	36	C h d	A criminal, hereditary pauper, and drunkard.
Sarah Truelove . . .	M	66	D z p	Drunken old woman of pauper associations.
John Curtis . . .	S	72	X z n	Single old man, withou any relations, who has had an accident.
Eliza Green . . .	Ch	4	O^1 d^2	Child whose father is dead and mother drinks.
Mary Carter . . .	W	59(?)	(dl) S n z	Elderly widow of good character for sobriety and industry, with no relations, and ill.
Eliza Knight . . .	M	60(?)	(dl) M^1 S	Husband insane. This woman, who is sick, has a good character for sobriety and industry.

In the summary which follows a few words of history are added, but it will be found that the alphabetical cipher gives the gist of each case.

SUMMARY OF STEPNEY STORIES

I.—*Indoor Relief.*

Note.— + implies longer period unknown. d = days. m = months. w = weeks.
Occupations in brackets those of husband or father.
(= Relations. { = Husband and wife.

No.	Sex.	Condition.	Age.	Occupation.	Cause of Pauperism.	Years Chargeable.	Story.	Known Pauper Relatives.
	(*Able-*	*bodied*)			(*Drink*)			
1	Male	Married	51	Pattern-maker	D	9	Wife had medicine in 1880. His family left him in 1884. Lost work through drink. In and out since.	Wife S d.[1]
2	Female	Widow	60	Lead worker	D p s	9	Drunken and immoral. Husband left her. Children are as bad. Often in and out of workhouse.	{ Son, S h d. Grandson, D^3c. Daughter, V s h. D'hter-in-law, H. w. v.
3	,,	,,	54	None	D w	11 +	Re-admitted in 1878. Had been sleeping in closets, on dust-heaps, and doorsteps. Drinks.	{ Late Husband, S. Brother, L m. Niece's Husband, No. 1036.
4	,,	,,	56	Needle-woman	D w	5	Husband died 1878. She sold his shop 18 months after for £20. Was passed from Poplar 1884, and has been chargeable to one or other parish since.	...
	(*Infirm*)							
5	Male	Married	68	Customs Officer	D	12	Dismissed for drink and theft. Partially paralysed. Wife lives with friends, who are comfortably off.	...
6	Female	Single	28	None	D	6 +	Chargeable many years. First record (1883) is that leave is stopped for returning drunk.	Brother, S.
7	Male	Widow'r	69	Carpenter	D	6	Seized with paralysis a few days before admission. Had been a great drinker.	...
8	,,	,,	81	General Labourer	D	8 +	Wife died in Sick Asylum (1881). Man was messenger at Relief Office, but drank too much.	{ Late wife, Sz. Sister-in-law, X.
9	,,	Married	61	,, (formerly School-master)	D	10	Had medical attendance from 1879 to 1887, when he was admitted. When out he lives at common lodging-houses and begs.	Wife, S d.[1]
(10	Male	Widow'r	42	Potman	D	11	Had medicine in 1879. Wife died in June 1888. Man was admitted to Sick Asylum with a bad leg in April 1889. His children became chargeable during the same month. His sister says poverty is due entirely to drink.	Late wife, No. 1072. Son, S.h.
11	Female (In	Child Schools)	13	...	D^1	11		Children, Nos. 11-13.
12	Male (In	Child Schools)	9	...	D^1	17d +		Sisters, Nos. 11, 13.
13	Female (In	Child Schools)	5	...	D^1	17d +		Father, No. 10.
{ 14	Male	Married	63	Cooper	D	9 +	First recorded application in 1875. In 1880 man said his wife was dead. She returned to him in 1881, and they have had medical and other relief since.	...
{ 15	Female	,,	69	None	Z d^1	7 +		...
(16	,,	Widow	66	Stallkeeper	D	9 m	Husband died 1873, and woman lived with her sons. Asked for relief in 1883. One son died in 1887, and was buried by Union. Mother and this son go into workhouse in 1888. Both drink to excess and use foul language.	...
(17	Male	Single	26	(Blind)	I d	9 m		...
(18	,,	,,	66	Coal work	D v e	9	Drunkard, has bad legs. Lived with No. 22 for 30 years. She left him in 1879.	{ Paramour, No. 22. Nephew's children, Nos. 19-21.
19	,,	Child	16	...	O^1 d^3 h	8	In 1881, the elder boy was sent to Smallpox Hospital with another brother and sister. Father died the same year, and mother got these three children into the schools.	Mother, No. 1006.
20	,,	,,	14	...	O^1 d^3 h	7		
21	Female	,,	13	...	O^1 d^3 h	7		
22	,,	Single	59	None	V p s	8	Had fits in 1881, and was admitted. Relieved several times since. Stays with daughters when out of workhouse.	Paramour, No. 18.
(23	,,	Child	5	...	D^3 v^3 h	5	These children have been frequently relieved with mother. Parents deserted them in April 1889, and they became chargeable. Father in prison for desertion.	Father, No. 1043. Grandmother, P d. Mother, D a.
(24	Male (In	,, Schools)	11	...	D^3 v^3 h	10		
25	,,	Widow'r	61	Coal backer	D v e	2	Drunken immoral family. Turned wife out in 1877; she died 1884. Admitted homeless in 1887.	Daughter, V d.

the children were ill, and several applications were made by the parents, the last being in November, 1888. This woman, Augusta Hendy, was the daughter of old Benjamin Hendy, known as "Red Ben," who is now in the workhouse, and every one of whose family has had relief. Benjamin Hendy, the younger, age thirty, a dock labourer, not married, was sent to the sick asylum at the end of 1880, and in 1884 went into Poplar Workhouse. Margaret, another of them, was a servant. In 1879 she hurt her face while staying with Augusta, and had medical aid. In November, 1883, she went into Poplar Workhouse and was confined of a male child (Robert), born in 1884. With this workhouse child we come at last to the end of the Rooney family and its connections.

8

EXPENDITURE AND STANDARD OF LIFE

WHEN a boy belonging to the working class in London has finished his schooling at thirteen or fourteen years of age, he readily finds work for which he is paid 4*s*, 5*s*, or 6*s* a week. As a general rule the poorer his future chances, the higher will be the immediate pay which he receives. In the already rare case of formal apprenticeship he usually foregoes all remuneration at the outset and, in addition, a premium will often have to be paid. In other cases the lad's earnings go to the man who teaches him, but this also is exceptional, and applies more commonly to father and son than to strangers. Thus for all practical purposes we may regard boys when they leave school as money-earners.

A boy usually hands over his money to his mother, who out of it gives him every morning pennies to be spent at lunch-time or needed for train or tramway fares, or allowed for pocket money. The rest of his earnings go towards the expenses of board, lodging, and clothes. It costs from 3*d* to 6*d* a day to feed a boy at home, including lunch, which, though generally eaten where he works, is prepared at home and carried in the pocket. The penny or so which may be added to be spent at the cocoa rooms would be additional.

As the boy grows older his weekly earnings rise. One who earned 5*s* when thirteen might be in receipt of any sum from 10*s* to 15*s* a week when he was eighteen years old, equal to a rise of from 1*s* to 2*s* each twelve months. After eighteen more and more divergence is shown, and by twenty or twenty-one some will be

---

Reprinted from "Industry Series," V, 319–25.

making men's wages while others are still earning no more than 14*s* or 15*s*. At some time between fourteen and eighteen years of age the arrangement between the boy and his mother will probably take a different shape. He prefers to keep his wages, and pay his mother for board and lodging. This change usually occur so soon as the mother would otherwise "make a profit" out of the boy; the same is true of girls also. Though it may savour more of business than the family tie, it is natural enough and has become customary.

The cost of keeping a young man in food varies a good deal, but depends mainly on the capacity of the housewife. A mother can satisfy her son more easily than others can, for it must be a very bad home if a lad does not prefer the food he obtains there to what he buys elsewhere. The money paid to the mother will vary from 5*s* to 10*s* a week, according to age and other circumstances, and out of this the boy or young man will obtain good value in board and lodging, washing and mending. On these terms, however small the profit may be, a mother is usually glad to have her son in the house. If the lad have no home, or for any other reason goes into lodgings, his living will cost him rather more. For the share of a room or, it may be, the half of a bed shared with some other young man, he would have to pay 3*s* or 3*s* 6 *d* a week, or about 4*s* if he have a small room to himself. This charge, besides furniture and bed linen, includes the use of the kitchen to sit in and the cooking and serving of meals, both of the simplest; the lodger finding the uncooked food himself. It may or may not cover ordinary washing and mending, but starched shirts and collars would, in any case, be extra, and are usually sent to a laundry. If cooked meals are provided, the charge for them will be 8*s* to 10*s* a week.

Altogether, living in this way would cost a young man 10*s* to 14*s* a week for board and lodging. This calculation assumes that substantially all meals are provided at home, being either eaten there or taken from there if eaten elsewhere. When meals are consumed away from the house, tea, coffee, cocoa, or beer will be bought in addition, and if food also is bought at a cook-shop or restaurant the expense of living is further increased.

A young man who is earning 15*s* a week has on this basis

over and above board and lodging, a small margin in hand—which is increased if he is living with his parents—with which to buy clothes and defray small charges;[1] and if his wages should be as much as 18*s* or 20*s* he is able to indulge in various pleasures. He may frequent the music-halls or pay for a bicycle by instalments, or take up any other pursuit, or indulge mildly in any extravagance to which his fancy turns, and may thus be considered well off. He might no doubt save money, but he rarely does so until he begins to look forward to marriage, and not always then. As he grows older his necessary weekly expenditures does not increase very much, while his pay, by the time he is twenty-two or twenty-three years old, rises to that of the full-grown man—to 20*s* or 30*s* or more, according to his trade. At this stage he generally marries and a new family life begins.

To pursue further this story of a working man's life, we will take the case of a man earning on the average 24*s* a week the whole year round, and suppose that he marries a young woman who has been earning 10*s* (out of which she probably has given her mother 7*s*, leaving 3*s* for her dress, &c.). When first married the wife will probably continue her work, and the married pair, living in lodgings with 34*s* a week joint income, are better off than they were when apart, and if careful will soon save money enough to furnish a home of their own. But if children are born, the wife can no longer earn money, and with growing expenditure and a diminished income pressure begins to be felt.

We will assume that there are two children and try to make up the budget of these people. Hitherto their income has been sufficient and they do not readily begin to stint themselves. Their food and firing will probably cost 14*s*; rent, lighting, and renewals of furniture, will not be less than 6*s*; and thus there will be about 4*s* a week (or £10 a year) left for clothes, tobacco, club money, doctor, and pleasure or holiday expenses.

It is evident that there is here no great margin for drink or

1 The margin that results from the economy of living at home may be at times absorbed by home claims of one kind or another, as for instance on account of widowed mothers, ailing fathers, or younger brothers and sisters; but pleasures probably count for less.

anything else; if drink is taken there will be so much the less money for other things. With three or four childern the position is naturally worse; but even so the income of this family would be 2*s or* 3*s a week above our supposed line of poverty*. With six or seven young children, and no increase of income, this household would fall below the line. The food obtained might still be sufficient, but the quantity of meat allowed must be small. Accommodation fully sufficient for four, and passing muster for five or six, would become very much crowded with eight or nine persons in the family. Clothes and furniture would become shabby, or go to pieces. Club payments would perhaps lapse; in case of illness, or trouble there would be nothing to fall back upon; and undoubted poverty, if not actual destitution, must supervene unless there is exceptionally good management on the part of the woman, and very helpful self-denying conduct on the part of the man. When these are present, results which would seem impossible are achieved.

Happily, in very many cases the earnings by this time have risen. They tend to rise as responsibilities increase, and a family of six or eight with 28*s* or 30*s* coming in may do nearly as well as one of four or five persons on 24*s*. Moreover, the extreme pressure passes as soon as the eldest children begin to earn money.

I have assumed that the wife does not work for money after her children are born, and it is at any rate evident that if she has several young children it could not be expected of her. She may, however, earn something by taking lodgers, forestalling in this way the position of a family with grown-up children. This resource, however, involves increased rent and more expenditure of capital for furniture than would be needed for the accommodation of elder children, and besides is subject to considerable risks from defaulting lodgers. In a lower class, amongst the chronically poor and very poor, when the man earns little or brings little home, and of course where there is no male bread-winner, the women almost always earn some money. The standard of life in many of these cases can be described only in negatives. It has rather been my aim to draw a rough picture of the most common lot—that of the fairly well fed and well clothed comfortable working class of London, and to indicate its risks and limitations.

Just as, starting from about 24*s* for a moderate family, each shilling a week less is a direct step into poverty, so each shilling a week more tells no less quickly in the opposite direction. As the weekly income rises from 20*s* to 22*s*, 24*s*, 26*s*, 28*s*, and 30*s*, not only does the whole standard of life gradually rise, but what goes for even more, that which is aimed at is attained. In this respect it is mainly the sum that regularly reaches the home that must be considered. What is done with the money, and the amount of comfort it yields, depends almost entirely on the wife. It may be said that habitual expenditure on extras of any kind, and even extravagance or squandering, if of such a description as can be laid aside at need, provide a kind of reserve. But wastefulness, whether on the part of the husband or the wife, affects the comfort of the home as much as, or perhaps more than, the presence of three or four additional children, so that with wasteful ways earnings of 24*s* or 28*s* become no more than 22*s* or 26*s*, or even less for any good they do.

This is no less true, though it may be less serious, when the money earned is 35*s*, 40*s*, or even 50*s*; and many a family which might be living in easy comfort is dragged down in this way. Otherwise a wide difference is standard of life, amounting almost to a class distinction, is noticeable between those who earn less and those who earn more than 35*s* a week, or thereabouts.

It is not possible to say with certainty or exactness what proportion of the population are living above, and what proportion below, this line, or any other line that might be chosen. The difficulties in the way of such calculations have been dwelt upon in the first part of this volume. Rates of wages are both incomplete and incorrect as records of income, because of the subsidiary earnings of children or wife, and because of periods out of work and other forms or irregularity of employment. Moreover, no returns that can be obtained represent fully the whole body of workers. We can, therefore, only arrive at an estimate. The result of all our inquiries make it reasonably sure that one-third of the population are on or about the line of poverty or are below it, having at most an income which one time with another averages 21*s* or 22*s* for a small family (or up to 25*s* or 26*s* for one of larger size), and in many cases falling much below this level. There may be another third who have perhaps 10*s* more, or, taking the year round, from 25*s* to 35*s* a week, among whom would be counted, in addition to wage-earners, many retail tradesmen and small masters; and the last third would include all who are better off. The first group, who are practically those who are living two or more persons to each room occupied, contains our classes A, B, C, and D. The next, with on the average nearly one room to each person, consists of Class E, with portions of F and G; while the final group includes the rest of F and G and all of Class H—that is, all those who employ servants as well as some of those who do not. Of the first, many are pinched by want and all live in poverty, if poverty be defined as having no surplus. The second enjoy solid working-class comfort, and of the third group the worst-off live in plenty and the best-off in luxury.

9

CROWDING AND APPARENT POVERTY

In the poorer parts of London most of the houses have a frontage of from 12 to 15 ft. only, and of this about 3 ft. is devoted to entrance passage and stairs. The front room on the first floor has usually two windows and occupies the whole breadth of the house. This may be repeated on the floor above. The other rooms are all somewhat smaller. The largest size commonly found is about 12 by 14 ft. and the smallest perhaps 8 ft. by 8 ft. The height from floor to ceiling varies from 8 to 10 ft.

It is with rooms of this character, containing on an average about 1000 cubic ft. of space, but varying among themselves to the extent indicated above, that we have usually to deal when the number of rooms occupied by a family is taken as a measure of poverty. Two or more persons making their home in one such room, or four or more in two such rooms, or six or more in three, are accounted crowded and therefore presumably poor; the assumption being that if they were not poor they would allow themselves more space. It is evident that this theory has many limitations, and affords but a rough test of poverty. Not only does the actual size of the room or rooms come into qeustion, but much depends on the meaning of "person." A mother and her baby count for two, but one room is all that they really require, whereas for two adults to eat, sleep and live in one room is a condition of crowding which would hardly be endured unless poverty compelled. Whether a family of four in two rooms is more crowded or less so than two families of two persons each occuping one room

Reprinted from "Industry Series," V, 3–12.

would probably depend on the management. With orderly arrangements the enlarged family might gain—but if disorder reigned the increase in numbers would undoubtedly aggravate discomfort. But in comparing large bodies of men one with another, such considerations may be ignored; for in almost every trade we shall find every description of family living in every kind of house in somewhat similar proportions.

Another irregularity springs from the greater difficulty found in obtaining house-room in some quarters than in others, and the consequent high rents paid by those who must give whatever is necessary to enable them to be near their work. These people, for workmen, may be well off, and quite beyond the pinch of poverty, yet they have to endure and make the best of very limited accommodation. A still more common case in which the test fails is where house-room is so plentiful and rents so low, or their payment so easily evaded, that even the poorest people need not be crowded in the rooms of which they make their homes. In such cases a low percentage of crowding may be combined with a high degree of poverty.

In spite of these divergencies, we are probably justified in assuming, that on the average crowding does provide a reasonably fair measure of poverty; and some support is given to this assumption by the fact that the total percentage of poverty indicated by this test agrees almost exactly with that reached in our previous inquiry by a different method, about 30 per cent. of poverty being shown in both ways. But the tests applied are very rough, and the results attained do not pretend to be more than an approximation to the truth.

The meaning attached throughout to the word "poverty," and the distinction drawn between the "poor" and the "very poor" must also be borne in mind. The "poor" have been defined or described as including alike those whose earnings are small because of irregularity of employment and those whose work though regular is ill-paid. They are further defined as those whose means are barely sufficient for decent independent life. Though not in actual "want," they would be the better for more of everything. Their lives are an unending struggle and lack comfort, but these people are neither ill-nourished nor ill-clad according to any standard that can reasonably be used. And finally, to come to figures, I have suggested 18*s* to 21*s* per week for a moderate-sized family as the income I have had in my mind. The "very poor"—who answer more or less to the very crowded, *i.e.* those living three or more to a room—are those who from any cause fall below this standard.

Although the average results may be fairly trustworthy, there is a very considerable difference according as the test of crowding is applied in the inner or in the outer circle of London. This difference, which we find in almost every trade, is largely due to the question of rent, but it also responds to the broad circumstance that the poorer representatives in nearly every trade live nearest to, and the better off furthest from, the centre of London.

It must be remembered moreover that we can only deal with *apparent* poverty. A man who earns good wages may spend but little of them on his home. Such is notoriously the case in trades where the rate of pay is high and the work intermittent, especially when wages are earned by great physical exertion, as for instance with the coal-porters. We are compelled by our method to treat the desire for sufficient house accommodation as a force acting uniformly or proportionately on all, but this is by no means always the case.

Taking into account so far as possible these considerations and limitations, we may proceed to compare the trades and groups of trades into which we have divided the people of London. It appears that, tested by the crowded conditions in which they live, street-sellers, coal-porters and dock-labourers are the poorest sections of the population (*see* Table I). On the whole, street-sellers take the lead, having, if we exclude those returned as employers, 69 per cent, of families living two or more persons in each room. Coal-porters come next with 65 per cent., followed closely by the 63 per cent. of dock-labourers. These two latter sections consist almost entirely of the employed class.

It is noteworthy that two-thirds of the costermongers and two-thirds of the dock-labourers live in the inner ring. As a rule these proportions are reversed: amongst coal-porters the homes of only one-third are in the inner ring.

The fact that crowded homes are not always a test of poverty where house accommodation is difficult to obtain and rents are high, does not apply to any very great extent in these sections. With costermongers the proportion rises to 71 per cent. in the inner, and falls to 55 per cent. in the outer circle; with coal-porters the comparative rates are 74 and 59 per cent.; while docks-labourers have about 62 per cent. of crowding wherever they live.

Finally, if we test these sections by the extreme cases of crowding, namely those in which three or more persons occupy each room, we find the same order. Street-sellers again lead with no less than 36 per cent., coal-porters come next with 30 per cent., and dock-labourers follow with 28½ per cent.

In no other occupations are the signs of poverty and discomfort quite so great, but the section of general labourers is not far behind in this unenviable competition. These labourers are, however, a selection of the poorest out of many employments, and therefore do not enter quite fairly into comparison. A large number of them are, indeed, actually employed as dock-labourers, coal-porters, or street-sellers, but being illiterate or without any special pride in their calling, put themselves down in the census schedule merely as "labouring men." That this must be so is certain, because the totals given in the census, especially for dock-labourers and costermongers, are undoubtedly very much below the true figures, and on the other hand the number of "general labourers" (returned as nearly eighty thousand) would not otherwise be accounted for. General labourers include also a proportion of loafers (though of these a large number would claim a trade), but for the rest are made up of contingents from many occupations, being usually men employed in unspecialized work who do not associate themselves—at any rate by name—with any particular trade, but are able to move from one kind of business to another, doing, wherever it may be required, labour of a rough character. To some extent, of course, this general heading may also comprise men whose work, though unskilled and simply called "labour," requires special practice. But when labourers are specially employed, and particularly when detailed to assist handicraftsmen, they are fully entitled and generally disposed to call themselves by the name of the trade in which they give assistance, as bricklayers' labourers, labourers in gasworks, or chemical labourers, &c. If returned in this way they cease, from the point of view of the census, to be "general labourer," and are included with bricklayers, gasworkers, &c. Some, however, return themselves in one way and some in the other, and the result is a confusion much to be deplored, but for which it is difficult to suggest any remedy, so long at least as the householder and not the enumerator is responsible for the correct filling up of the schedule.

Of the eighty thousand general labourers, those who are assistants in skilled trades are better off than the rest, and most of them will be found living in the outer circle, where are situated the factories at which they work. On the whole, the section shows 58½ per cent. of crowding, or omitting a few employers (returned, we suppose, as "master labourers"), 59½ per cent. This rate rises to 70 per cent. in the inner, but falls to 51½ per cent. in the outer ring. Of extreme crowding there is 26 per cent.

Next in order of apparent poverty comes the great body of carmen with 56 per cent. of crowded families, or 58 per cent. if employers are omitted. The percentage of crowding is 62 in the inner and 50 in the outer circle, and amongst them there is 27 per cent. of extreme crowding.

These five sections—street-sellers, coal-porters, dock-labourers, general labourers and carmen—together include 88,469 heads of families, or a total of 399,690 persons, of whom no less than 235,281 exist under crowded conditions, while 109,390 are so crowded as to be living three or more persons to a room. Even in the outer circle, where rents are comparatively moderate, over 114,000 of these people are to be found living two or more persons to each room occupied.

After allowing for all possible limitations, these figures indicate an appalling amount of poverty and discomfort among those engaged in these occupations.

The second grade in the comparison we are attempting to make is occupied by a group from the building trades—bricklayers (including scaffolders and labourers), plasterers (including whitewashers) and painters, of whom many are very irregularly em-

TABLE I.—*Sections arranged in order of apparent poverty of heads of families* (1891).

SECTIONS.	PERCENTAGE OF CROWDING.		SECTIONS.	PERCENTAGE OF CROWDING.	
	All Families.	Excluding Employers.		All Families.	Excluding Employers.
Costers and street-sellers	65	69	Millers, &c.	34	39½
Coal-porters	64	65	Plumbers	34	39
Dock-labourers	62½	63	Tobacco workers	33	42
General labourers	58½	59½	India-rubber, &c.	33	39½
Carmen	56	58	Musical instruments, &c.	32½	37
Bricklayers	53½	55	Carpenters and joiners	31½	33
Municipal labour, &c.	53	54½	Hatters	30½	36½
Plasterers & paperhangers	51	53	Seamen	30½	33
Paper manufactures	49	55	Chemicals	29½	36
Painters and glaziers	49	52½	Dyers and cleaners	28½	37
Hemp, jute, and fibre	47	52½	Soap, candles, and glue	28½	34
Masons	45½	49	Railway service	28	28
Cab and omnibus service	45½	48	Engineering, &c.	27½	29
Cabinet makers, &c.	45	52	Silk and fancy textiles	27	33
Boot and shoe-makers	45	52	Bakers and confectioners	26½	38
Woollens and carpets	45	51½	Surgical, &c., instruments	26	30
Warehousemen, &c.	45	46	Police, &c.	26	26
Gasworks service	44	44½	Dock and wharf service	25½	27½
Glass and earthenware	43	48	Dress-makers, &c.	24½	29½
Brass, copper, tin, lead, &c.	42½	47	Butchers & fishmongers	23½	34
Machinists	42½	44	Gardeners, &c.	23½	26
Railway labour	42	43	Jewellers, &c.	22½	28
Blacksmiths	41½	45	Milk-sellers	22	30
Bookbinders	41½	44	Shipwrights, &c.	22	24
Factory labour (undef.)	41½	42	Watches and clocks	21	28
General shop-keepers	40½	47	Art and amusement	19½	23½
Extra service	40½	45	Builders	19	35½
Brush-makers	40½	46	Coal, wood, & corn dealers	18½	32
Tailors	40	47	Stationers	17½	25
Locksmiths, &c.	39½	43½	Grocers, &c.	15	24½
Country labour	38½	44½	Ironmongers, &c.	15	24
			Booksellers, &c.	15	20½
Sundry workers in iron and steel	38	42	Civil & municipal service	14	15
			Medicine	13	20
Brewers and mineral water makers	37½	42½	Army and navy	10½	15
Carriage building	37	41	Commercial clerks	10½	11½
Leather dressing, &c.	36½	43	Publicans	10	22½
Engine drivers (undef.)	36½	38	Drapers	10	15½
Coopers	36	38	Literature and science	7	9½
Trimmings, &c.	35½	43	Religion	6½	9
			Merchants, brokers, &c.	6	13
Shirt-makers and seamstresses	35½	37½	Education	5½	6½
Lightermen	35	37	Lodging & coffee-houses	5	10
Printers	34½	37	Law	5	9½
Saddlery, harness, &c.	34	41	Architects, &c.	4	7

NOTE.—As in previous volumes, the deductions for employers and thei families have been made on the assumption that they will live under bette conditions than the bulk of those they employ.

ployed. To these we have added those engaged in drainage, &c., including scavengers and others employed in the care of the streets. Bricklayers have 55 per cent., municipal labour 54½ per cent., plasterers 53 per cent., and painters 52½ per cent. of crowding, employers being omitted in each case. To this group may be added, as of kindred employment, the masons and their labourers, although they are somewhat better off, showing only 49 per cent. of crowding. In these sections taken together we find 50,842 heads of families (including employers) and a population of 238,229 persons, of whom 120,045 live under crowded conditions, 51,554 being very crowded. In this case 75,000 of the crowded live in the outer circle, where there is least excuse for so unfavourable a condition of life.

Having now dealt with the sections which include the great bulk of the labourers, we pass to manufacture and other employments in which the proportion of those living in crowded homes falls gradually from 50 to less than 5 per cent. This is shown in the summary in which both employers and employed are included.

Fully one-half of the population (omitting inmates of institutions) show from 30 to 65 per cent. of crowding, and in this half are included by far the greater number of ordinary industrial occupations. Engine and machine makers and those engaged in the manufacture of chemicals or in dyeing and cleaning (all very modern trades) fall just below 30 per cent. Lower rates apply to the professional classes, shop-keepers, commercial clerks, police, and a few old established highly skilled employments, such as silk weaving and watch making. It may be that in these cases there is less apparent crowding because the accommodation sometimes includes the workshop. If employees only are considered, the list of occupations with less than 30 per cent. of crowding would be still further restricted.

The question then arises, who are all these people in every trade who lead so pinched an existence, and why is it that their means are so restricted or their standard of house room so low?

Before any complete answer can be given to these questions it will be necessary to sum up and bring to a point much of the in-

TABLE II.—*Summary Statement.* (*Arranged in order of crowding.*)

OCCUPATIONS. [Figures in parentheses indicate proportion of crowding.]	Families.	Population.	Crowded 2 or more in each room.	Percentage crowded.
Costers and street-sellers (65·2), coal-porters (63·9), dock-labourers (62·5), general labourers (58·5), carmen (56·2)	88,469	399,690	235,281	65 to 55
Bricklayers (53·7), municipal labour (53·1), plasterers (50·8), painters (48·8), masons (45·7)	50,842	238,229	120,045	55 to 50
Paper (49·0), hemp (46·8), warehouse-men (45·2), woollens, &c. (45·0)	23,223	99,945	45,707	50 to 45
Cab and omnibus service (45·7)	32,588	144,237	65,877	45
Cabinet-makers (45·2), boot and shoe-makers (44·9), machinists (42·5), tailors (40·0)	74,110	333,898	145,685	45 to 40
Glass and earthenware (43·1), brass, tin, lead, &c. (42·7), factory labour undefined (41·7), book-binders (41·3), extra service (40·5), brush-makers (40·3)	61,993	229,991	94,513	do.
Gasworks service (43·9), railway labour (42·1), blacksmiths (41·6), general shop-keepers (40·3), locksmiths (39.6)	25,743	120,045	49,699	do.
Iron and steel-workers (38·2), carriage building (36·8), leather dressing, &c. (36·7), coopers (35·9), saddlers (34·2), plumbers (33·9), tobacco workers (33·0), india-rubber, &c. (32·9), musical instruments and toys (32·4), carpenters (31·5)	66,700	312,631	106,122	40 to 30
Country labour (38·7), brewers and mineral water makers (37·6), engine drivers, &c., undef. (36·7), shirt-makers, &c. (35·6), trimmings, &c. (35·5), lightermen (35·0), printers (34·3), millers (34·1), hatters (30·5), seamen (30·6)	56,796	242,641	84,993	do.
Chemicals (29·3), soap, candles, &c. (28·7), dyers and cleaners (28·5), engineering (27·5), silk (26·9), surgical, &c., instruments (26·1), dressmakers, &c., (24·3), jewellers, &c. (22·4), shipwrights (22·1), watches and clocks (21·0)	50,460	203,793	52,358	30 to 20
Railway service (27·8), bakers, &c. (26·3), police (25·9), dock service (25·3), gardeners (23·6), butchers and fishmongers (23·4), milk-sellers (22·2)	65,914	310,576	78,153	do.
Art and amusement (19·3), civil and municipal service (13·8), medicine (12·6), army and navy (10·4), literature (7·0), religion (6·3), education (5·3), law (5·2)	60,040	270,793	30,190	20 and under
Builders (19·1), clerks (10·6), merchants (6·1), architects (4·0)	64,566	308,582	31,318	do.
Corn, &c., dealers (18·5), stationers (17·3), ironmongers, &c. (15·3), grocers, &c. (15·2), booksellers (14·9), drapers (9·9), publicans (9·9), lodging-house keepers (4·9)	59,161	294,248	36,399	do.
Total	780,665	3,509,299	1,176,340	33
Domestic service *	19,224	70,453		
Pensioners, means, institutions and servants in charge	126,877	631,991		
Total of families and population	926,766	4,211,743		

* Includes only those occupied in service who have homes of their own; the others are enumerated with the families they serve.

formation gathered together in the preceding volumes of this work. As a first step, we may carry forward our comparisons into earnings and into the relation between standard of earnings and standard of life.

III. Religious Influences Series

10

AN EXAMPLE: WESTMINSTER AND SOUTH PIMLICO

Old Westminster

BEFORE passing to the wealth and fashion of the streets and squares surrounding Hyde Park and Kensington Gardens, and before we are led on through these portals to the problems of the Outer West, we may pause for a moment at Westminster where we have a district hardly less remarkable than the City of London itself: the centre and citadel not of London indeed, but of the Empire.

The Abbey is the nucleus round which modern Westminster has grown up, and it is the Abbey which, with its associations and monuments, remains the Valhalla and Mecca of our race. Near it Royal Palaces were erected, succeeded by the present Houses of Parliament, to which, stately though the later buildings be, the Great Hall, dating from the time of William Rufus, lends a dignity unequalled in anything that has been added; and near it, too, have sprung up the public buildings and offices of British rule. In the forefront is the parish of St. Margaret, which, with the adjacent portion of St. Martin's-in-the-Fields, is packed full of public buildings and palaces. Here there are hardly any residents, and the business done is practically confined to the Public Service. The main duties of the police are to guard the national buildings and monuments; those of the Church to maintain the sanctity of the Abbey, to fulfil some occasional parliamentary functions, and to welcome at St. Margaret's Church a fashionable congregation.

Reprinted from "Religious Influences," III, 73–91.

This seat of Empire is approached by three great thoroughfares: Westminster Bridge, from the further end of which radiate wide roads South and East; Whitehall, connecting Westminster through Trafalgar Square with the heart of London; and Victoria Street, through which we reach the wealthy district to be described in our next chapter. From the actual South, along the riverside, there is at present no very good approach; but an extension of Grosvenor Road to the Houses of Parliament by means of the widening of Millbank Street is sanctioned, and the acquisition of the river-bank will surely form a part of any scheme of improvements that may be arranged.

Behind the Abbey and Dean's Yard to the South, is found a group of poor streets, the condition of which forms the principal subject of this chapter. This little district of ancient poverty lies mainly within the parishes of St. John, St. Matthew, and St. Stephen, but to it must be added part of Christ Church, for under the influence of demolitions the poor are now occupying new ground further South. To the South-West, in the portion of Pimlico included in our sketch map, the conditions are, by comparison, entirely modern, but present an admixture of shabby gentility and vice, hardly less depressing than the low life of the old slums; and both areas suggest homilies when contrasted with the wealth and fashion of Belgravia and Mayfair.

Residential Westminster as a whole is being subjected to all the changes which accompany rebuilding; of which much has already taken place, whilst more is contemplated. In the older parts, at any rate, the area of poverty is diminishing; but the final results are still doubtful. Nothing so systematic as the action of the late Duke of Westminster in Mayfair is in progress, or could perhaps be expected. The Ecclesiastical Commissioners, who are the greatest landholders, are either less enterprising or, it may be, have less control; but it is thought that their duty as trustees is not incompatible with a wide outlook for the public good; they might, it is suggested, take more advantage of the opportunities obtained when leases fall in, or in the more flagrant cases of neglectful ownership might use their power to exercise some pressure upon the leaseholders in advance. There have been schemes before

Parliament for dealing with the river front, but so far they have come to nothing. Something more complete and far-reaching is needed, and could be secured perhaps by some public improvement scheme, if undertaken by the new Borough of Westminster.

At present the changes progress without any general plan. In some cases, when old houses are replaced by flats built for an altogether different class of occupant, the poor remain in the adjacent houses alongside of the rich; but when this is so there seems to be no sign that they have any effect on each other. A mixture of class is realized, but without any advantage arising from it. Moreover, the present state of things is transitory. The poor will leave; old houses in which they live are doomed, and it is unlikely that many of them will be accommodated in the new buildings to be erected. The new population will be of a different character; but it is very much to be hoped that it will include a considerable working-class element.

Apart from the well-to-do, the population as it exists consists mainly of two classes; the larger and increasing section being working people, as contrasted with the less reputable inhabitants of such a spot as Great Peter Street and the hangers on of charity. Among the working section there are "brewers" men, policemen, postmen, and railway employees; a good many waiters engaged at clubs, men working at the Army and Navy Stores, and mechanics of various kinds. It is such inhabitants as these that Westminster should if possible retain. There are also many respectable widows employed as office cleaners who would rightly find here their home.

In the district of ancient poverty just mentioned we have a very large area demanding reconstruction, much of which is, at any rate, extremely well suited for permanent working-class accommodation. The process of rebuilding is going on piecemeal, and only requires a guidance and an encouragement in that direction, to be arranged with fair prospect of profit for working-class dwellings of the block type, which, without being so costly and high in rental as to exclude the regularly employed among the present inhabitants, might yet do something to raise the standard of health and happiness in Westminster.

In no neighbourhood would such dwellings be more useful, or more likely, if well designed and well built, to be permanently profitable. For no other purpose is a considerable portion of the district equally suitable. It is not so subject as are the parts of London which surround the City, to enhancement of values from the competition of business premises (the extension of the Army and Navy Stores is exceptional); nor is much of it so suitable or so likely to be used for rich men's houses as Upper Chelsea. The area required for offices and chambers will always be limited; and though it is difficult to forecast the ways of fashion, it is perhaps not likely that the area so occupied will extend far from the frontages provided by Victoria Street on the one side, and the river embankment on the other. Elsewhere, in the less desirable situations, if flats are built, but are not well tenanted, there is the danger, almost amounting to certainty, that unsatisfactory characters will get in, as has so largely happened in the adjoining district to the South and West of Vauxhall Bridge Road.

Thus the future of this area may be largely governed by the way in which it is laid out; by the class of building encouraged by the public authority, and by the possibility of bringing the owners of property into line on some scheme advantageous to all.

At present the disreputable classes are still very much in evidence in Westmister. This is especially the case in the parishes of St. Matthew and St. John, but even St. Margaret's, although mostly given up to public buildings, still contains in Lewisham Street one rather black spot. A very bad name is given to this street by the police and those accustomed to visit it, and it is rather extraordinary that such a place should exist here, so near to where fashion lingers in Queen Anne's Gate. The church has, with remarkable and commendable enterprise, secured the lease (with twenty-one years to run) of seventeen houses in this street; and the clergy hope, by combining the power of ownership with the exercise of other influence, to change its character. They admit that in the process some of the old inhabitants will have to go, but hope to retain most. It is a very interesting experiment. The length of lease gives it full scope, otherwise the special situation is such that this property, if it were available, would almost surely be taken for other purposes than working-class dwellings.

There is nothing much lower to be found anywhere in London than the life led in some of the Westminster courts and streets. The doors of the houses standing open disclose bare passages and stairways; dirty women congregate on the doorsteps, dirty children play in the gutter, and larrikins loaf at the street corners; there is always a great deal of drinking, and there is some crime. The common lodging-houses accommodate the lowest classes, both male and female. If these people are disturbed by the demolitions, clearances and evictions in one part, they reappear in another, and they carry their manners and customs into the new quarters wherever they live.

Nor does low life furnish the only disreputable people. There are blocks of mansions containing very "dubious occupants"; women whose "sole claim to respectability is that they are well dressed"; not alone "kept women," who may be very careful in behaviour, but also many stylish prostitutes. These elegant people are even less amenable to religious influence than their rough sisters of the low streets "who have never known what virtue is."

Nor is it the disreputable classes only with whom the churches find it difficult to deal. The fashionable dwellers in flats are seldom seen at church, and are not easily approached. Even if not of the "vagrant" class—those whose rooms are let and re-let time and again without number; who come and go, no one knowing who or what they are—even if of the highest respectability, these flat-dwellers are continually on the move in and out of town, and cannot be relied on to share in either the worship or work of the churches. Finally, the working classes, though they are civil enough and quite accessible to visits, "don't care." The binding together of such elements is like "twisting a rope of sand." Even the Roman Catholic priest speaks of the difficulties of the task as regards many of his flock; for ever "hunting, hunting, hunting," confronted by leaden indifference.

On the whole, the numbers of the disreputable poor have decreased. Besides being shuffled from street to street, and parish to parish, within the district, there has been a considerable exodus, partly into Lambeth, but mainly to Battersea and to Fulham, where a new Alsatia is being found.

The churches are, however, alive, and, in spite of the difficulties I have referred to, are fairly filled, both morning and evening, with congregations collected partly from outside and partly from amongst the upper working-class dwellers in some of the new buildings. The church services are extremely attractive. In several instances the eloquence of the preaching is remarkable and far-famed, and in at least one the music given is exquisite. The work done amongst the poor has little connection with any of this. The services neither attract the poor themselves, nor do they form the bond amongst those who from religious motives seek to minister to their wants. Services are held in special mission rooms, in the hope of reaching those who do not come to church, but to very little purpose. Women will go where they are helped, and in some of these a rather debased form of piety is aroused. Men seldom attend at all. It is the old story of middle-class residents, the few there are in this locality are probably Nonconformists.

There is much systematic visitation, and on this rests the value of the religious work of the churches among their parishioners; there are also some notable social organizations. In St. Stephen's parish, where there were already large schools, a Technical Institute was established, which obtained six hundred students, and has recently been taken over by the Technical Education Board. There is also a large club which is made the centre of much social work, including a "self-help" organization, based on a modified system of co-operation, in which ordinary retail shops are dealt with, the special discounts for cash being paid over to the Society for periodical distribution among the members. The success of the Society has been so remarkable that operations have had to be strictly limited to the parish, for they threatened to grow beyond all bounds, and much detailed work is involved which is given voluntarily. Herein lies the difficulty of such efforts; the amount of social work falling on the clergy becomes overwhelming. Compared to it, "Sunday is child's play." At St. Matthew's, too, the activity is great and the work unceasing. In a letter to his parishioners, the vicar deprecates the idea that the multiplicity of organizations are any true test of progress, which, he writes, is something that "the world's coarse thumb and finger" fails to measure; but the organizations exist and are full of life. The parish magazine is largely occupied with the accounts of concerts and entertainments. Much effort is made, much money is raised and spent, the pressure of their work on the clergy is great, and the results are disappointing.

The work of the Church of England is by far the most important in Westminster, but there are two or three undenominational missions, and some City Missionaries, who obtain a measure of support from the better working class though they also fail to rouse any genuine religious response among the poor. Common lodging-houses are visited and services held therein, but, from a religious point of view, no effect can be traced. That a certain friendliness results is, however, indicated by a cricket match we hear of between eleven men from one of these houses and eleven missionaries. There is as great difficulty in touching the lowest stratum by anything the missionaries can do as by the "numerous and varied" social organizations of the churches. For instance, it is said, no club really gets the rough boys as a class, though in every club there may be some tamed specimens, caught and gradually educated. Take it all in all, little spiritual progress can be claimed. It is honestly confessed to be "terribly slow work."

The story of one of these missions is remarkable. It began as a ragged school, to which were added a working men's club and youths' institute. All these have passed away. The men were allowed to manage the club, but three secretaries in succession misappropriated money. The youths' institute died with the lady who managed and subsidized it, and the Ragged Day school was killed by the introduction of Board schools. There still remain the Sunday school and mothers' meeting, and, in addition, scantily-attended services are held. The distinctive work lies in the management of a large block of buildings, built with money borrowed at 3 per cent., and let at low, but economic rents. The tenants are not selected in regard to any personal connection with the mission work, but it is their landlord, and makes their welfare its main object. This work has been largely the employment of one man's spare hours; a professional man retired from active work and growing old.

The Baptists have a church in which, as usual, we find a gathering of small tradesmen and clerks, with a larger proportion of the working class than is seen elsewhere. But the total numbers of the congregation are small. Many of its members come from a distance, being former residents who have moved away. This church is not of the austere order of Baptist, and gives "Pleasant Saturday Evenings" for the people, which are "always full, and sometimes crammed"; its temperance work, too, is enlivened with entertainments, and amongst the young people the work of mutual improvement includes gymnastics, football, and other games. The church seeks to do its duty by the poor who live near with open-air services and by visitation. To this end a band of twenty visitors has been organized, who call at seven hundred dwellings on Sunday, or during the week—no doubt to leave some printed matter.

The Wesleyans have a large, but not very well filled church, partly connected with, and partly overshadowed by, their great college in Horseferry Road. It is situated close to the blackest street in Westminster. They, too, attempt systematic visiting, and have Saturday night entertainments to attract the people. The congregation, beyond the students from the college, who fill it up in term time, consists mostly of shop assistants, and others of the same regularly employed, respectable, well-dressed class.

All alike—churches, chapels, and missions—have their mothers' meetings and Sunday schools, and the churches have also large day schools. Nothing is wanting. Attractive and varied services, eloquent preaching, systematic visiting, eagerness to meet and help the poor, the children taught and the mothers sought, no lack of means, a pouring out of energy concentrated on some small group of streets within a quarter of a mile of Westminster Abbey and the Houses of Parliament; and yet it can hardly be denied that such improvement as can be traced in the morals or habits of the people is mainly due, not to all this, but to structural alterations; and that it is to these physical changes, to the destruction of bad property, combined with better policing and improved sanitary supervision, and not to religion or even education, that we have chiefly to look for further improvement in the future.

This part of Westminster still contains over two thousand Roman Catholics in charge of a settlement of Jesuit Fathers, who in this case undertake parish work. Their flock is, however, decreasing with the displacement of the poor, who were largely Irish or Cockney Irish. A better class are coming in, but they are not Catholics. To the remaining poor a good deal goes in charity. "They are awful beggars," and even by the Roman Catholics the danger is felt here of the people learning to look upon the priest as a person who may be expected to give.

The parishes of St. Mary, St. James the Less, and Holy Trinity, with the southern portion of St. John, contain the overflowings of the poor, and in them we encounter the same problems, only (except as regards St. John's) in a less acute form. We find also a quiet, though not less earnest, effort to cope with them; but, to see how small a part religious observance plays in the lives of the people, one need only compare the numbers who attend the services at the three churches first mentioned, to which no outsiders come, and where consequently the nakedness of the land is visible, with the total population for whose spiritual wants the churches are supposed to provide.

The prospects and conditions are much the same throughout. Changes impending, leases falling in, slums to be cleared, and the principal ground landlord the Ecclesiastical Commissioners.

This portion of the district, though not yet scheduled for destruction to the same extent, nevertheless falls in with the great opportunities that offer for carrying out the noble plan of reconstruction afforded by the river front, and can contribute as its share the large open space resulting from the destruction of Millbank Penitentiary, already partly occupied by the Tate Gallery, by a building for the Army Service Corps, and, further from the river, by blocks of County Council dwellings.

In the district at large, to whatever combination of causes it may be set down, it is recognised that there has been improvement. As to crime, so far as the amelioration is local, it is undoubtedly due to clearances, and some effect is attributed to the destruction of the prison, round about which the discharged prisoners and ticket-of-leave men were, it is said, apt to linger. In addition, Westminster has fully shared in improved police administration, and though one of the missionaries speaks of daylight robberies occurring in Great Peter Street quite recently, he also says that lady cyclists now pass through, a thing they would not have ventured to do a few years ago. As to drink, many public-houses have been closed mainly through the action of the Ecclesiastical Commissioners, but I do not gather that there is any less drinking. "More amongst women, less among men," is the usual opinion—and here, as elsewhere, the changed attitude of women generally, in that they now enter the public-house without any feeling of shame, is mentioned.

The poverty remains. Its causes lie deep. The funds available for its relief are large, and where poverty is endowed, it is apt to persist. The administration of relief is, perhaps, as good as can be expected. The clergy claim that they follow Charity Organization principles "as far as possible," holding, as it is whimsically expressed, that there are cases which, on these principles, may quite rightly be refused by the good Samaritan, yet which "the priest and Levite cannot pass by."

On the whole things are better than they were. The area of poverty is more circumscribed; there is less violence and less brutality, and in these directions the improvement is likely to go on and go further.

South Pimlico

Between Victoria Station and Lupus Street, bounded on the East by Tachbrook Street, there is a singularly unsatisfactory district. In our map part of it is tinted yellow, but that portion of it is diminishing; the remainder is partly red and partly pink, including many streets in which the status of the inhabitants is indicated by the mixture of pink with a bar of red. Of purple and of blue there is hardly any. In other words, there is an absence of marked poverty, and every indication throughout of working or middle-class comfort, and of what aims at fashion and may pass for wealth in the squares and principal streets.

These yellow or lately yellow streets and squares, tend year by year to become shabbier. Even the well-to-do occupants seem often to take little pride in their houses. At best it is a depressing district, passing, as regards much of it, from the shabbiness of shabby gentility to the gradual decay and grimy dilapidation which is apt to overtake houses built for another class, and altogether unsuited for their present occupants: short of paint, the plaster peeling and cracking; sordid and degraded dwellings, they remain a nightmare in the memory.

South of Lupus Street red becomes pink and pink purple, and, if the process of decay continues, purple will soon become blue; while the one patch of blue shown on the map of 1889 has, in the interval, acquired a black line. But even here there is no squalor, no striking poverty.

It is not the shabby gentility of the one part, nor the increasing poverty of the other, that is the main trouble, but the fact that the whole district swarms with prostitutes. The streets near Victoria Station are their home parade; the small hotels in Vauxhall Bridge Road their houses of accommodation, and the pink streets barred with red their dwelling place. These young women usually room two together and are satisfactory as lodgers. If they ply their trade altogether away from their abodes little can be said, and, with regard to their way of life, an eye is shut. Even if the good rule that maintains the respectability of the home is broken, if hansoms drive up at night, it is difficult for the authorities to take action so long as the neighbours make no complaint. And where there is so much of this kind of vice—in a number of streets every third house is said to be affected by it—public opinion becomes lax.

There is more hope of improvement in the poor part to the South. Half this area is occupied by great works, for so long as the wharves remain it is well-situated for trade; and it contains some of the best model dwellings in London. St. George's Square, too, has an out of the way charm of its own which, making little pretence after fashion, seems to defy decay; while the river frontage offers many advantages. Thus it may be hoped that some healthy development will check the spread in this direction of the disreputable and decaying condition of the district to the North, and prevent any further influx of squalid poverty and disorder from the evictions in Westminster.

A portion of this district is included with the rich parish of St. Peter, Eaton Square, which has a second church, St. John, on the south side of Victoria Station, but the bulk of it is divided between St. Gabriel's and St. Saviour's. In the churches of both of these parishes the ritual is High, and in St. Saviour's especially so. They are both fairly active, and they combine forces in carrying on day schools. Though not full, they have considerable congregations. Both speak of the decline of the neighbourhood, but their people are not to be accounted poor, and some of them, we are told, in one case, resented the introduction of a curate because he came from the East End and therefore could not be a suitable man for them. To be told that the very best men were sent to the East End was no satisfaction. So, too, the Methodist minister tries to visit, but finds the people very shy; "hiding their poverty," which he thinks is greater than appears. The services at his chapel are very poorly attended, its supporters having left. The Wesleyans do better, but, compared to the size of their chapel, the membership is small, and they also lose members by removal. The Congregationalists have two churches and they, too, find it difficult to hold their members. Young people who marry, dislike to live in "buildings," and are apt to leave. Those who attend regularly form a small inner circle. On occasion these two chapels combine forces. They are situated very near together, and one would seem to be enough. There is also a Baptist Mission which uses a building owned by the Wesleyans.

The parish of St. Andrew, lying to the north of the district we have been describing, comprises a more satisfactory area, but here, as elsewhere, the residents in flats are of little good to the church; workers are not easily found and are hard to keep. The Congregationalists have a great and empty church: the shell of a popular preacher, who has passed on, and whose place it is not easy to fill. In this parish, also, the Roman Catholics have their great English centre. Here resides the Cardinal Archbishop, and here is building the great cathedral, to the services in which Catholics will come from all parts; but the neighbouring mission church

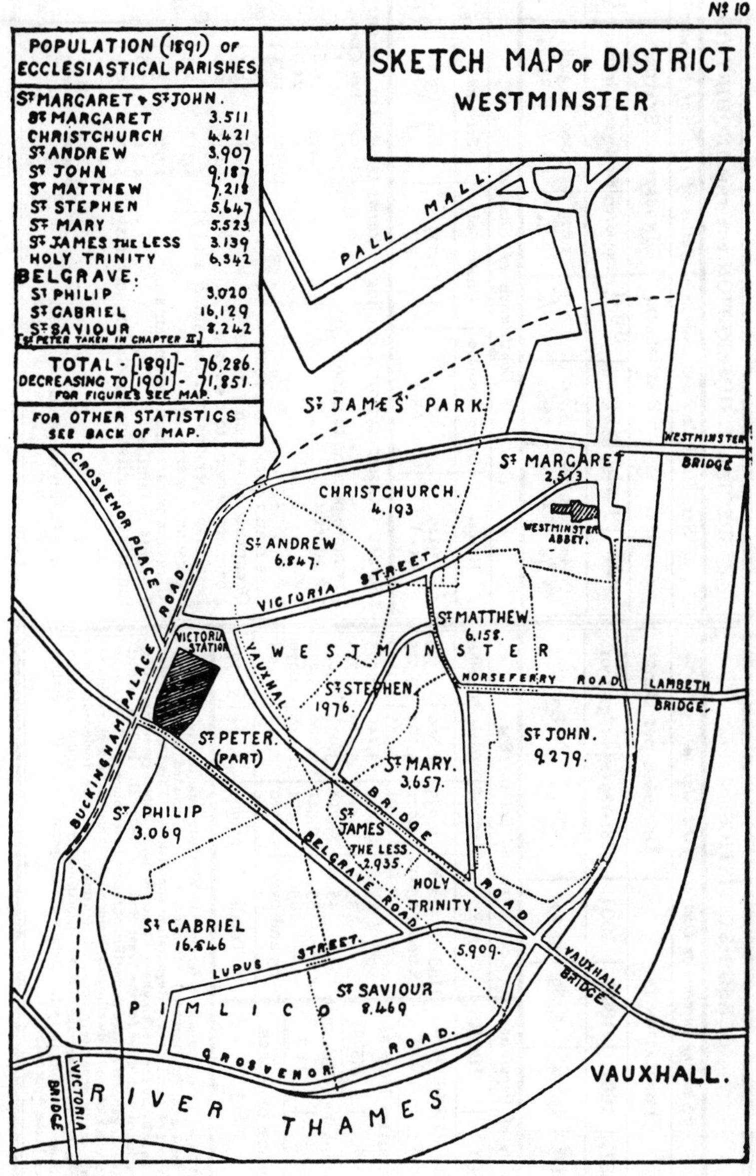

Nº 10
SKETCH MAP OF DISTRICT
WESTMINSTER
POPULATION (1891) OF ECCLESIASTICAL PARISHES
ST MARGARET & ST JOHN.
ST MARGARET 3.511
CHRISTCHURCH 4.421
ST ANDREW 3.907
ST JOHN 9.187
ST MATTHEW 7.218
ST STEPHEN 5.647
ST MARY 5.523
ST JAMES THE LESS 3.139
HOLY TRINITY 6.342
BELGRAVE.
ST PHILIP 3.020
ST GABRIEL 16.129
ST SAVIOUR 8.242
[ST PETER TAKEN IN CHAPTER II]
TOTAL - [1891] - 76.286.
DECREASING TO [1901] - 71.851.
FOR FIGURES SEE MAP.
FOR OTHER STATISTICS SEE BACK OF MAP.
PALL MALL.
ST JAMES' PARK.
WESTMINSTER BRIDGE
ST MARGARET 2.513.
CHRISTCHURCH. 4.193
WESTMINSTER ABBEY.
ST ANDREW 6.847.
VICTORIA STREET
GROSVENOR PLACE ROAD.
ST MATTHEW. 6.158.
VICTORIA STATION
W E S T M I N S T E R
VAUXHAL
HORSEFERRY ROAD
LAMBETH BRIDGE.
ST STEPHEN. 1976.
ST PETER. (PART)
ST JOHN. 9.279.
BUCKINGHAM PALACE
ST MARY. 3.657.
BRIDGE
ST PHILIP 3.069
ST JAMES THE LESS. 2.935.
BELGRAVE ROAD
HOLY TRINITY.
ROAD
ST GABRIEL 16.646
LUPUS STREET.
5.909.
VAUXHALL BRIDGE
ST SAVIOUR 8.469
P I M L I C O
ROAD.
GROSVENOR
VAUXHALL.
VICTORIA BRIDGE
RIVER THAMES

STATISTICS *bearing on the* AREA INCLUDED IN SKETCH MAP NO. 10.

CENSUS STATISTICS.

Showing Increase or Decrease of Population.

Population in				Decrease per Cent.	
1881.	**1891.**	**1896.**	**1901.**	1881-1891.	1891-1901.
60,175	55,774	53,589	51,299	**7·3 %**	**8·0 %**

Density of Population.

1891.	1901.
Persons per Acre.	
67·8	66·1
Inhabited Houses.	
5,608	4,563
Persons per House.	
9·9	11·2
Number of Acres.	
823	

Age and Sex in 1891.

Age.	Males.	Females.	Together.
Under 5 years	2,733	2,866	5,599
5 & under 15 yrs	4,721	4,794	9,515
— 20 ,,	2,704	2,455	5,159
— 25 ,,	3,625	3,140	6,765
— 35 ,,	5,441	5,330	10,771
— 45 ,,	3,718	3,936	7,654
— 55 ,,	2,541	2,688	5,229
— 65 ,,	1,431	1,648	3,079
65 and over	786	1,217	2,003
Totals ...	27,700	28,074	55,774

NOTE.—These Statistics refer only to Westminster (the civil parishes of St. John and St. Margaret). Pimlico, which is included in the sketch map, is part of the Belgrave Registration sub-district. This area is divided almost equally by the Buckingham Palace Road, and the figures respecting it are included with those for the West End in Chapter II. In this district block dwellings form a large proportion of the occupied houses. The Census counts a block of model dwellings or residential mansions as a single house although many separately occupied tenements may be included. This unduly increases the average numbers of persons per house, and may explain the increased crowding in 1901. Details of the Special Family Enumeration are given in the Appendix.

SPECIAL ENUMERATION for this INQUIRY (1891).

Sex, Birthplace and Industrial Status of Heads of Families.

Sex.		Birthplace.		Industrial Status.			Total Heads.
Male.	Female.	In London.	Out of London.	Employers	Employees	Neither.	
9,944 76 %	3,166 24 %	5,807 44 %	7,303 56 %	1,023 8 %	9,000 69 %	3,087 23 %	13,110 100 %

Constitution of Families.

Heads.	Others Occupied.	Unoccupied.	Servants.	Total in Families.
13,110 (1·0)	10,435 (·80)	23,009 (1·75)	4,147 (·32)	50,701 (3·87)

Social Classification according to *Rooms Occupied* or *Servants Kept.*

	Persons.	Per Cent.	
4 or more persons to a room	3,964	7·1	Crowded 38·6 %
3 & under 4 ,, ,,	5,343	9·6	
2 & ,, 3 ,, ,,	12,225	21·9	
1 & ,, 2 ,, ,,	12,322	22·1	Not Crowded 61·4 %
Less than 1 person to a room	1,671	3·0	
Occupying more than 4 rooms	6,089	10·9	
4 or more persons to 1 servant	1,637	2·9	
Less than 4 persons to 1 servant & 4 to 7 persons to 2 servants	1,317	2·3	
All others with 2 or more servants	1,986	3·5	
Servants in families	4,147	7·6	
Inmates of Institutions (including servants)	5,073	9·1	
Total	55,774	100	

Living in Poverty (as estimated in 1889)	34·3 %	100 %
,, in Comfort (,, ,,)	65·7 %	

has lost the bulk of its old congregation, for the Catholic poor have gone.

DESCRIPTIVE NOTES. MAP L. (VOL. III., PART II., CHAPTER I.)

Westminster and South Pimlico.

General Character. — The map comprises the district of Westminster (St. John), and the greater part of Pimlico. A Royal palace, a large public school, Westminster Abbey, the Houses of Parliament, as well as several public offices, are within the map; Wellington Barracks is just within the northern, and Chelsea Barracks just without the western boundary. The range of colour is from yellow, through every grade of red and blue, to black. Buckingham Palace is included, as well as Chadwick Street (black). Between St. James's Park and Victoria Street there is wealth mixed with comfortable working-class streets, and a few very small patches of poverty. Between Victoria Street and the river there is wealth, chiefly in flats, with a large working-class area containing great poverty and vice of old standing. In Pimlico, to the West, there are the remains of wealth, and a number of lodging-house streets, notorious for the prostitutes who live in them (*vide* p. 87).

Poverty Areas. — Old standing poverty is found in small patches in Lewisham Street (*vide* p. 79); off Great Peter Street, where are situated low-class lodging-houses for men and for women; off Tufton Street, and off Regency Street, where it is connected with gasworkers and loafers. The amount of great poverty is decreasing, owing to the demolition of slums and the removal of Millbank prison, which gave a bad name to the district.

Employments. — Brewers' men, policemen, postmen and railway men; many waiters engaged at the clubs; also men working at the Army and Navy Stores, and piano makers and other mechanics. The women are domestic servants, office cleaners, shop assistants, machinists and flower sellers. There are many prostitutes. The poorest are the common lodging-house population of cadgers and loafers and the gasworkers, and a few riverside workers and builders' labourers. The chief centres of employment in the district are Victoria Railway Station, Watney's Brewery, the Army and Navy Stores, the gasworks, Broadwood's piano works, the Government clothing factory, and several riverside wharves. Large numbers, both of men and women, come in daily to their work.

Housing and Rents. — The flats off Victoria Street are rented at from £300. a year downwards, the prices in Victoria Street itself being rather higher. Working-class tenements of two to four rooms with a scullery, fetch 6*s* 3*d* to 10*s* 6*d*. In a 'black' street, the houses (which have three storeys, contain six rooms each, and are in bad repair) are mostly let in furnished rooms, the rent of one room being 5*s*. In Pimlico, where the houses have mostly three and a half storeys, and 16-ft. frontage, the rent for single rooms is 3*s* 6*d*. In a 'light blue barred with black' street the rent is 4*s* for a single room (1898-99).

Markets. — Strutton Ground and the east end of Warwick Street are working-class markets. The rich buy at the Army and Navy Stores and in Buckingham Palace Road.

Public-houses are found in plenty over the whole district, being most numerous in Westminster; a large portion of them are fully licensed.

Places of Amusement. — The Royal Aquarium, with a theatre next to it (the sites of which have been recently acquired by the Wesleyans for their central establishment in London), and a music-hall in Victoria Street, are the chief local places of Amusement.

Open Spaces. — Public open spaces are St. James's Park in the North, St. John's Garden and Victoria Tower Gardens in Westminster, and St. George's Gardens and some open space by the river front in the South. There are also a fair number of private squares in Pimlico; and Dean's Yard, Vincent Square, the garden of the Grey Coat Hospital, and the open ground round the Tate Gallery, and the river, give, on the whole, a sufficiency of air space. The darkest and most airless streets are those on either side of Victoria Street, over-shadowed by high buildings.

Health. — Health is moderate, and the sanitary conditions unsatisfactory in the older parts of Westminster. The ground is low, and the greater part of the district is on blue clay.

Changes of Population. — Changes are due to the building of a large number of flats and offices round Victoria Street, the demolition of slum areas, and the migration of fashion from Pimlico. The rich migrants have gone to Chelsea and Kensington, the poor to Fulham, Lambeth and Battersea. Those who have come in are rich vagrants and bachelors, and Members of Parliament, to whom flats near the centre of official and fashionable London are a convenience; and fairly comfortable artisans, drawn from the surrounding streets and also from outside.

Means of Locomotion. — Victoria Station is the only large terminus in the map; the Metropolitan Railway touches the northern part of the district at Victoria and St. James's Park stations. The only tramway—a slow one along Vauxhall Bridge Road—will, it is to be hoped, when the new Vauxhall Bridge is finished, be converted from horse traction to electricity, and continued across the river into South London. Several omnibus routes traverse the district, most of them converging on Victoria Station. A line of trams is needed along the Thames front from Westminster Bridge to Chelsea, but is strongly opposed by the rich inhabitants on the line of route, who fear the noise and a possible inrush of traffic.

PLACES OF WORSHIP.

List of Parish Churches in the district described in Chapter I. (Vol. III., Part II.), with other Places of Worship grouped in their ecclesiastical parishes.

Christ Church, Westminster.
- Wellington Barracks' Chapel.

Holy Trinity, Vauxhall Bridge Rd.
- Bessboro' Place Mission.
- L. C. Miss., Dorset St.

St. Andrew, Westminster.
- Westminster Chapel (Cong.), James St.
- St. Peter and St. Edward (R.C.), Palace St.

St. Gabriel, Pimlico.
- All Saints', Grosvenor Rd.
- U. Meth. Free Ch., Westmoreland St.
- Brethren's Meeting Room, 6, Sutherland Terrace.
- Old Bapt. Union Miss., 57, Winchester St.

St. James the Less, Upper Garden St.

St. John, Smith Square.
- St. John's Miss., Horseferry Rd.
- Bapt. Ch., Romney St.

St. Margaret, Westminster.
- Westminster Abbey.
- St. Margaret's Miss., New Tothill St.
- Dartmouth Hall, Lewisham St.

St. Mary, Tothill Fields.
- Salv. Army Hall, Regency St.

St. Matthew, Westminster.
- Miss. of Good Shepherd, St. Matthew St.
- Wesl. Ch., Horseferry Rd.
- St. Mary's (R.C.), Horseferry Rd.

11

THE POSITION OF RELIGION IN LONDON

The Attitude of the Religious Bodies to the People

THE ATTITUDE of the religious bodies in London to religion, to their own religious duties, and, amongst themselves to the members of their own congregations, has been set forth in the earlier chapters of the present and exhibited in great detail in the six preceding volumes; but as to the attitude of these bodies towards the people at large, something more may be said by way of introduction to the converse subject of the attitude of the people towards them and towards religion generally.

In speaking of the attitude of a religious body, the reference is limited, on some issues, solely to the clergy and ministers, and almost always to those who, inspired by the doctrines of a particular church, share in its work: those who are not only convinced that they themselves hold the truth, but who feel constrained to spread the knowledge of what perhaps seems to them to be the one hope for every individual soul, and for the regeneration of the world. On them, in the providence of God, this task has been laid.

Those who take up their religion in this spirit are comparatively few in number, but the amount of work which they do is marvellous, and its influence on the lives of the whole population, very great. It is hardly surprising if, in the hurly burly of work, and with the intensity of the feelings and beliefs which inspire it, there should be some lack of the sense of proportion or perspective, some distortion of view, some failure to understand the position of

---

Reprinted from "Religious Influences," VII, 414–29.

others and their own in relation thereto. Yet on a true perception of these points the success of their efforts must largely depend.

Outside of these inner religious circles comes the much larger body of those who, without possessing such intensity of conviction or such ardent zeal, do from many motives support the church to which they belong.

This outer circle of adherents and supporters forms the first and most readily responsive public. They probably come of a religious stock, their souls still affected by bygone spiritual experiences on their own part or that of their forebears. Such people can very likely be roused, at least for a time, to fervour, and from them mainly the inner body is recruited. The action and reaction that result constitute a large part of the life of every active church.

The successes achieved amongst such as these serve to strengthen the optimistic delusion common among religious bodies, which regards all men as open to receive the Gospel they offer to the world; and thus the attitude of these bodies to the people is largely based on a misconception of the attitude of the people towards them. One of the clergy suggests that London should be treated as entirely heathen and worked as a mission from one centre. London, says another, "is thirsting for visitation; no place so lonely; hundreds of young men and women longing for sympathy," by which he means religious sympathy and visitation in the name and cause of religion. The same kind of prepossession is reflected in the suggestion that the people might be won over if the Bishop of Stepney had a palace in the East End, or in the view expressed by a leading Congregationalist in another part of London, that to catch the working man it was a fine building that was needed, "for they do not care to go to what they describe as a '———old iron shed.' " Others think that it is the shyness of the public that has to be overcome, and point to the men who, they say, "will lean against a fence and smoke as they listen; but who have not pluck enough to go to church, though they will purposely attend open-air meetings." This seems to me to be a pure delusion. But the same idea is shown everywhere in the building of special missions and the holding of special services in them. Others again think there is need for a change in the form of the "presentment of the truth," if it is to be listened to: new words must be found and the old ones dropped. Many of the Church of England clergy attribute lack of success to the inadaptability of the church services to different classes, holding that they are only suitable for the instructed. And the belief that novelty is the one thing needed, is reflected in the remark of one who said he was "too old to learn new tricks," and in the need felt everywhere for young clergy to keep up the pace. The lack of all power of concentration is constantly dwelt upon, and the "Tit Bits style" is thought to be necessary even for sermons; while the common position of those whom the churches make such efforts to reach is stated to be "just carelessness," in death as well as in life. Thus, while optimistic as to possibilities, the view is often almost despairing as to results; and in the main the attitude of the churches to the people is one of surprise at the rejection of the teachings of religion by so many of those to whom they are offered.

The belief is easily fostered that if the people at large were better as men, they would be more attentive to religious observance, and, conversely, that if more constant at church they would become better men; but if we accept the ordinary social view of good and bad, there is no certainty that either statement is true. The words of St. Paul are very commonly quoted, and by nearly every sect, for almost all endeavour, and even claim to be, "all things to all men, that some may be saved"; whereas in fact they are only *all things* to themselves, and *something* to a quite narrow circle of sympathisers. It may be that in their narrowness lies their strength. They approach the rest of the world in a spirit of undying hope, indeed, and of faith in the ultimate triumph of "God's Word," but meanwhile of amazement at what seems to them wilful blindness and obstinate unbelief, and this attitude often applies almost as much to the wrongheadedness of other religious bodies, as to that of the irreligious.

If the religious bodies would awaken energy for furthering the welfare of others, and would keep it pure, what they propose must be untainted, alike by the struggle of competition or by ignoring the work that others do, by magnifying their own office, by exaggeration of statement, or by bribery in all its subtle forms. But to avoid all this needs self control besides humility of spirit, for all these things do in a certain low but definite manner "pay," and result in a melancholy success. Highly coloured appeals bring in a golden return, treats and blankets swell the lists of mothers and children on the books of the undertaking, and, above all, the sectarian spirit binds and braces together the energies of the band of workers.

But if religious propaganda and denominational appeals are apt to be tainted in these ways so far as their own adherents are concerned, the risks are far greater as regards those whom the religious bodies aim to serve. When the poor are made the subjects of such ignoble competition, the result is apt to show itself in cringing poverty with all its evils: lack of independence, hypocrisy, and lies, accompanied by the contempt of those who stand aside.

Moreover, there is often an uneasy internal sense of rivalry, accompanied by the consciousness that the inability of the religious bodies to present a united front to the world, strengthens the ground of the unbeliever. General approval can only be won by aims that are felt to make for the general welfare, and in so far as denominations appear to regard themselves as of intrinsic individual importance they are apt to lose moral status in the public view.

The general attitude of the religious bodies towards the people does much to create that of the people towards them. There is on both sides a lack of respect. On both sides the terms of approach seem to be wrong. If the churches, instead of demanding of the people "how can we help you?" were to ask, even of the poorest and the worst, "how can you help us?" a road might open out; and the battle would be won if it were found, as perhaps it would be, that the people, even the poorest and the worst, would claim their right to share the work on equal terms, asking for their part, not "how can you help me?" but "how can I help you?"

The Attitude of the Religious Bodies to Each Other

The discomforts that exist in the relation between the various bodies, but especially between the Church of England and the Nonconformists, can be best indicated by extracts from the remarks made to us. It is a case in which evidence can hardly go astray, for the question is largely concerned with what is felt, irrespective of the degree of justification; and although there are some pleasant exceptions, there is not a little bitterness of feeling.

An Evangelical Churchman of position told us that for his part he was willing to preside at Nonconformist meetings if asked, and often had done so at temperance meetings; but added that he could not invite any of the Nonconformist ministers to preside at his meetings:—"They are to me as laymen, while I am a specially ordained priest; they may be better as laymen than I am, but in my eyes they are not ordained clergymen." Another Evangelical mentions meeting Nonconformists on such occasions as "The Soldiers and Sailors' Wives' War Fund Committee," or "The Children's Country Holiday Fund," and of speaking for them on one occasion at a temperance meeting; but none of them had ever spoken at his meetings. And another, also Low rather than High Church, complained of the tendency of his flock to go astray. "You spend half your time," was his expression, "in warning them against false sects." Those belonging to the High Church take up yet stronger ground, and even tell those who are working independently that such as they "have no right to be there without leave." The responsibility, it is held, rests upon the clergy, and all the workers must be communicants at their church.

The Nonconformists tell the same story from the other side. The Church clergy, we hear, hold themselves aloof. "In the eighteen months I have been here, I have not spoken to one of them," said a Wesleyan minister. "It is their fault," he added. "We would gladly meet them and work with them, but it must be on terms of equality. We will not abate one jot or title of our ministerial position." A Baptist says the same. He would be delighted to work with the clergy of the Establishment if on level ground. "No patronage." It is not only toleration that they demand, it is respect.

Meanwhile, naturally, there is very little co-operation of any kind. A Congregationalist stated that he found it difficult to work on Charity Organization committees because of the "frequently offensive behaviour" of the clergy, who are usually in force on these committees. "I do not like," he added, "being patronized by some boy, merely because he has 'orders' on which I, certainly, lay little store." There are, however, instances of cordial co-operation; this last witness himself mentioned one, but its spirit could not be presumed on, for when he wrote to the successor of the man whose co-operation he had enjoyed, hoping that the relations of the past might be continued, he called forth a reply of many pages telling him he was living in schism, and that no dealings with him were possible unless he joined the Church.

"The Church of England clergy look down on the Nonconformists; at most they tolerate us," says another Baptist, who cannot understand why it should be so; while a Wesleyan missionary simply says, "We never see the Church of England"; adding, kindly, "In London you seem to be absorbed in your own work"; and that there was practical co-operation in this case was evidenced by the advantage taken of Church of England institutions on the part of his mission.

Presbyterian ministers in especial resent the name of "Dissenters," and do not even call themselves "Nonconformists." They are ordained in very regular fashion, and do not forget that in Scotland they represent the Establishment. This may tend to separate them from other Nonconformists, and whatever the cause the position they assume is very independent.

Though among the various Nonconformist churches it is difficult to maintain any very effective co-operation, there is seldom any ill-feeling. Independent missions are, however, in a different position, and sometimes complain of, and sometimes are complained of by, all the others. The superintendent of one such mission told us that he received neither help nor sympathy from the local churches of whatever denomination, and that there was no co-operation even with other missions. His view was that he was ignored by the "reverend gentlemen" because they considered that his organization was going beyond its proper sphere, and thus trenching upon theirs. It is clear that underlying all these jealousies, personal and sectional, is the stress of competition; though surely there is room for all.

We have, however, heard in more than one quarter that the divisions between the Nonconformist denominations are breaking down. A minister of the United Methodist Free Church in an outlying part of London, where the population is much scattered, claimed to have Baptists, Congregationalists, Wesleyans and Presbyterians in his congregation; and a Wesleyan, whose congregation is of similar mixed character, makes an interesting reflection when he says that if members of his congregation leave him it is quite possible that they revert to their old connexion. They may thus only appear to lapse, and are not necessarily lost to Christianity though they may be to Wesleyanism.

Some Nonconformists are no more willing than the Church to recognise "unauthorized preaching," or to accept the theory advanced by one of themselves whom they had slighted, that "each one of us speaks with authority as he has it from above"; but the main trouble lies between the Established Church and those who cannot submit to her authority and pretensions. To her the complaints mainly apply, and hers is the opportunity to rise above sectional ideas and assume the leadership. I do not hesitate to affirm that in London it lies neglected at her feet. To attain it, doctrinal authority which she is powerless to wield, and mediæval pretensions which may well be left to Rome, must, indeed, be abandoned. It would be a new departure, I grant, but no new organization is required. To give to others their place would be to fill her own, and this not in London only, but as the Mother Church of all the English speaking nations.

The Attitude of the People to Religion

It may be said of the inhabitants of London, as of the people of England, that they are distinctly Christian in the sense that they would all (except the Jews) repudiate the imputation of belonging to any other of the great religions of the world. Which of them would not laugh in the face of an inquirer who gravely demanded of him whether he were Mahommedan, Buddhist, Brahmanist, Zoroastrian, or Christian? To such a question there can be no doubt as to the reply. Furthermore, it may be said that though the mass of the people may not understand the exact force and bearing of the various doctrines of which the Christian system is built up, they are acquainted with them in a general way. The doctrines of the Incarnation, the Atonement, the Resurrection, are fairly well known to them, and though many would say they did not well understand them, there would be no general disposition to question their truth. It would be mainly among the very intelligent, educated members of the more highly paid working class that formal disagreement would find expression.

But something more is demanded than a mere acquiescence which is often felt to amount to little more than "not being prepared not to believe," and such sentences as "It is heathen London still"; "It is heathen London with which we have to deal"; "The rich have purses but no souls"; "You may write indifference across it all"; are familiar in the mouths of the ministers of religion.

There is, however, another point of view. According to many, including not a few of the clergy themselves, everything that is beneficial may be brought under the aegis of religion. "Only that which is harmful is irreligious," says one, while some go so far as to "recognise no distinction between the sacred and the secular," in which case all moral life could be accepted as religious, and of moral conscientious life in London there is much.

If, however, religion is not simply a moral mode of life, neither is it merely a devotional expression; religion is also an impulse and a persistent attitude, an intimate possession of the soul, perhaps not understood even by the individual, and very difficult of interpretation by others. But if we consider the recognition of the divine and the spiritual in life to be the distinctive characteristic of religion, judgment is still obscured. In this sense men are often more religious than is known. The most religious may be those whose professions are fewest; who may give no sign to the world of their inner spiritual life. The form of reserve that hates to display feeling is a national quality.

Although it is thus difficult to form any definite judgment as to the religious character of London, the fact must be admitted that the great masses of the people remain apart from all forms of religious communion, apparently untouched by the Gospel that, with various differences of interpretation and application, is preached from every pulpit.

Of the effect of age, sex and class on this aloofness much has been said. Children cannot be regarded as having any attitude of their own in this matter, save that of willing acceptance of anything pleasant that may come within their reach. It is not doctrine or ritual, but the measure of kindly welcome and the rewards, that determine the direction of their feet. And taking London as a whole, it is the young children alone who in the mass are responsive. Though easily won they are held with difficulty, and there is little continuity in their religious training. The habit of the home is stronger than the precepts of the school, or the influence of the churches. Girls are more amenable than boys, and throughout London the female sex forms the mainstay of every religious assembly of whatever class. Otherwise the palpable distinctions are those of means. Fashionable and "yellow" districts secure, at the least, prosperous churches and large morning congregations on Sunday. For the rest, what was written of North London holds good throughout. "Where the streets are 'red' we find a vigorous middle class religious development combined with active social life. Where 'pink' there is as regards organized religion a comparative blank. Where 'blue' we have the missions, and step by step as it deepens to black, the more hopeless becomes the task. The map thus seems to give the key. . . . . . From these broad conclusions there is no escape."

Among the working classes there is less hostility to, and perhaps even less criticism of the Churches than in the past. The Secularist propaganda, though not suspended, is not a very powerful influence. Pronounced atheism is rare. There is evidence that a wave of such feeling did pass over London nearly a generation ago, but the last twenty years have witnessed a notable change in this respect. The success at the polls, whether for Boards of Guardians, Borough Councils, or the School Board, of men and women who in the name of religion are giving their lives to the service of the people, is one of the noteworthy facts in democratic rule. The sub-warden of a Congregational mission sits as Mayor of Southwark to-day.

While there has been this change of attitude towards the Churches, they also have been changing alike in the breadth of their sympathies and the scope of their work. Direct response was doubtless looked for and might have been expected, but there is little sign of it in the sense of an increased acceptance of the particular teaching of the Churches, and at this disappointment is felt. The humanitarianism of the clergy and others is approved of, but their doctrinal teaching carries no weight. The fact that working men are more friendly, more tolerant perhaps of clerical pretensions and in a sense more sympathetic, makes them no more religious in anything approaching to the accepted meaning of the word. And to this we must add that a liberalised form of Christianity, as preached by some, makes no better headway; the fact, indeed, remains that in those chapels and missions in which the greatest proportion of really attached working men are found, the teaching is strictly and even narrowly orthodox.

What then is happening? If the working classes are not becoming more religious, what direction does development take? It is claimed that changes making for improvement are in progress among them, that habits are becoming softened, that the influence of education is making itself felt, that intelligence is spreading, that the range of interests is widening: are, then, their interests becoming more political, or more social, more intellectual or more material? No conclusive answer can be given. We only know that such interests as trade unions and friendly societies, co-operative effort, temperance propaganda and politics (including Socialism) with newspapers and even books, are filling, in the mental life of the average working man, a larger space than in the past, and with some may be taking a place which might have been otherwise occupied by religious interests; but this usurpation and engrossment of the mind may probably be asserted much more confidently of pleasure, amusement, hospitality and sport. In these matters a measure of the demand is found in the facility of the supply, and for all the last-named the facilities readily keep pace.

For most wage earners the claims of the working day are not so exacting as in the past. The great mass of men have more leisure, but the time freed goes in some of these other directions; religion hardly gains. One who fought hard for the Saturday half-holiday, hoping that Sunday would then be given to God, sadly admits his mistake. The maw of pleasure is not easy to fill. The appetite grows. Sunday is increasingly regarded as a day of mere recreation. Nationally we have yet to learn how to use the day. The old "dulness" which one witness regarded as "our salvation, physically as well as spiritually," has been rejected; but the full force and the best form of alternative interests and attractions are not yet realized.

Apart from the Sunday question, the other interests mentioned are, however, not in themselves absolutely incompatible with the maintenance of active religious connexions. In practice the associations of the public-house, the music-hall or the race-course conflict with those of church and chapel, but there is nothing inherently or theoretically inconsistent between the two sets of interests. There is nothing that is found so in Roman Catholic countries, nor among ourselves, by many middle-class families who are able to enjoy the theatre on Saturday and yet join in active Christian communion on the following day. The conflict arises from the character with which these amusements have acquired, and the spirit in which they are sought, both of which religion, if accepted, might successfully modify. We therefore turn rather to the special obstacles which in the case of the working classes prevent church going. These have been largely studied in the preceding volumes, and may be taken as constituting the attitude of these classes to religion.

The churches have come to be regarded as the resorts of the well-to-do, and of those who are willing to accept the charity and patronage of people better off than themselves. It is felt that the tone of the services, especially in the Church of England, is opposed to the idea of advancement; inculcating rather contentment with, and the necessity for the doing of duty in, that station of life to which it has pleased god to call a man. The spirit of self-sacrifice, inculcated in theory, is not observed among, or believed to be practised by, the members of these churches in any particular degree, and this inconsistency is very critically and severely judged. Phrasing it somewhat differently, the working man would doubtless heartily endorse the opinion of one of the clergy themselves, that "what we want for the recovery of the lapsed masses is not more but better Christians."

There is also an incompatibility of moral temper. The average working man of to-day thinks more of his rights or of his wrongs than of his duties and his failures to perform them. Humility and the consciousness of sin, and the attitude of worship, are perhaps not natural to him. He is not helped by calling himself a miserable sinner and would probably feel the abasement somewhat exaggerated, and, in the same way, perhaps, triumphant praise strikes in him no sympathetic note.

"The dawn of hope for the working man, who has begun to realize that he has ample opportunities to improve his position," was regarded by one of our witnesses, himself a clergyman of the Church of England, as "the main factor in the improved moral tone of the present day," due otherwise to a combination of causes —religious, educational, and administrative. But how does the ordinary religious service fit in with this ideal? Neither the Prayer Book nor the New Testament itself give any prominence to the idea of progress, either for the community or for the individual, except in so far as it is involved in the ideas of moral and spiritual regeneration. It may, indeed, be urged, that with these all true progress will be ensured, and without them none, but it is difficult for those below to regard the matter in this light.

As to religious truth, among many teachers, the inquirer in the end is thrown back upon himself to form conclusions as best he may, and, in most instances, finding no satisfactory solution he puts the issue by. Amongst all the reasons for abstaining from public worship, genuine, conscientious, reasoned unbelief takes a very small place.

The clergy and ministers have no authority that is recognised, but their professional character remains, and owing to it they perhaps lose influence. It is accounted their business to preach, they being paid to do it; and their manner, though accepted as a pose necessary to the part they play, is somewhat resented. No prestige covers them—"they are no better than other men." In the case of the Roman Catholic priesthood alone do we find the desired combination of professionalism and authority, safeguarded because accepted, and resting not on the individual but on the Church he serves; and where most nearly approached, it is by the saintly lives of some of the High Church clergy. To live a life of voluntary poverty seems to be the only road to the confidence of the people in this matter.

To the reasons adduced to account for the abstention of the working classes may be added the habit of detachment itself, bringing a feeling of discomfort in unaccustomed surroundings if this habit be at any time broken through; and answering to this we have the recognition that it is to warmth of welcome that success is mostly to be attributed when success is secured at all.

Finally, it may be said that London surroundings bring little or no pressure to bear in the direction of conventional church-going. Even men who have been churchwardens in the country feel, we are told, no obligation to attend church here, and the ordinary resident knows that, in this respect, his conduct, so far as non-attendance goes, is for the most part free from observation, and, if observed, from comment. Among the working classes the pressure exerted is apt to be on the opposite side, such as in the "ragging" of the workshop, or the sneers of neighbours who connect religious observance with cupboard love. But in a general way, London life secures for all men the maximum freedom of conduct. Even criminals find it their best hiding-place. To ask no questions is commonly regarded as the highest form of neighbourliness.

12

ILLUSTRATIONS (Inner South London)

IN THE Spring of 1900, I visited a large number of the churches and chapels in this district, and the four sections that follow contain extracts from notes made at the time. I take this occasion to renew my warning that these and the other extracts given in the following chapters must be regarded as illustrations only, not as in themselves a sufficient basis for any conclusions.

St. Saviour's. — One descends from the street to the old level on which the church stands, and the entrance is far away to the west. In the interior the impression is quite that of a cathedral: sightseers wandering about while morning prayer went on in the Lady Chapel; and the interest of the sightseers duly considered by the labelling of points of interest—as "Norman Doorway," "Norman Recess," &c. At the same time attention is called to projected improvements—painted glass it is desired to insert of which the design is exhibited in order to attract gifts. The Sunday morning congregation in the Lady Chapel consisted mainly of school children.

St. Olave's is a stately old-fashioned Georgian building, with great fluted columns carrying roof and galleries. It is fitted with pews even in the galleries. Below they are very high, and some are of the old-fashioned square pattern. The centre aisle is wide and was set out with benches. It was a chilly Sunday morning in February, and no one yet had come. The gas was burning to warm the air. Later, I found a congregation of six adults, with some charity children, seated in the aisle.

Roman Catholic Church of the Most Precious Blood. — A bare, undecorated building, walls left rough inside, colour-washed with a painted dado for the sake of cleanliness. For early Mass there were

"Reprinted from "Religious Influences," IV, 171–77.

present about one hundred adults and the school children—quite poor people, and, as is often the case with the Catholics, there were others in the street and hanging about the door who evidently belonged to the congregation. In the evening the adult attendance was again about one hundred. The congregation made the responses very well. This bare church, with curious canopied altar, produces a very striking effect.

All Hallows, which I also visited, is no less remarkable, and much larger, a really grandly proportioned church, also in the bare style. It makes no show outside, and one may walk all round it before finding the door. It was quite empty, the morning service not having begun, and looked exactly like a Roman Catholic place of worship, even to the figure of a minor kind of priest or brother, in cassock and biretta, seated in a corner reading out of a red-letter breviary. In one part of the church is a great Calvary set upon rocks, and in front space for kneeling in private prayer. In the central aisle a man was slowly pulling the rope of the bell and the school children began to come in, shepherded by the Sisters in their nun-like garb. A good many other worshippers followed. The service is announced as "a solemn Mass with sermon: 11.15." In the evening there was a fair gathering, mainly young people and children, who seemed to belong to the church. There is a bookcase near the door, and it is the custom for those who come to take from it their prayer and hymn books and to return them to the shelves on going out .A Sister was present, but not in charge. All seemed to reflect a loving familiarity with the church, making of it a religious home.

At *St. Michael's* on Sunday morning there were ten to fifteen adults and thirty to forty children, besides the choir. In the evening the little church was fairly filled. The vicar preached, and all he said was simple and to the point. The morning lesson had told of Adam's fall, and he read it again "because so few could come—that is, get out of bed soon enough—to come to morning service." The Bible story, he said, might be taken as of a particular man or as of human nature generally, and in speaking of temptation and sin he always used the pronoun "we." He took for his text God's searching words, "Where art thou, Adam?" as addressed to every one of us. We are all Adams and Eves. We have some knowledge and want other things —we all disobey and all fall, and should not blame Adam for it.

St. Alphege, with a darkened church and a great suspended Christ on the cross, produces a very beautiful effect, and the air was filled with incense. In the morning some adults were there and a large number of school children. The regular evening service was abandoned, and in place of it there was to be a procession at 8.15. I saw it start in a drizzling rain. It consisted of a small body of choir and clergy all in white surplices, getting very wet and limp, escorted by men bearing lanterns of a mediæval type hanging from short poles. They gathered in the street, made a false start with a hymn, stopped, started again, and I saw them wend their way watched by eight or ten of the populace. Within the church there was a small weather-bound congregation who, awaiting the return of the procession, were encouraged to occupy the time by singing hymns. If the weather had been fine all would have been in the street no doubt, and many others would have enjoyed the show.

Charterhouse Mission is a very singular building. Entering by steps leading down into a basement, a visitor finds himself in a striking and lofty church, divided into three parts by columns supporting arches and a flat roof, the latter forming the floor of the club rooms above. In the church hang sacred pictures and a crucifix and there is an altar bearing candles and decked with embroidery. At the morning service there were school children and young persons, male and female, all behaving well, and the priest in his robes attended by acolytes and choristers. In the evening the numbers were larger. The sermon was preached by a stranger who, when he had done his part, rushed off to catch his train while the congregation sang a hymn and the collection was taken up. We then sang another hymn as the procession wound slowly round the church, the priest in splendid robes, out of which he quickly slipped in order to bid us each good night at the door. The stranger's sermon was noteworthy and attentively listened to, though the interest was hardly sufficient to stop coughing. It was on the power of the will of man to defeat God's purpose, leading up to the scheme of salvation; and laid stress on the part played in this by the Virgin Mary, and our consequent adoration of her. She was set up as an example of complete submission to the will of God. As Christ was the new Adam, so she was the new Eve, and the hymn we sang was addressed to B. V. Mary, the Mother of God.

The Working Men's Mission. — When I reached the place, a religious procession was approaching with lights and music. The missionary led, followed by the band, a few other men, some women and some children, about thirty in all. Halting at the chapel door they doused their flaring lights and entered the building, inviting strangers in, but I was the only one who entered with them. There were some other people already inside, and with an audience of perhaps sixty the square room was about one-fourth filled. The missionary was supported on the platform by two other men, and by his son, who not only played the harmonium and sang a solo, but also preached the sermon. The father, a seemingly illiterate man, with hardly an H in his vocabulary, told us how pleased he should himself be to listen to his son, and hoped that the words might be blessed. He spoke, too, of other members of his family, mentioning three of his children who had given themselves to Christ's work, and asked our prayers for his wife who was ill and in suffering.

The young man began by saying that he had studied the Bible all the week without being able to find an inspiration, but that while he sat there one had come to him; he however admitted (very candidly) that it was a subject on which he had spoken before, and he evidently had it by him to use, failing any other inspiration. It was on Pilate's words "Behold the man," and was perhaps the reflection of some sermon he had heard. He described first Pilate and his position and cowardice, then the people Pilate addressed and the aims of their leaders, and lastly the Man who stood there. It was the scheme of a great oratorical effect—without the orator.

The Roman Catholic Church of St. Joseph (*Bermondsey*) was quite full on Sunday morning with school children and adults. Every seat was occupied and a crowd standing behind. When I entered it was that period of the Mass when, the principal priest being busied at the altar, the kneeling congregation sing in a subdued tone, with very devotional effect. Meanwhile another priest, a big man, took the opportunity of walking up and down the centre aisle, looking right and left as, with book in hand, he appeared to tick off those who were present or absent. In the evening there was a fair, but much smaller congregation, all adults. A young priest was reading the lesson. It was, I noticed, the same portion of the Gospel that is appointed to be read in the Church of England service of the day.

Holy Trinity (*R. C.*), *Dockhead.*—It was 10.30; I suppose there would be High Mass at 11. Meanwhile the church was largely filled with children who were being specially addressed. They occupied the front and centre, adults sitting at the sides and behind, and many, both adults and children, were standing at the back waiting to take their seats. The priest stood at the altar-rail, and talked to the children at his feet in an easy familiar style. He referred to the Blessed Virgin chosen of God for her high office and of her naturally great influence in heaven, with great simplicity, and passed on to St. Joseph who had been selected as foster father and who, working for his living as a carpenter, had supported both Mary and her son; doing thus his duty; and he referred also to the influence that St. Joseph could not but have gained. And then he turned his discourse to the practical lesson for his hearers, most of whom would have to earn their bread with their hands, that honest work would be approved of God.

In the evening this church was crowded to the doors (Sunday, 13th May, 1900). I do not know what the occasion may have been, but a sacred procession passed round the aisles to the intense delight of a church full of poor people and children on their knees. In the procession were seventy or eighty girls of all ages veiled in white muslin. Some were quite little things, and these, walking backwards, strewed flowers in front of the priest, who carried the host under a canopy. The canopy was held by four rough-looking men. I watched the people as they left the church. They seemed to be there by families and were of all classes found in Bermondsey, but especially the poor. They looked well fed—better fed than dressed—a characteristic with the Roman Catholic poor.

From this scene I went to Mr. Davis's railway arch mission. The service there is put late. The building was full, with perhaps two hundred and fifty, all adults, and mostly working or lower middle class, and some seemingly quite poor. They were appealed to as those whose duty it was to spread the Gospel and to help in every way those not so well off as themselves. The appeal as regards money is doubtless ultimately to the rich, and the funds a raised from the West End, but those who attend also give. The address began at 8.35, and when nine struck some began to slip out, so the preacher hurried to a conclusion, and the final hymn was sung in the confusion of a general break up of the party. There is much that is rough and little that is reverent about such services, but they are homely and the people find satisfaction in them, counting themselves as servants of Christ, doing God's work on earth and hastening the coming of His kingdom.

The junction of Bermondsey New Road and the Old Kent Road is a very favourite pitch for out-door services, and probably its occupation at stated times by certain bodies is understood. When I reached the spot one Sunday morning the Salvationists were there: a group of about twelve men, women, and boys, with musical instruments. The speaker, an earnest, pallid man, with a very harsh voice, was declaiming our need of salvation before we die. He was more forcible and real and less conventional in what he said than usual; but had no outside audience. At the Grange Road end of the street was another Salvation Army meeting, still smaller, conducted by women speaking with low voices; quite as effective, perhaps, as the other, or at least not less so. The people in the street were marketing—the idlers were not yet out in any numbers.

The Haddon Hall Baptists followed the Salvationists on the first pitch, which they held till 1 o'clock, carrying on a regular service, with harmonium, at the same time as that in their hall close by. They had brought a party of their school children to sing in the street, and at the end, after 12.30, there was a considerable gathering round them, but at that time the street swarmed with idlers and those bound homewards from other services. Earlier, they spoke and sang to the air.

IV. Final Volume

13

SUNDAYS, HOLIDAYS AND AMUSEMENTS

Many accounts have been given us concerning life on Sunday, both in the streets in the homes. "The day," says one, speaking of his own poor neighbourhood, "is comparatively quiet but for the costers shouting all day long in the poor streets. The shops, with few exceptions, are shut or only partly open. In the homes the men lie abed all the morning, mend rabbit hutches and pigeon lofts in the afternoon, and go for a walk in the evening. "Their objection to going to church," this witness adds, "is stronger than ever." "Those of a rather better stamp take the 'kids' for a ride on the tram"; and for these and some of a rather higher class too, a picture is drawn of the man in bed with his paper on Sunday morning and his wife cooking the dinner. A deacon of a Congregational church gives the following description of the people in his neighbourhood: "They get up at nine or ten, and as he passes to his chapel he sees them sitting at breakfast half-dressed or lounging in the window reading *Lloyd's Weekly Newspaper*. After they are washed and dressed the men wait about until the public-houses open, and then stay within their doors till three o'clock, when they go home to dinner, which meanwhile the women have been preparing. At half-past twelve, as he returns from chapel after the morning service, the minister often meets women laden with baskets of provisions from the street-market near by, on their way home to cook the dinner. After dinner the men, if they have drunk much, may go to bed, but the better sort take a stroll.

Reprinted from "Final Volume," pp. 47–56.

In the evening the young people pair off for walking out, while the elders may perhaps go to a concert or Sunday League lecture."

Here is another more summary description: "The church bell, they say, wakes them: they get up, adjourn to the public-house from one to three, dine soon after three, sleep, and either go again to the public-house in the evening or to the Park." This comes from Mile End, but is echoed almost exactly from Stockwell (*vis à vis* on the map): "Up at twelve to be ready for the "pubs.,' which open at one; dinner any time between two and four, then sleep, and then off with wife and children to hear the band on the Common."

By way of contrast I may add the account given by a Baptist minister in South London of the churgoers' Sunday: "The evening service is best attended; families come then. In the morning the man often comes without the wife, leaving her at home to cook the dinner. Sunday dinner, the meal of the week with his people, for which all the family are gathered together, takes place between 1 and 2.30. Some children are late for Sunday school at three because dinner lasts so long. After dinner, when the children go to school, the men sleep, though this has been broken into to some extent by the men's P.S.A.[1] meeting lately inaugurated, to which fifty to seventy come, over a hundred being on the books. [The P.S.A. is an Evangelistic service, with instrumental and vocal music, hymns, solos and a short address.] Tea at five, and then the evening service, which all attend."

Secular amusements on Sunday are said to have increased to such an extent as to have become a nuisance to those who like a quiet rest on that day. The brakes that drive past laden with pleasure-seekers have generally each their cornet-player, and this custom has gone so far that some suburban local authorities are making by-laws to check it.

The decent occupations, interests and pleasures encouraged, or provided, by the efforts of the "Sunday Society" are even more directly aimed at the improvement of the uses to be made of the Sunday holiday than are the efforts of the religious bodies, and they have been rewarded with considerable success. The victory

1 Pleasant Sunday Afternoon.

won over the narrower Sabbatarian has been attested by the success of the Society in securing the opening of public museums on Sunday afternoons. Crowded audiences of respectable non-churchgoing people welcome the Sunday concerts and other entertainments offered by the National Sunday League; whilst the Sunday Lecture Society's meetings are well attended, as are also the Ethical Society's lectures and concerts. The concerts given at the Albert Hall and at the Alexandra Palace draw crowds. Moreover the clubs provide Sunday amusement for some thirty or forty thousand people in winter.

In the way of Sunday pleasuring much is spent on themselves alone by the men, who leave their wives and children at home. The thoughtless selfishness and indifference of men of all classes are denounced, and the consequent lack of home life is mentioned as a blot. The clergy hold the upper classes especially responsible for sapping the foundations of religion by making Sunday a day of pleasure. "Sunday is becoming the great holiday," said one of them, and mentioned the stream of bicyclists, but at the same time bore witness as to his own following that "our faithful people are very faithful, and our earnest people very earnest."

A more agreeable and perhaps quite as true a view of the life of the people is that "Sunday is the great day for visiting; families go off to see their relations, whilst others are receiving theirs at home." "In the morning they do not get up in time for church; in the evening they receive or visit their friends, and in summer go to the park or the common." With some of a different class we hear that "Sunday is spent in lounging about or gardening, and in the evening you hear the tinkle of the piano and the mandoline."

Holiday making is spoken of as "one of the most remarkable changes in habits in the last ten years," and the statement is applicable to all classes. "The amount saved by working men is little compared to what is spent in this way" and yet, in the opinion of this witness (a superintendent of police), "they save more than they used to." "The district" (says one of the Hackney clergy) "is almost deserted on Bank Holiday. The women go off as well as the men." "A great change," says another witness, "has come over the people"; instead of spending so much in the public-houses, they go for "excursions of all kinds" and the result is recognised as a distinct improvement. But it is partly in connection with this that the public-houses have acquired a new use, it having become customary for young men to take young women there, when out on pleasure together. The change of habit in holiday making has thus helped to introduce a practice that was formerly never thought of —a change in fashion as regards what it is proper to do corresponding to that as regards smoking in the streets, which fifty years ago was inadmissible. This use of the public-houses has been fostered by the fact that other places of refreshment are usually closed on general holidays as well as on Sundays, but there are some signs that a change is coming in this matter; tea rooms having been opened, as many of them certainly should be.

Excursions in brakes are without end. One of these noted consisted of sixteen vehicles, containing all the girls from some large works with their young men, as to whom all that the milkman, who was looking on, could say, was, "Well, they dress better, but their manners are about the same." The manager of another large works at which many girls are employed, said: "It is useless to open the works on the day after Bank Holiday, or even for two days." Very rarely does one hear a good word for the Bank Holidays. The more common view is that they are a curse, and, as already stated, the mischievous results from a sexual point of view due to a general abandonment of restraint, are frequently noted in our evidence. But the rough crush must act as a safeguard of a kind, although "nothing," says one witness, "can surpass the scenes of depravity and indecency" that sometimes result. From other points of view, too, there is some reason to think that their establishment was a step in a wrong direction. The religious festivals at Christmas and Easter, with perhaps one national day (which among them all we have not got), make perhaps a sufficiency of fixed points. Beyond these it would certainly be far better that each trade, or each business establishment, should arrange holidays to suit its own convenience and the seasons of its work, and this freedom might even be extended to each individual. The spirit of pleasure in London does not appear to need fostering so much as wise guidance. It is only as enforcing holidays when otherwise they might not be taken at all, that the atmosphere of a general holiday may be accounted as good.

"To keep the Sabbath holy" is worth a great effort; and for this purpose Sunday labour should cease, so far as possible, but when this high reason does not apply it seems folly to plan that all, except those whose work is such that they are over pressed to meet the needs of the holiday makers, should take holiday on the same day. Those who cater for amusements, and the sellers of drink, are busier than ever; but other shops are closed very inconveniently, and it is said that though drink is always obtainable, food, too often, is not.

The closing of banks on these fixed days is inconvenient and quite unnecessary. The staff of every bank is arranged on a scale which allows for holiday absences.

The convergence on Saturday as a weekly half-holiday is on another footing, and though it may be abused, as in the case of men who spend half their week's wages before coming home, it more properly and more generally enables the wife to do her week's marketing in good time and still have leisure and money left for the evening's enjoyment; shops and markets in the poor districts and places of amusement everywhere being in full train of activity. With a richer class this half-holiday is valued as making "week end" outings possible.

The demand for amusement is not less noticeable than that for holidays, and supply follows. To "What shall we eat, what drink, and wherewithal shall we be clothed?" must now be added the question, "How shall we be amused?" To this an answer has to be found. Even to the police it has presented a problem. "What," they ask, "is to be done with young fellows? Every evening crowds of them come back from their work and loaf about the streets; they join in with whatever is forward, and are an embarrassment if there are no places of amusement for them to go to."

And from something more than the police point of view, what can be made of it? "It is a good thing for people to clean themselves up and go out," says a vestryman of long standing, who holds that not half enough local amusement is provided, and who declines to accept as adequate the efforts of the religious bodies in this direction. Unmistakably, taste is more critical, and, beyond this, any attempt to "improve the occasion" is resented. "Concerts and entertainments given by the Church are poorly attended," said a North-West London vicar, but added that if let for some benefit, when a concert of the usual music-hall type would be given, the hall was always crammed.

Passing by the ordinary mission entertainment, of which the failure is patent, and considering only professional work, there has been a great development and improvement upon the usual public-house sing-song, as to the low character and bad influence of which there are not two opinions. The story of progress in this respect may be traced in many of the existing places which, from a bar parlour and a piano, to an accompaniment on which friends "obliged with a song," have passed through every stage to that of music hall; the presiding chairman being still occasionally, and the call for drinks in almost every case, retained. But the character of the songs on the whole is better, and other things are offered: it becomes a "variety" entertainment. The audiences are prevailingly youthful. They seek amusement and are easily pleased. No encouragement to vice can be attributed to these local music halls. The increase in the number, as well as size of these halls, has been rapid. The profits made by the proprietors have been great, and the favourite performers, being able to appear before a succession of audiences, passing rapidly with their repertoire from hall to hall, can be and are very highly remunerated. The performances also can be continually varied, for the supply of artistes is without end. The taste becomes a habit, and new halls are opened every year: soon no district will be without one. Then theatres follow. But meanwhile, and especially in poor neighbourhoods, the old-fashioned style of sing-song still continues in force.

In the central districts all places of amusement are very largely supported by the rich or by strangers visiting London. People from the outskirts come occasionally, but it is the music hall or theatre of their own neighbourhood that they frequent, and of which the influence has mainly to be considered. It is, perhaps, too much to ask that the influence of music halls and theatres should be positively and entirely good; at any rate no one claims that it is so. If it is not directly, or on the whole, evil, or if one can hope that it takes the place of something worse, a measure of improvement may be indicated. This can, I think, be claimed. It is not very much. A tendency in the direction of the drama, which is certainly an advance, may be noticed in music-hall performances, and it is to be regretted that questions arising from the separate licensing of play-houses should check the freedom of development in this direction amongst the halls. Excluding the dramatic pieces or "sketches," the production of which is hampered in this way, the attractions most usually offered are those of a low form of art or of blatant national sentiment, neither of which can be carried further without becoming worse; or of displays of physical strength and skill on the part of acrobats and gymnasts, or of performing animals; all representing, indeed, a background of patient and unwearied effort, but involving, it cannot but be supposed, not a little cruelty in the training of children and animals necessary to secure the rewards of popularity. But the "variety" of the entertainments increases. In addition to conjuring and ventriloquism, which are old fashioned, we have now, for instance, the cinematograph and various forms of the phonograph, and there has been much development in the forms of stage dancing.

Limitations in the form of entertainment apply less to the halls in Central London, where, for instance, beautiful and elaborate ballets are produced. These fashionable resorts have the best of everything that can be offered, and the performances, consequently, reach a perfection which silences criticism in that respect, though in some cases there may remain ground for attack on the score of encouraging vice. In these palaces of amusement even music is not neglected. The orchestra at the Alhambra is very famous, whilst those at the Empire and the Palace are also excellent. But in the minor halls, development is never in the direction of music. Strange as it may sound, anything that can rightly be called music is seldom produced at a local music hall. The only exceptions I call to mind are a performance of Lancashire bell ringers and the vagaries of a musical clown on his violin. In this respect, the efforts of negro minstrelsy have been far superior.

Perhaps music might some day find its way in through operatic sketches, if these were encouraged.

The taste for music, and for good music, in all classes, is undoubted. "People" (says a London County Councillor) "will not put up with any sort of music; they appreciate good music, and insist on having it." "They appreciate the best music you can give them," remarks the Superintendent of a Wesleyan Mission. They may not be so ready to pay for it, but they find pleasure in hearing it, will take trouble to go where it is given, and will pay a little—will pay to enter the enclosure near the band stand, or for a reserved seat when the rest are free. Good music would seem to be amongst the things which can with safety be supplied collectively, and in this matter, as in others, the London County Council are showing the way. Voluntary effort in the same direction is exemplified by the People's Concert Society and by the choral societies and orchestras connected with many of the churches, Polytechnics and Settlements.

Over this matter Sunday becomes the bone of contention. On the one side it is said that to supply such attractions outside tends to empty the churches, or if given inside to lower the flag of religion; and on the other that the churches can, without going beyond their *rôle*, "hold their own," and never will do more, and that it is from the delights of the public-houses and the charms of the streets, and from homes that fail to delight and lack all charm, that the people are drawn to Sunday concerts or to the parks when the band plays. In confirmation of the latter view we were told at Greenwich that at the outset publicans readily set forth in their windows the bills announcing the times at which the band performaces took place, but that they do so no longer. One of them (it was added) had said that his takings had been reduced £7 or £8. But we have also heard much of the increasing difficulty of holding the young people at church or Bible-class when the band is playing, and some, no doubt, are drawn from both directions.

The Bibliography of Charles Booth

"Occupations of the People of the United Kingdom, 1801–81," *Journal of the Royal Statistical Society*, 49 (June, 1886) : 314–444.

"The Inhabitants of Tower Hamlets (School Board Division), their Condition and Occupations," *Journal of the Royal Statistical Society*, 50 (June, 1887) : 326–401.

"Condition and Occupations of the People of East London and Hackney, 1887," *Journal of the Royal Statistical Society*, 51 (June, 1888) : 276–339.

Labour and Life of the People. Vol. I: *East London*. London: Williams & Norgate, 1889.

Labour and Life of the People. Vol. II: *London Continued*. London: Williams & Norgate, 1891.

Labour and Life of the People. Appendix to Volume II. London: Williams & Norgate, 1891.

"Enumeration and Classification of Paupers, and State Pensions for the Aged," *Journal of the Royal Statistical Society*, 54 (December, 1891) : 600–643.

Pauperism, a Picture, and the Endowment of Old Age, an Argument. London: Macmillan & Co., 1892.

Life and Labour of the People in London. 2d ed. 9 vols. London: Macmillan & Co., 1882–97.

"The Innaugural Address of Charles Booth, Esq., President of the Royal Statistical Society. Session 1892–93" ("Dock and Wharf Labour"), *Journal of the Royal Statistical Society*, 55 (December, 1892) : 521–58.

"Life and Labour of the People in London: First Results of an Inquiry based on the 1891 Census," *Journal of the Royal Statistical Society*, 56 (December, 1893) : 557–96.

The "Booth Collection," consisting of the original materials which formed the basis of all editions of his classic study and involving over 400 items, is located at the British Library of Political and Economic Science in the London School of Economics.

The Aged Poor in England and Wales: Condition. London: Macmillan & Co., 1894.

"Statistics of Pauperism in Old Age," *Journal of the Royal Statistical Society*, 57 (June, 1894) : 235–53.

Old Age Pensions and the Aged Poor: A Proposal. London: Macmillan & Co., 1899.

Improved Means of Locomotion as a First Step towards the Cure for Housing Difficulties in London. Pamphlet. London: Macmillan & Co., 1901.

Life and Labour of the People in London. First Series: "Poverty"; Second Series: "Industry"; Third Series: "Religious Influences"; Final Volume: "Notes on Social Influences and Conclusions." 3rd ed. 17 vols. London: Macmillan & Co., 1902–3.

Poor Law Reform. London: Macmillan & Co., 1910.

Reform of the Poor Law by the Adaptation of the Existing Poor Law Areas, and Their Administration. London: Macmillan & Co., 1910.

Comments on Proposals for the Reform of the Poor Laws. With note by Sir Arthur Downes. London: Macmillan & Co., 1911.

Industrial Unrest and Trade Union Policy. London: Macmillan & Co., 1913.